A PASSAGE TO SWORD BEACH

A PASSAGE TO SWORD BEACH

Minesweeping in the Royal Navy

BRENDAN A. MAHER

NAVAL INSTITUTE PRESS
ANNAPOLIS, MARYLAND

LIBRARY OF CONGRESS CATALOGING-IN-PUBLICATION DATA

Maher, Brendan A. (Brendan Arnold), 1924–
  A passage to Sword Beach : minesweeping in the Royal Navy / Brendan A.
Maher.
      p.   cm.
  Includes bibliographical references (p.   ) and index.
  ISBN 1-55750-572-1
  1. Maher, Brendan A. (Brendan Arnold), 1924–   . 2. World War, 1939–
1945—Campaigns—France—Normandy. 3. Operation Neptune. 4. Normandy
(France)—History, Military. 5. World War, 1939–1945—Naval operations,
British. 6. World War, 1939–1945—Personal narratives, British. 7. Seamen—
Great Britain—Biography. 8. Great Britain. Royal Navy—Biography. I. Title.
D756.5.N6M24   1996
940.54′5941—dc20   95-24424

Printed in the United States of America on acid-free paper ⊚

03 02 01 00 99 98 97 96   9 8 7 6 5 4 3 2
First printing

Quotation on page 25 from Comdr. Justin Richardson, RNVR, "RNVR," in *Wavy
Navy*, J. Lennox Kerr and David James, eds., London: George Harrap, 1946.
Reprinted by permission of Eric Dobby Publishing, Ltd., Orpington, Kent,
England.

Quotation on page 35 from Lt. Comdr. Hugh Campbell, untitled poem, in
Gordon Holman, *Stand By to Beach*, London: Hodder & Stoughton, 1944.
Reprinted by permission of Hodder Headline, PLC.

Quotation on page 217 from Lt. Comdr. John Moore, RNVR, "Sonnet for Dead
Comrades," in *Wavy Navy*, J. Lennox Kerr and David James, eds., London: George
Harrap, 1946. Reprinted by permission of Eric Dobby Publishing, Ltd.,
Orpington, Kent, England.

Frontispiece: ML137 leaving Tough's Yard, Teddington, Middlesex, June
1945. (Photo, in possession of author, taken by a friend)

To the memory of the men and women who made the passage to this and other beaches and there paid the price of the peace that they could not come home to share

Contents

Preface

I had the good fortune to participate in one of the greatest actions of naval history, the invasion of Normandy in 1944. Now, more than fifty years later, I feel compelled to share my recollections of that experience with others.

In late 1942, at the age of eighteen, I joined the Royal Navy as an ordinary seaman and was commissioned as a midshipman in 1943. I served primarily in minesweepers. Until the end of the war in Europe, I maintained an irregular written record of experiences in the Navy. These experiences included rehearsal for, and participation in, Operation Neptune, the naval part of the invasion of Normandy on 6 June 1944. My assignment was that of navigating officer in the leading minesweeper of the Fifth Minesweeping Flotilla for one of the assault channels to Sword Beach. Behind us came the remaining minesweepers of the flotilla, followed by assault forces of the Canadian Army. We later took a major part in the minesweeping of Cherbourg and Brest in the zone of operations of the U.S. forces. My record includes accounts of convoy escort duties during the same period, the minesweeping of the waterways of Holland immediately after the German surrender, and my periods in hospitals as a result of wounds received in those operations.

One part of the record consists of my Midshipman's Journal, a daily log of activities and observations kept while serving as a midshipman in HMS *Jason*, a fleet minesweeper of the First Minesweeping Flotilla. Such journals were required of midshipmen in peacetime; they were periodically examined and countersigned by the commanding officer, typically once a week. The practice of requiring midshipmen to keep journals was generally suspended during World War II; however, Comdr. T. G. P. Crick, RN, commanding officer of the *Jason*, required that I observe the practice. This I did until I was promoted to sub-lieutenant and transferred from the *Jason* to HM *ML137*, of the Fifth Motor Launch Flotilla. During the whole period, I also maintained a personal diary, some of which overlapped with the content of the journal, but it included matters that would have been inappropriate for the journal, particularly for inspection by the commanding officer. Conditions during and after the Normandy invasion made it impossible to keep a daily diary, and so portions of it were written later as circumstances permitted.

In this book, I include the entries from my Midshipman's Journal and from my diary exactly as written. Overlap between the two documents has been avoided where this consisted of exact duplications. Where the material is taken directly from these documents, I have retained the British usage in which they were written. In the interest of archival authenticity, I have also retained the variations of spelling and inconsistencies of usage that they contained. The remainder of the continuous text is presented in U.S. usage, and with an intended consistency of style and format.

The documents included in this work present events as they were seen through the eyes of a young man not yet twenty-one years old. By the time that they occurred, Britain had been at war for more than three years. Manchester, my home town, had been badly damaged by German air raids, and numbers of its citizens had been killed. The early German terror raids on Warsaw, Rotterdam, and Belgrade and the continuing raids on Britain, especially on London, formed a background for our individual and national determination to defeat the enemy completely. The desperate days of 1940 and 1941 were behind us. We were no longer alone, and the power and resources of the United States were daily more evident. We in the Navy knew that the preparations for the Second Front were well advanced, and we hoped that we would take part in it.

It is perhaps unnecessary to remark that participants in actions seen at sea level do not usually have the benefit of understanding the grand plan of which their own tasks are a very small part. Rather than correct any of my own misperceptions by reference to later historical accounts, I have used such sources to describe the broad context but have left the original naiveté of my journal and diary unchanged. Rereading them now, I recognize some attitudes and opinions that the passage of time has modified. One opinion that remains unchanged is that World War II was a justified war against a terrible evil.

During the half century since D-Day, many of the people mentioned in this work have died. The survivors are no doubt scattered to many parts of the world. Out of respect for possible wishes for privacy, where I cannot locate the individuals concerned, I have changed some names or used nicknames. Some names remain unchanged, either because the presence of the individuals concerned at an action is a matter of public record, or where I wish to pay tribute to a fine shipmate.

In 1993, my wife, Winifred Barbara Maher, made a copy of my Midshipman's Journal and diary. As she did so, she reminded me of various anecdotes that I had recounted to her over the years. In addition, she questioned me carefully about the meaning of terms and concepts that might not be familiar to persons unacquainted with naval service. This material, together with a number of recollections of other events not recorded in the original journal and diary, is incorporated into this book. I have added clear explanations of naval practices and techniques, familiar to experienced mariners, that might be new to the interested general reader. Also included are some excerpts from contemporary published accounts of the naval operations in which I took part. These accounts provide a wider perspective than is possible for someone directly engaged in the actions.

That this book has been assembled, organized, and annotated is entirely due to my wife. Her perceptive questioning about the events described in the original documents, her inquiries about the meaning of terms and the otherwise cryptic sets of initials that are employed in the naval service, her elicitation of additional recollections of periods not described in the diary, and her keen eye for the relevance of other published accounts of the same events have all combined to give this work its present continuity and coherence. Completion of the manuscript was largely due to her energy and dedication. This is truly a collaborative work.

A debt of gratitude is due to my children who encouraged me, and to many friends whose enthusiasm and support were important during the writing. Particular thanks go to my brother John Maher for crucial logistic support in the checking of sources, to Jim Clark for his astute editorial comments, to John Fox, Pat Patullo, and John Roche. Thanks are due to the anonymous reviewers of previous drafts of the manuscript. Special thanks are due to Anne Collier for her calm, professional editorial advice and her steady support for the development of this work, and to Terry Belanger for her outstanding work on the task of copyediting.

Abbreviations

AA antiaircraft
AFO Admiralty Fleet Order
ARP Air Raid Precautions
A/S anti-submarine
asdic sonar (from initials of the Allied Submarine Detection Investigation Committee)
ATS Auxiliary Territorial Service
AVGO auxiliary vessel gunnery officer
BAMS British auxiliary minesweeper
BBC British Broadcasting Corporation
Bosun boatswain
BYMS British yard minesweeper
CB confidential book
CO commanding officer
CPO chief petty officer
Cox'n coxswain
CSA smoke-producing apparatus, named for the chemical used to produce the smoke

CW commission or warrant
CWO commissioned warrant officer
CWS Cooperative Wholesale Society
D/C depth charge
D/G degaussing range
DSC Distinguished Service Cross
DUKW amphibious truck (also called "Duck"); origin, U.S. Army code:
         D for year of design (1942), U for amphibious vehicle, K for
         all-wheel drive, W for dual rear axles
ENSA Entertainment National Service Association
FOIC flag officer in charge
FXLE forecastle, or fo'c'sle
HF/DF high-frequency direction finder
HM His Majesty's
HMT His Majesty's trawler
IoW Isle of Wight
kmh kilometers per hour
KR King's Regulation
KR and AI King's Regulations and Admiralty Instructions
L/A low angle
LBK landing barge kitchen
LCA landing craft assault
LCI landing craft infantry
LCT landing craft tank
LSH landing ship headquarters
LSI landing ship infantry
LSL landing ship large
LST landing ship tank
MA/STU mobile anti-submarine training unit
MGB motor gunboat
ML motor launch
MMS motor minesweeper
MRU "much regret unable" signal
M/S or MS minesweeper, minesweeping
MSF minesweeping flotilla
MTB motor torpedo boat
NAAFI Navy, Army, and Air Force Institutes
NOIC naval officer in charge
OCTU officer cadet training unit
OLQ officerlike quality

OOD officer of the day
OOW officer of the watch
O/S ordinary seaman
P&O Peninsular & Orient
P/O petty officer
PPI position-plotting indicator
RAD rear-admiral dockyard
RAF Royal Air Force
RCN Royal Canadian Navy
revs revolutions
RFA Royal Fleet Auxiliary
RN Royal Navy
RNAH Royal Naval auxiliary hospital
RNAS Royal Naval air station
RNB Royal Naval barracks
RNR Royal Naval Reserve
RNVR Royal Naval Volunteer Reserve
RPC "request the pleasure of your company" signal
RPO regulating petty officer
S/O senior officer (i.e., ship in flotilla commanded by the most senior officer)
WAAF Women's Auxiliary Air Force
WMP "with much pleasure" signal
W/O warrant officer
Wren member of WRNS
WRNS Women's Royal Naval Service
YMS yard minesweeper

A PASSAGE TO SWORD BEACH

Prologue: The First Clouds

It is a foolish thing to make a long prologue, and to be short in the story itself.—THE SECOND BOOK OF THE MACCABEES

The Basque children brought us the first faint stirrings of apprehension about the possibility that there was going to be a war. They had come to Manchester, England, in 1937 as refugees from the Spanish Civil War and were housed in Saint Joseph's Home, a rather austere convent orphanage attached to my father's school. He had invited three of them to spend Sunday with us. They had little English, but responded with vivid gestures whenever they understood our questions. We played in the back garden of our house—throwing a ball, leapfrogging, and other such things. Somebody asked about air raids. The playing stopped. The oldest of the three raised his hands to the sky and moved them up and down vigorously, while he turned in a slow circle as if to say, "The bombs came down all the time and all around." He finished abruptly. Then he drew his finger slowly across his throat. Nobody seemed to want to resume our games, so we went indoors and waited for Sunday tea. When the scones and crumpets were eaten and the iced cake reduced to crumbs, our guests left to return to the convent. We did not see them again.

My father, Thomas Francis Maher, was the headmaster of a Catholic elementary school, St. Gilbert's, in the town of Eccles, an industrial suburb of Manchester. He was born in Clonmel in County Tipperary in Ireland and had married my mother, Agnes Power, who was a school-teacher from Carrick-on-Suir in the same county. I was the third of five children, all boys, of whom two had died in infancy. My older brother, John Desmond, was always called "Des" by the family, but he preferred his first name and became John when he entered the Royal Navy during the war. I have followed his preference in this narrative, except when quoting from documents where the family's habit prevailed. My younger brother, Ciaran Patrick, was known as "Kerry." John and I were students at De La Salle College in the town of Salford nearby, while Kerry attended St. Gilbert's.

Although my parents' choice of Irish names for all of their children reflected a core of national pride, we boys all felt ourselves to be English. We had been born in the town of Widnes in Lancashire and knew little about Ireland and even less about Irish history. What little we did know about our family history was that one uncle, my father's brother John, had been killed near Loos in 1916 while serving in Leinster Regiment and that another uncle, my mother's brother Arnold, had served in the British Merchant Navy in the same war.

For most of our childhood, we had grown up with the notion that major wars were things of the past. The Great War, as World War I was then called, had been surely the apocalyptic termination of modern war. Men of our neighborhood drew part of their identity from what they had done in that war, and the more so because they had taken part in what most believed to be the historic closing chapter of a kind of catastrophic human folly that would never be repeated. At least, that was how the grown-ups spoke of it. Initially, few people expressed concern about Italian or German fascism; fewer still seemed to perceive the omens that were beginning to appear. The Spanish Civil War gradually began to disturb complacency about the future. In the North of England, popular sympathy generally lay with the Spanish government, and there was some unease at the possible emergence of a third dictator on the European continent. The intrusion of German and Italian fascists on the side of the fascist rebel General Francisco Franco, made possible by the nonintervention policies of Britain and France, added to the feelings of unease. Nevertheless, these problems seemed remote from the quiet of British life and much less pressing than the continuing problems of the Great Depression.

By March 1938, matters had changed considerably. The bargain struck at Munich between Neville Chamberlain and Adolf Hitler was to be the hinge of history. German expansionist ambition seemed to know no limit. The next German demand would lead to war; the only question was when it would begin. Preparations began with the formation of the civil defense service, known as the Air Raid Precautions (ARP). The tacit expectation was that when war broke out there would be massive air raids almost immediately and that, quite likely, poison gas would be used. Air raid sirens were installed, volunteers recruited for the fire service, and provision made for a special constabulary and all of the other needs that would arise when the bombs began to drop. A volunteer, going from house to house, measured us all for gas masks. Each person tried one on for size, the volunteer made notations, and a few days later delivered the masks. The masks came in individual cardboard boxes; each box had a cord to hang the box around the neck. Pamphlets came that instructed the householder on how to install blackout curtains over the windows and how to crisscross the windowpanes with tape to minimize the risks from flying glass should bombs explode nearby. All of this was both alarming and yet seemed quite unreal. Fortunately, the gas masks were never required, but the blackout became a permanent feature of the war years.

My mother, to our mild surprise, decided to volunteer as an ambulance driver. She had had the rare experience of going through air raids during World War I. At that time, she was a student at a convent boarding school near the East Coast city of Hull in Yorkshire. Zeppelins, bombing by night, had raided the area several times. When a raid began, the nuns roused the girls from the dormitory and led them, muffled in overcoats against the cold, to the shelter of the deep ditches that lay along both sides of a nearby main road. There they huddled and shivered until the raid was over. My mother spoke of all this in matter-of-fact tones and once described the flaming fall and crash of a Zeppelin that had been hit by flak, vivid and flaring against the night sky.

Her training as an ambulance driver took place on weekends. As there were no ambulances available, the trainee drivers practiced driving large heavy-duty garbage trucks around the area on Sundays. One of our neighbors came by to inquire discreetly about this, having formed the opinion that my mother must be training to be a garbage driver, perhaps because of some financial stringency. He was visibly relieved when he discovered that his offer of help was unnecessary. She drove her ambulance during most of the major bombing raids on Manchester. In one of these raids, she and her codriver were blown out of the ambulance cab by the blast of a nearby bomb. Both got back in and carried on with their work. We learned of this incident only when her driving partner later described it.

Matters were calmer as 1938 gave way to 1939. International tensions seemed to diminish. At school, we were mostly preoccupied with the feared Matriculation examination, the results of which would determine our future prospects for admission to a university. The summer came, the results were published, and all was well. Time had come to relax, and the family went for a few weeks to the Isle of Anglesey, off the coast of North Wales.

One day, while picnicking on a grassy headland, we noticed a gradual gathering of ships in Liverpool Bay at a position not far to the north of our vantage point. Some emergency was taking place there, but we could not see any sign of a vessel in distress. Later the same evening, the BBC news reported that a new submarine, HMS *Thetis*, had sunk during her sea trials. Desperate efforts were in progress to rescue the crew and civilian engineers trapped inside. Unhappily, the efforts failed. The German Navy sent a message of sympathy and a wreath for the funeral service held for the ninety-nine men who had been lost. Simplemindedly, I was reassured. How could we worry about a war with a potential enemy who offered such gestures of sympathy? As for the *Thetis* herself, she was raised soon afterward, refitted, and renamed *Thunderbolt*. In this incarnation, she was credited with sinking an Italian destroyer in 1940. Later, in 1943, she was reported overdue and presumed lost in the Mediterranean.

As the summer wore on, German demands on Poland escalated. The storm began to gather. The news that Germany and the Soviet Union had signed a mutual nonaggression pact came as a sickening shock. The die had now been cast; this time there would be no negotiation. If Hitler marched, there would be war. Ultimatums were delivered and received, and although nothing was certain until deadlines passed, there was no optimism or doubt in anybody's mind.

On 1 September 1939, two days before the declaration of war itself, instructions came for my schoolfellows and me to gather at school to be evacuated from the city of Manchester to an area thought less likely to be bombed in the opening days of the coming war. My father's school was not included in the evacuation plan because it was judged to be sufficiently distant from the city to escape major bombing. As a safety precaution, my parents had sent Kerry to stay with our grandmother in Ireland. John had already graduated from De La Salle and was working near Manchester.

Each child to be evacuated had been instructed to bring a brown paper bag containing an apple, an orange, a banana, a bar of chocolate, and a can of corned beef. These were to be given to the hosts, in whose homes we were to be billeted, to tide us over until billeting arrangements were completed and ration coupons supplied. With our gas masks in their cardboard containers slung around our necks by a piece of cord, we went to the station. Only when we boarded the train did we learn that we were to go to Accrington, a mill town on the edge of the Lancashire moors.

In Accrington, buses were waiting at the station to distribute us to our assigned billets throughout the town. Clipboard in hand, our accompanying billeting officer hung onto the platform handbars of the bus as it swayed its way up and down the narrow streets. From time to time, he stopped the bus and beckoned one or two boys to follow him to a selected house, there to be deposited as uninvited guests. One of my classmates, being rather taller than the rest of us, was rejected by the first householder with the peevish remark: "He's too big. We'd rather have a smaller one. You'll have to take him back to the bus." He came back to the bus, shamefaced at this summary rejection. He looked much like a dog that had been returned to a pet store because of some defect.

Eventually, all of us were placed. We handed the bags of rations to our hosts and tried to adjust to this strange turn of events. Two days later, the war started and nothing ever would be quite the same again.

Evacuation of schools had seemed like a good idea. Air raids were expected momentarily. Gas masks were waiting, blackout curtains were already in place in most homes, and trellises of tape crisscrossed the windows of every house. Barrage balloons, floating like jelly-boned elephants at the end of their cables, began to appear over the cities. Surely, it would be only a matter of days, or perhaps even hours, before the raids began.

In fact, none of this was yet to happen. We went to Accrington Grammar School in the mornings by sharing the use of the building with its normal occupants, who took their turns in the afternoons. Having the afternoons free, we wandered on the edge of the moors or through the town. Once, we went to the movies to see *Hell's Angels*. Perhaps the sight of dogfighting biplanes looping and diving over Flanders was thought to be in keeping with the general wartime mood that was developing.

My classmates and I had passed the Northern Universities Matriculation examination in the spring of 1939, and we anticipated that the school year would be one in which the tensions generated by the pressures of the ominous examination would give way to a more relaxed attitude. The excitement of the war added to our impatience with studies; being in school at all seemed to be a pale alternative to experiencing what was happening in the real world outside. Our studies were spasmodic, we were away from home, and the looming landscape of dark mills and the russet ambience of the autumn moors held a hint of foreboding and adventure that fitted our mood.

As for the war itself, little seemed to be happening. The Royal Air Force (RAF) dropped leaflets over Germany, while the British troops in France waited, perhaps secure in the belief that the Maginot Line, the trench to end all trenches, would protect against any sudden incursions by the enemy. Entertainers on the radio sang, "We're Going to Hang Out the Washing on the Siegfried Line" and "Run, Rabbit, Run." Posters by Fougasse appeared to warn against spies—"Be like Dad. Keep Mum." In short, we saw all of the signs of a country at war, without actual warfare.

Only from the sea came reports of action. October brought the loss of the battleship *Royal Oak*, sunk with the loss of many of the ship's company while at anchor at Scapa Flow, Scotland, during a bold attack by a German U-boat. The national dismay caused by this was offset by the defeat of the German pocket battleship *Graf Spee* in December at the Battle of the River Plate in Uruguay. Submarine warfare was being waged in the Atlantic, but details were sparse.

But all of these events were far away, having reality only in the nightly news broadcasts of the BBC. Closer to home, the school arrangements were not working very well; the presence of billeted strangers was a strain in many homes. One by one, parents began to reclaim their children. Evacuation came to an end, and we returned home to Manchester and our own school in early 1940.

Once back, we settled down to studies in preparation for the next examination hurdle—the Higher School Certificate. Our sense of stability and routine was gone, however, and the war news became increasingly threatening. There were still no air raids, but, as the school year came to an end in the spring of 1940, the naval battles in the fjords of Norway were followed by the blitzkrieg. The rapid German advance through the Low Countries, the ruthlessness of the attacks on civilian populations, and the total futility of the Maginot Line defense came as a succession of shocks. During the first days of the blitzkrieg, it was not uncommon to hear the old soldiers of World War I speculating cheerfully that the whole withdrawal was a ruse designed to draw the Germans into some clever trap. The evacuation of Dunkirk put an end to all that. It told us that the war had now begun in earnest and that we faced great dangers. Conscription speeded up. Our older schools friends, not long gone from the sixth form, began to reappear as occasional visitors, uniformed and waiting to go into action at a time and place yet unknown. If there had been any delusion that the war was going to be brief and that victory was certain, it now disappeared. It was going to be a long haul, and we might even be defeated—an outcome that was obviously possible but was defiantly dismissed by the majority of the population.

There was, in fact, a rather extraordinary mood of relief—almost an atmosphere of exaltation. Somehow, it was as if being required to stand alone against Germany had brought the realities of our circumstances into sharper focus, and determination had replaced doubts and ambiguities. Prime Minister Winston Churchill was the voice of the country when he spoke of fighting on the beaches and in the cities until victory came. Matters had come to the sticking point. Plans for postwar careers were now irrelevant. Staying on at school seemed impossibly pointless, and so, not yet sixteen, I left school at the close of the school year in June 1940 to take a position as junior clerk at the Manchester office of the Legal and General Assurance Society.

The Legal and General Assurance Society was, and still is, an insurance company headquartered in London, with branches all over the country. The Manchester office was at 38 John Dalton Street in the middle of the city. I replaced a predecessor who had been called into the RAF. For the next two and one-half years, I remained in this job and learned the elements of insurance law, actuarial tables, account-keeping, and so forth. When I began my clerkship, the war in France was still something that existed only in the newspapers and the BBC broadcasts; as the summer lengthened into autumn and the Battle of Britain was fought in the skies of the southern counties, we knew that it would not take long to reach our own streets.

Preparations were made. In some parts of the country, signposts were removed or obliterated to prevent enemy parachutists from finding their way. All of the Legal and General office staff, male and female, were sent for a day to a Civil Defense center to be trained as "firewatchers"—a duty that involved learning how to extinguish an incendiary bomb by crawling toward it with a heat-proof shield and spraying it with water pumped by hand from a bucket.

A schedule of office fire-watching duties was arranged. In the manager's office—the only one with any degree of privacy—camp beds were installed. A retired military pensioner, Sergeant Tudor, was hired for permanent duty, and two staff members joined him each night. For this duty, each staff member was paid a small cash allowance. When the air raid siren sounded, the firewatchers hurried up to the rooftop and waited, bucket and pump at the ready, for incendiary bombs to fall.

Manchester was to suffer through several major air raids, notably during the days of Christmas in 1940 and then periodically afterward. Among its other effects, the first major raid on the city paralyzed most of the public transportation system. I walked the five miles into work, along streets filled with rubble and fires still raging throughout the ruined buildings. At one point, a bomb had broken the gas main under the street and flames flared from the center of the crater. People on the way to work walked in a long file winding its way around the craters and piles of rubble. Most of these people were dressed as always, some with brief cases and black bowler hats, as if the surroundings were a nuisance but not much more. Already, some shops displayed handwritten signs defiantly declaring "Business as usual." Buildings on either side of our office were hit by bombs, but the Legal and General somehow survived. The only damage was done by the fire brigade when it had to smash the large plate glass front window to get at the building next door that was ablaze.

As the air raids on Manchester intensified through 1941 and 1942, the decision was made to move much of the office staff and operations into the suburbs. The company leased a large house in Altrincham, Cheshire, about thirty minutes by train from central Manchester, and we moved there. The John Dalton Street office remained open with a minimal staff as a convenience for customers making claims, paying premiums, and transacting other business. We continued our fire-watching routine there, and I spent memorable nights on the rooftop, as I watched searchlight beams sweeping across the night sky and listened to the roar of bomb explosions and the flat banging of the antiaircraft barrage. The original office was still in place in 1992, although the Legal and General had moved to larger quarters in the city.

At the Legal and General, I had become good friends with two other young men of my age. We shared fire-watching duty together from time to time and generally engaged in office larks that centered on being subtly impertinent to our elders and betters. In due course, we reached the age at which military service was imminent. One of my friends, Ted Russell, joined the RAF and served as a navigator in bombers; the other, Sidney Walton, entered the Royal Navy in the Fleet Air Arm. I did not see Ted again until after the war, but I did have a brief meeting with Sidney in Portsmouth in early 1944.

The young men entering the various services were informally "adopted" by women staff members, who sent occasional packages with cake and knitted gloves and balaclava helmets. One of these was Peggy Banks, a young woman whose brother Jimmy was a signalman in the minesweeper *Fraserburgh*. He and I met once in the Navy during a rehearsal for D-Day. The Banks family was very hospitable, and I spent several pleasant evenings with them when on leave.

Rationing led to the development of various schemes designed to increase the supply of food. Citizens were urged to "dig for victory" by planting vegetable gardens. Every patch was cultivated, even the grassy slopes of railroad embankments. Whale meat made its first appearance in the meat ration. One plausible source of meat was the rabbit; the Ministry of Food created local rabbit clubs so that groups of people raising rabbits were eligible for an allowance of rabbit fodder. There was also a small ration of gasoline for the club organizer to collect the bags of fodder from the warehouse and deliver them to the individual members.

By a process still unclear to me, my mother became the organizer and chair of a rabbit club. She held meetings in our dining room at which minutes were read and votes taken, and I once heard the treasurer announce a balance of threepence-halfpenny in the bank. We acquired two or three rabbits for breeding. They were quite pretty creatures—Dutch rabbits with black-and-white coats and one, an English rabbit, white-coated with a line of dark spots setting off its beauty in geometric fashion. With fatal results for our anticipated diet of rabbit meat, the rabbits were given names. I cannot recall these names but have a dim remembrance that they were the names of famous racehorses. The naming of the rabbits was their salvation. I accompanied my mother as she drove to the warehouse to pick up the supply of rabbit fodder and deliver it door to door to club members. Occasionally, she delivered one of the offspring of the rabbit-racehorses to a buyer, but my memory is quite clear that we never had rabbit meat on our table.

By autumn of 1942 and the approach of my eighteenth birthday, I decided that the time had come to volunteer to join the Navy. Ships and the sea had fascinated me from a very early age. During summer vacations, we had often visited Ireland to spend time with my maternal grandmother, Mary Power, in her home, Three Bridges House, near Carrick-on-Suir. We took passage in one of the freighters of the Clyde Shipping Company—the steamers *Rockabill*, *Tuskar Rock*, or *Skerries*. The freighters carried mixed cargoes between Liverpool and Waterford—machinery and manufactured goods of all kinds to Ireland, and cattle, agricultural products, and the like to England. Under Board of Trade regulations, the ships could carry no more than twelve passengers. We slept in double cabins and dined with the master and mates in the shared dining saloon. Once clear of the River Mersey and past the Crosby Lightship, the master of the *Rockabill*, Captain Roberts, invited my brother John and me to come on the bridge and watch the work of the watchkeeping officer and the quarter-master at the wheel. Once, a thrill to remember, when the ship was well out to sea, I was allowed to take the wheel for a few minutes, with strict instructions not to turn it one way or the other.

My boyhood reading had included a major ration of nautical adventure stories. The works of Captain Marryat, Stevenson, and others formed images of a life of adventure, at once compelling and impossibly remote. I read and re-read *The Three Midshipmen, The Three Lieutenants, Mr. Midshipman Easy, Treasure Island, Kidnapped*—anything that spoke of rigging and anchors, the reek of tar and rope, of strange coastlines seen from the sea, palm fronds floating on tropical waters, the creaking of blocks and spars, the sight of distant and mysterious sails, the long stern chase, and the boom of cannon. To me, even the sea scenes in *Tom and the Water-Babies* hinted of the myths and mystery of the ocean.

We were not a traditionally nautical family, although there were links. My older brother John had already joined the Navy as a supply assistant. He was ultimately promoted through the petty officer ranks to the rank of paymaster sub-lieutenant. An American cousin, John O'Toole, was already in the U.S. Navy and serving in an observation blimp patrolling the East Coast for U-boats. Uncle Arnold, my mother's brother, who had served as a radio officer for the Marconi Company in the British Merchant Navy during World War I, had survived two sinkings by torpedo. One of these had happened while he was serving in a hospital ship in the Gallipoli campaign. The survivors were rescued from their lifeboats after two or three days in the open—long enough for Arnold to draw a pencil sketch of the sinking ship. He kept the sketch in a diary that he maintained. I have since wondered whether early recollections of that diary, which was given to my mother, influenced my own decision to keep a written record of my naval service.

In Albert Square, not far from the offices of the Legal and General, lay the recruiting office of the Royal Navy. From time to time, a lunchtime stroll or other small errand brought me past its windows. Peacetime posters, now fading, were still in the windows. One poster portrayed sailors, in crisp white uniforms, smiling and relaxed but ready for anything. Beyond the immaculate decks of their ship rose a background of

Malta, where terraced villas climbed the hill behind the harbor. On another poster, a biplane came to a perfect three-point landing on an aircraft carrier. In yet another, still-smiling seamen sat down to dinner, served apparently by white-aproned cooks. This was the life, said the posters.

For all of these reasons, it seemed inconceivable to me that anybody would want to serve in any service other than the Navy. At the age of eighteen, military service would be compulsory. As my own time to serve approached, the decision was obvious: join the Navy.

1

Becoming a Sailor

I am the gate toward the sea: O sailor men, pass out
   from me
I hear you high on Lebanon, singing the marvels of
   the sea
The dragon-green, the luminous, the dark, the
   serpent-haunted sea
The snow-besprinkled wine of earth, the white-and-
   blue-flower foaming sea

—JAMES ELROY FLECKER, "GATES OF DAMASCUS"

My entry into the Navy was not entirely smooth. I first went to the Royal
Naval recruiting office in Manchester to volunteer in September 1942,
shortly before my eighteenth birthday. After taking various written tests,
I was briefly interviewed by a petty officer, who then informed that I
could not be accepted because I stuttered. He went on to explain that
clear speech was a crucial requirement. He reminded me that, when the
communications system of the cruiser *Exeter* had been put out of action
at the Battle of the River Plate, the gunnery commands had to be given
by a relay of crew members repeating them by voice. The *Exeter*, with the
cruisers *Achilles* and *Ajax*, had been responsible for the defeat and destruction of the German pocket battleship *Graf Spee* in December 1939.

I went home, but I was determined that I would get into the Navy
somehow. I hid my disappointment and embarrassment by telling people
simply that I was to go back for a second interview. After waiting a few
weeks, with the hope that the rotation of staff in the recruiting office
would keep me from meeting up with the same petty officer again, I went
back. I knew what to expect and had practiced my answers until I had
gained better control over my speech. This time, the testing and inter-

view went off smoothly. My test results and education led them to classify me as a potential officer cadet. To confirm the classification, it was now necessary for me to go through a much more detailed set of tests, physical examinations, and interviews at a naval center in Crewe, Cheshire. Crewe had absolutely no connection with the sea and was best known as a major railway junction; it must have been chosen by the Admiralty because it was easy to get there from almost anywhere.

In due course, I was summoned to Crewe. For some reason—now incomprehensible to me—I believed that I wanted to be a naval pilot in the Fleet Air Arm. Quite apprehensive about the possibility that stuttering would catch up with me again, I went through another interview, more tests, and a complex physical examination. At the end of this examination, I was told that my blood pressure was not quite at the standard the Navy required for pilots and I might go into "blackouts" in a diving plane. The problem was marginal, and they wanted me to come back in two months for a repeat of the physical. This I did, on 18 December 1942. The result was essentially the same: they informed me that I was in good shape for service as a seaman branch officer but not for flying. That was the end of my brief flirtation with flying. I was officially enlisted into the Navy as of that date and classified as a volunteer and member of the officer candidate program (known as the "Y" scheme). After getting one day's pay for my "service" at Crewe, I went home and waited for orders. The entry on my service certificate reads, "Volunteered for the period 'Until the end of the present emergency.'" Until I was called into the service, I continued to work at the Legal and General.

HMS Raleigh

I was ordered to report on 10 February 1943 to HMS Raleigh, a training base in Devon, located near the village of Torpoint, three or four miles west of Plymouth. HMS Raleigh, as were most naval bases, was known as a "stone frigate"—a naval shore base given a ship's name preceded by the initials HMS (His Majesty's Ship). This dates back to the time when ratings (a term equivalent to the U.S. term, enlisted persons), before being sent to a seagoing ship, were housed in dismasted hulks that served as barracks in port. During the course of my naval career, I was attached at one time or another to various stone frigates (see list of stone frigates in Appendix B).

My rank was O/S (ordinary seaman). On the evening of 9 February, I left Manchester on the midnight train to Plymouth. Wally Eaton, one of the older salesmen from the Legal and General, was waiting to see me off at London Road station. Wally had served as an artillery captain in the campaign in Mesopotamia during World War I. Although he had the partial deafness that afflicted many artillerymen, he had an enduring loyalty to the service. Wally made a practice of taking out for a drink each young man in the Legal and General who was leaving for the war. I had the impression that there was an element of nostalgia in this, a kind of looking back at his own departure so many years ago.

The train was packed with men my age. Dim lights lit the interior of the darkened carriage; cigarette smoke swirled slowly in their faint beams. Some of my fellow travelers were laughing and talking boisterously; others sat quietly and perhaps apprehensively as we clicketty-clacked along the rails to Plymouth and the Navy.

When we arrived, we were met by a rating and assembled to await a truck to take us to Raleigh. As we waited in the station parking area, a group of sailors going on leave from a ship in the dockyard saw us and began to cheer and chant, "You'll be sorry, mate," and "Why don't you go back home now before you're really in the Andrew?" (The Navy was often referred to colloquially as "the Andrew." The origin of this term is not clear, although the common story is that an eighteenth-century press-gang officer, Lieutenant Andrew, had pressed so many men into involuntary service that he had created the Navy all by himself.) Our truck arrived at that point, and away we went.

My messmates in Raleigh were largely from Glasgow, plus a few from Lancashire and the Midlands. Soon after arrival, we went through an intake procedure and were issued a kit bag, a small fiberboard attaché case, two blue uniforms (each consisting of bell-bottom trousers, jumper, black silk scarf, and a separate broad denim collar edged with three white tapes), two pairs of black ankle boots, an oilskin coat, a blue greatcoat, a blue raincoat, two dungaree suits, a hammock stamped with the owner's name, one blanket, a "housewife" (a small sewing kit), a block of thick yellow soap, and woolen underwear that looked and felt as if it had been woven out of hairy oatmeal. The kit bag and hammock were carried by the sailor whenever he was transferred from one place or ship to another. The uniform of bell-bottom trousers and jumper was colloquially known as a "square rig," in contrast with the "fore-and-aft rig" of collar and tie, visored cap, and normal trousers worn by petty officers, writers, and others. Some effort was spent on instructing the new recruit in the proper manner of folding the uniform. Bell-bottomed trousers were to be turned inside out and then folded in concertina fashion into seven horizontal folds. Once compressed in this way, the trousers were to be tied into a roll with two short strings ("stops"). Aspects of the sailor's uniform were explained in traditional, but probably apocryphal, terms: three tapes on the collar for three victories of Nelson (Trafalgar, Copenhagen, and the Nile), seven folds of the trousers for the Seven Seas, the black scarf in the mourning for the death of Nelson, and so on.

We slept on metal-frame bunks in a wooden hut, warmed unreliably by a potbellied stove. Raleigh consisted of many rows of these huts; a parade ground; a ship's mast with signal yardarm and ratline ladders (with a safety net underneath to catch those who fell off in the compulsory mast-climbing exercise); and buildings that contained, among other things, classrooms, a huge mess hall, two chapels, and a sick bay.

During the time at Raleigh, I completed basic training, which included rowing, seamanship, knot tying, riflery, lifesaving, signaling, gunnery—all at a fairly elementary level. Those individuals unable to complete the basic training satisfactorily were discharged as unfit to perform naval duty and returned home.

I was appointed class leader—an inevitable consequence of being the only potential officer candidate in the hut. With this came the privileges of wearing an armband with a crown and anchor on it and of appointing a deputy leader. Careful inspection of the musculature, manners, and language of my messmates convinced me that it would be wise to pick the biggest and strongest looking, thereby putting him on my side, so to speak, in the difficult task of keeping order in a group of tough Glaswegians. Gordon Sutherland proved to be the right choice, and things went smoothly thereafter.

We were taught rowing in a naval cutter firmly embedded in a large sand-filled base. We sat in this as we dragged oars through the sand and pretended that we were on the water. After several of these experiences, we were finally taken to Plymouth harbor, where we repeated the exercise in real water and had the fun of seeing the boat actually move forward.

Once a week, we assembled on the parade ground, in our best (No. 1) uniforms, to be inspected. A great deal of maneuvering took place, with a close inspection of uniforms by an officer, and much marching and countermarching. All of this was done with music provided by an accompanying band. The repertoire was heavily World War I, so we wheeled, advanced, turned about, saluted "eyes right," slow-marched, and then quick-marched to "There's a Long, Long, Trail A-Winding," "Keep the Home Fires Burning," and (with particular inappropriateness) "Where Are the Boys of the Old Brigade?" These rather lugubrious musical accompaniments were enlivened from time to time with "Hearts of Oak," "A Life on the Ocean Wave," and other more nautical pieces. Once, there was a Strauss waltz.

An Ulster gunner's mate taught us rifle drill. We were learning the salute, "Present arms," a maneuver at the end of which one should be holding the rifle vertically, absolutely upright, in front of chest and face. Contemptuous of the tentative way we went about this, our instructor sneered in his aggrieved Belfast tones, "Stop holdin' the roifle like a sprig o' parssley! Grarsp it firmly by the lower baand."

Being a new recruit in the Navy was seen by each of us as something of a problem, one to be concealed as much as possible. Concealment was largely sought by trying to "age" the official uniform. The dark blue denim collar would gradually fade to pale blue after months of wear and washing. Hence, much effort was spent applying the yellow soap to one of the collars in an effort to make it fade quickly. Army and Navy stores in Plymouth sold "prefaded" collars, as well as other stylish (and prohibited) variations of the uniform. Favorite items were jumpers with the V-front opening down nearly to the navel, black scarf ribbons that dangled well below the waist, and trousers with unusually large bell-bottoms. All of these were "illegal" and could not be worn on the base, but we squirreled them away for wear ashore. On the first home leave, it would be possible, perhaps, to impress the neighbors with the trappings of an old sea dog.

Our immediate supervisor, teacher, and general sea-daddy was Petty Officer O'Shea. He had served in the regular Navy, retired to his home in Cork, and returned to serve again when the war broke out. He was a decent man, well versed in the ways of the Navy, including how to get around the more inconvenient rules and customs. At the end of training, we were to be examined on our knowledge of knots, gunnery, and all of the things that we had supposedly learned. One day Petty Officer O'Shea explained to me that there was to be a new kind of examination in which "they give you the question, and several answers, and you have to pick the right one." This was meaningless to me; I had never seen a multiple-choice examination. However, Petty Officer O'Shea had somehow come into possession of the examination questions (although not the answers) and he communicated them to me, with the instruction to pass them on to my messmates. Presumably, our resultant stunning performance would reflect well on all of us, including him.

Examination passing was not a dominant concern for many of my messmates, and the information was of little interest to them. When the time came to take the examination, the items proved to be so simple that the whole preparatory enterprise appeared rather pointless. I can remember the first question, which read "The hollow inside the lead in a lead line is filled with (a) bacon fat; (b) tallow; (c) sand; and (d) nothing" and so on. Given that (a), (c), and (d) were so obviously absurd, it was no great feat to choose tallow. The class did quite well, which I took to be testimonial to the simplemindedness of the test, rather than any great ability on our part. The powers that be were suspicious about it all, however, and spent some time interrogating us one by one. Petty Officer O'Shea was a little tense about this but nothing came of it, and they continued to use the test.

One of the pieces of information that we had to learn was the recognition of ranks and badges. To this end, O'Shea produced a stack of armbands made of canvas painted black, with stripes of various ranks and badges of rating painted on them. A number of men were called out from the group and told to put these on. Then, O'Shea called on one of us and said: "Go to the lieutenant commander and salute," "Report to the chief bosun's Mate,"[1] and so on. It was very reminiscent of the way a dog is trained to "fetch" the newspaper or to lie down. After some initial confusion, in which an "Admiral" was mistaken for a "Chaplain" (a mistake that would never be made in real life by any seaman of even the meanest intelligence), we learned what was required, together with the approved manner of address.

During this period, I received a parcel from my mother's sister, Sister Mary Xavier (Sister "Mary Save-me," as we had called her at home). It contained a collection of rosary beads, crucifixes, medals, and other items designed to protect me from the dangers ahead and with enough spares to equip the rest of my hut-mates, if I had wished to do so. I managed to conceal them successfully, but I was called in by the Catholic chaplain and asked to assist as an acolyte at Mass—something that I had never done in my life and did not know how to do. I explained this, and he reluctantly agreed to find somebody else, but he added that he would expect to see me at Mass and that he had received a letter expressing the special interest of Sister Mary Save-me in my spiritual welfare.

So, the next Sunday I went to Mass. By special dispensation, Catholics were permitted to eat breakfast at a second sitting after Mass and after the others had all eaten. It was a small congregation, maybe ten people.

1. Bosun: boatswain, a warrant officer in the seaman branch, usually found only on large ships.

When we got to the dining hall later, we found that the catering was always done on the assumption of a much larger attendance—hence we had, for once, unlimited bacon and eggs. I happened to mention this when I returned to my hut. The news had an immediate impact. Next Sunday and thereafter, the little chapel was overflowing with bacon-and-egg Catholics. The chaplain was happy.

Although there was no home leave during basic training, we did have occasional liberty to leave Raleigh. Nautical terminology was used wherever possible; to go into Plymouth was to "go ashore." Contrary to legendary expectations of wild times in port, the possibilities in Plymouth were quite modest. The cinema and the pub comprised the spectrum of entertainment that lay within our means; there were no bright lights in the blacked-out city, and the necessity of getting back to Raleigh in time precluded any disreputable adventures. Some of my Glasgow messmates had discovered a church mission, in which a combination of meat pie, tea, and hymn singing was provided free but the components were not available separately. After allowing enough time afterward for a short visit to the pub, they returned to the hut—singing cheerily and beerily, "Jesus wants me for a sunbeam, O what a sunbeam I will be."

At the end of the training, we were given a few days of leave. With our little brown attaché cases, kit bags, and hammocks, we assembled at the station to take trains home. Once in a train, the prefaded collars and other illegal uniform items came out of hiding; the new sea dogs were ready to begin life as "real" sailors—or at least try to convince their friends and families that they were.

Only once did I meet one of my Raleigh messmates after leaving there. This was in Harwich, many months later. We met by chance on the street and exchanged a few words. He told me that two of our former messmates had been lost at sea, but he knew nothing of the others.

On 20 April, I was assigned to the Royal Naval Barracks (RNB), Devonport, the main naval barracks of Plymouth, also known as HMS Drake. My time there was basically idling, waiting for a posting to a ship, and I was occupied by morning parades, working parties to load things, and generally "make work." Here, we slept in Nissen huts and were wakened each morning by a bugler who did not know how to play the bugle. He had solved the problem by putting a bellows into the mouthpiece of a bugle, from which he pumped a hideous sequence of blasts as he walked up and down between the bunk beds.

HMS *Cardiff*

I left Drake on May 4 by train to Glasgow to join HMS *Cardiff*, a C-class light cruiser. Built in December 1917, the *Cardiff* was more than twenty-five years old when I joined her. She displaced 4,190 tons, was 425 feet long, 43 feet in the beam, and armed with five 6-inch and two 3-inch guns, plus 20-mm Oerlikon rapid-fire machine guns and 40-mm Bofors antiaircraft guns. She had served in the 6th Light Cruiser Squadron during World War I and had participated in actions off Heligoland, Germany, and a major raid in the Kattegat Strait. Her wartime service culminated with the honor of leading the German Grand Fleet into Scapa Flow after the German surrender in 1918. In accordance with the terms of the Armistice, the Germans had agreed to turn over their fleet to the British. Once their ships anchored in Scapa Flow, however, the Germans scuttled them. The smaller ships were completed submerged, but some of the larger ones turned turtle and remained half-submerged during the subsequent years. One or two of them still could be seen in Scapa when I arrived there in the *Jason* in 1944—on the upturned hulls were the huts of workmen still engaged in salvaging the metal. In 1921, the *Cardiff* received as a passenger the abdicated Austro-Hungarian Emperor Karl following his surrender to Senior Naval Officer (Danube) in HMS *Glowworm*.

During World War II, the *Cardiff* had taken part in a bombardment of Cherbourg, France, in 1940 and later had been assigned to duty as a gunnery training ship in the Firth of Clyde in Scotland. Each week, a group of gunnery specialists, officers and men, arrived from various naval bases to shoot at towed targets at sea. As the specialists were employed in the skilled tasks of laying and training the guns, seamen of the *Cardiff*'s crew performed the unskilled and more laborious tasks of loading ammunition from the magazine into the hoists that lifted the explosive charges and shells up to the guns and the manhandling of these into the guns.

I served in the *Cardiff* until 5 July 1943. My duties were the traditional deck duties of an ordinary seaman—cleaning, scraping, painting, swabbing decks, loading shells and explosives from the ammunition barges into the magazines, performing lookout duties, serving as a member of the crew of a 6-inch gun, and doing galley chores. I was one of a group of eighteen potential officer candidates, officially known as CW (commission or warrant) candidates (i.e., ratings who had been selected for likely admission to the officer training establishment). The group had been sent to the *Cardiff* at the same time; in the ship, we were under the direct supervision of a petty officer, who was our instructor. We were treated somewhat differently from the rest of the crew. When other ratings were given liberty, we spent the time learning elements of small-boat sailing in the whalers that were carried by the *Cardiff* and became familiarized with the engine room, signaling, and other skills. In flag signaling, we learned the use of code flags, semaphore, and Morse code. Groups of code flags are hoisted in a vertical sequence up to the yardarm. Semaphore is a form of manual signaling—the signalman takes a highly visible position on top of some part of the ship's superstructure and holds a red-and-yellow flag on a stick in each hand. Various positions of the flags made by movements of the arms indicate letters of the alphabet. Morse code was signaled with controlled flashes of a signal lantern. We spent many hours of practice at this on board ship and do would do many more when we went to King Alfred.

When circumstances permitted, the bosun's mate piped the order "Hands to make and mend clothing"; the wording of the order dated back to the days of sail when ratings were provided with material with which they had to make their own clothing. By this time, the order indicated that all of the crew except the duty watch were excused from normal ship's work and could catch up with personal chores, writing letters, repairing their clothing if necessary—or napping. CW candidates rarely had the opportunity to do any of these things, as we were assigned to training of one kind or another during "make and mend" periods.

Once, to our collective astonishment, came the pipe "Hands to dance and skylark." This was a traditional order for hands to take a break for spontaneous exercise. In the days of sail, seamen actually danced, usually to the music of a fiddle. Dancing long had been regarded as a good form of exercise, a practical one in the confined spaces of a ship. Long weeks at sea called for exercise breaks such as these. In the *Cardiff*, we did not dance nor did I see much skylarking, but the order did give us a chance to walk the decks without the usual necessity of appearing to work. Skylarking was normally frowned upon. To be found "skylarking on watch" was an offense that sometimes led to disciplinary charges.

The *Cardiff* was less modern in most respects than other warships of the time. One of the repeated pipes from the bosun's mate was "Clear lower deck to hoist boat." The task was to lift a heavy boat (a twenty-seven–foot wooden whaler) out of the water up to the davits on which it would be secured. Many ships did this the easy way by running the ropes around a power winch and doing most of the hoisting that way. We did it the old way. At the sound of the pipe, all ratings—seamen, cooks, stokers off duty—assembled on deck and were divided into two groups. Each group took hold of a thick rope (the fall) much like people lined onto a rope in tug o' war, except that we faced into the rope and each man's hands crossed over the hands of the man on either side. Down at sea level, the boat was attached to hooks at the end of each fall. At the order "Haul taut singly," we hoisted the rope until it began to take the strain of the weight of the boat. Each fall was hauled in this way until the boat was out of the water and hanging level. Then the pipe shrilled again, and the command "Marry the falls" was shouted. Now both groups joined the ropes and stamped away along the deck as before, with men peeling off the end of the rope as they reached the end of the ship and dashing back to take position in the space near the davit. All that was missing was a sea chantey. If the boat tilted out of level, the order came to "Separate the falls," followed by an order for one or the other of the falls to be hoisted until level was restored. When the boat was hauled almost to the top of the davits, the petty officer in charge shouted, "High enough." This was followed by the report that the falls were "chock-a-block," meaning that the two pulleys (blocks) were now tight together and could be pulled no farther. The task was complete.

Food for each mess in the *Cardiff* was prepared for cooking by two ratings from the mess. The duty rotated throughout the members of the mess, who were responsible for deciding the menu, peeling potatoes and any other such chores, and then delivering the food to the ship's galley, where it was cooked by the regular cooks. As an inevitable consequence of the steady rotation of pairs of incompetents, the meals left much to be desired, especially in the matter of variety. The cost of the food was charged against a victualing allowance. Each officer and man in the Navy was allocated a victualing allowance. This money was offset against the cost of food drawn from the paymaster's store. I think that the sum was on the order of one shilling and tenpence-halfpenny per day.

Each mess, typically about twenty men, decided what the members would eat each day and drew the food from the paymaster. On any given day, different messes in a ship might be eating slightly different meals. I say "slightly" because the culinary imagination of sailors did not usually go much beyond meat, potatoes, vegetables, and steamed puddings, and, in any case, the paymaster's stores did not offer a selection of gourmet items! At the end of the month, there was a reckoning, which might result in a debit or credit to the mess concerned. Food was charged at cost, so that it was quite possible for a mess to live plainly but adequately and have a little money left over. These "mess savings" could be divided up as cash by the members of the mess or could be used for a better-than-usual menu during the following month. A debit created a "mess bill," although usually not of catastrophic amounts, which could be either paid then or worked off by an even plainer menu during the following month. In the *Cardiff*, we varied between mess savings and mess bills, never more than a few shillings in either case. Larger ships were run along different lines, with central catering and no mess bills for ratings.

For officers, the same principle applied, but it worked out quite differently in practice. Later, when I served as a midshipman in the *Jason*, my mess bill averaged about one pound (four dollars at the rate of exchange at that time) a month, plus the wine bill, which was separate. If the president of the wardroom mess (usually the first lieutenant) was given to extravagance, each member of the wardroom would find himself with a heavy mess bill. Wardroom mess matters were supposed to be settled by democratic votes of the members, but this was not easily achieved in practice. Midshipmen were limited by regulation to a wine bill of ten shillings a month and were also prohibited from drinking spirits, so that the wine bill was always for either wine or beer.

One tot (a third of a gill of rum diluted with two parts water) was issued to ratings over the age of eighteen, and one tot of straight rum was issued to petty officers. The mixture of water and rum was known as "grog," after an Admiral Vernon (nicknamed "Grogram" after the coat that he wore) who had introduced this practice into the Navy. Rum was issued at noon daily in a ritual known as "Up Spirits." Any rating who was eligible for grog but requested to be classed as "temperance" was given a daily allowance of three pence in lieu of the ration. Officers were not eligible for the rum ration but could order a limited amount of duty-free liquor, with the charge put on their mess bills. The limit was six fifths of liquor—rum, gin, whisky, or other spirits—per officer per month. Drinking at sea was restricted; however, duty-free spirits, such as Scotch whisky, sold for a mere four or five shillings a bottle (compared with thirty to thirty-five shillings ashore) and it was possible for an officer of rank above midshipman to consume quite a lot of liquor when in port.

U.S. Navy ships were completely "dry." When we worked with these ships, we invited the officers over for drinks when that was feasible. They reciprocated, when possible, by inviting us over to eat with them. As the U.S. Navy generally had much better food than we did, this worked out well for both groups.

At night, hammocks were slung from overhead hooks and, packed much like sardines in a can, lay side by side in overlapping rows across the interior of the mess deck. Getting into and out of a hammock and learning how to sleep in one took a little practice. The hammock, as issued, did not include anything to keep it stretched in the open position once it was hung up. When a sailor climbed into the hammock, it closed over the occupant into a suffocating sausage shape. This could be easily prevented by placing a short wooden stick to spread the ropes at the head end. No such stick was issued, so it was necessary to acquire one somehow; for some suitable trade in tobacco or rum, the shipwright's shop could meet the need.

Accommodation for ratings in a man-of-war was designed for a ship's company of the size necessary to work the ship in peacetime. Wartime demanded larger crews. Mess tables and hammock hooks adequate for peacetime could not accommodate the numbers. As a result, sailors slept in any vacant cranny that could be found and often ate their meals while sitting on flat portions of machinery big enough to provide a seat.

No lights were allowed at night, and heavy canvas curtains screened the exits to the open deck. After a few hours, the air became very thick, a factor that combined with heavy weather and stodgy food to produce seasickness in those unlucky enough to have sensitive stomachs. At midnight and 0400 (4 A.M.), watchkeepers came in to waken sailors scheduled for the next watch. This occasioned some violent shaking of hammocks, bad language, and general stumbling around. At first, this disturbance added to the difficulties in sleeping that plagued the greenhand sailor. After a few days at sea, fatigue provided an effective cure; nothing disturbed our sleep, and we learned to sleep anywhere and anytime the opportunity came up.

Our main shore liberty was to the town of Lamlash in the Island of Aran. There were only two things to do in Lamlash. One was to walk out of town into the hills and admire the scenery, which was beautiful in the stark way that Scottish scenery so often is. The other was to visit the Church of Scotland hut, a Nissen hut canteen that offered tea, large bricklike sections of pound cake, a dart board and a gramophone—no beer, but hymns on the Sabbath. When the weather permitted, the scenery was the better option.

On one occasion, the *Cardiff* went up the Clyde to Greenock to replace the barrels of the 6-inch guns. The rifling had been worn smooth by our constant practice firings. For some reason, the removal of the old and the installation of the new barrels took place without the benefit of the power of the ship's engines to move the *Cardiff* into position under the crane that was to lower the barrels into place. As there were five barrels to be installed into five different mounts and the crane was fixed, the entire crew was called out to stand on the dockside, lay on to a thick wire hawser, and haul the *Cardiff*, all 4,000 tons of her, for each move. This maneuver, "shifting ship" it was called, took place in a steady downpour. It could have been done by tugboat, but the *Cardiff* preferred the old ways.

At the end of this period in the *Cardiff*, two in my group of eighteen officer candidates were judged unsuitable for officer rank, and one more was discharged from the Navy as physically unfit. The latter had unaccountably slung his hammock from two immediately adjacent hooks so it hung down in a U, like a hairpin. Repeated advice to adopt the normal method of suspension had no effect. From sleeping in that position every night, he had developed a urinary problem.

2

Temporary Gentleman

The naval quip has dubbed us gentlemen
Essaying to be sailors. We'll not ask
A better name, not know a fairer task
—JUSTIN RICHARDSON, "RNVR"

HMS King Alfred

On 5 July 1943, the remaining fifteen officer candidates from the *Cardiff* were drafted to HMS "King Alfred," the officer cadet training unit (OCTU) in Sussex. We entered King Alfred on 6 July. I was commissioned on 30 September with the rank of Midshipman RNVR (Royal Navy Volunteer Reserve). The system of reserves in the Royal Navy at that time was rather complicated. The permanent RNVR consisted of prewar civilian volunteers trained on a part-time basis as "weekend sailors." With the outbreak of war, all of these men were called into active duty. People, such as myself, who were commissioned during the war were officially designated as "temporary." Thus, my midshipman's commission was as Temporary Midshipman RNVR. There were no temporary RNVR ratings and only a small number of permanent RNVR ratings, these being men who had joined the reserve in peacetime and had been called into active duty when the war started. All newly joined ratings were RN. When commissioned, I moved from being an ordinary seaman, RN, to a temporary officer, RNVR. Officers in the RNVR wore wavy gold lace stripes of rank on their cuffs, unlike regular RN officers with straight stripes. This circumstance led to the RNVR being known colloquially as the "Wavy Navy," and sometimes to the RN being known as the "Straight Navy."

A second major division of the reserves was the Royal Naval Reserve (RNR). Here, the officers and men came from the career seamen of the Merchant Navy. Like members of the RNVR, they had undertaken part-time training in peace and the obligation to serve in time of war. Most often, the officers came from the major passenger lines, such as the Cunard, P&O (Peninsular & Orient), and Royal Mail Line. The cuff stripes worn by RNR officers were in the form of two thin bands of gold lace crisscrossed into a braid; each braid was the equivalent of a single stripe. In 1952, the traditional wavy or braided stripes were replaced by the regular straight stripes of the Royal Navy, with the letter "R" in the loop of the uppermost stripe to indicate that the wearer was a reserve officer. By 1958, the two reserves were merged into a single Royal Naval Reserve, and the RNVR came to an end. A common joke during World War II was the "RN officers are gentlemen trying to be sailors, RNR officers are sailors trying to be gentlemen, and RNVR officers are neither, trying to be both."

Training in King Alfred was divided into three phases at different locations. First, we went to Brighton for about two weeks. The main purpose of this phase was to conduct a final screening of the candidates before proceeding to the main training course. The first phase took place on the premises of a former preparatory school requisitioned for the purpose, but we were billeted in local households. Our hosts had been acting in this capacity for some years and were used to the repeated departures and new arrivals that were a feature of their lives. During the day, we spent a lot of time on drill, plus some elementary navigation classes, rifle training, and so on.

The major event of this period was the final interview by a board of senior officers to determine if one was still regarded as suitable for entry into officer training. Failure in the interview meant returning to sea as an ordinary seaman. We were all very nervous about this, and there were many rumors about what "they" would ask, and what "they" were looking for. Much reference was made to a nebulous concept known as OLQ—officerlike qualities. It was quite unclear what this was—maybe accent, maybe standing up straight at all times, maybe being neat and smartly groomed. One odd bit of lore accepted as a mark of OLQ was that one should not accept a light or offer to light a cigarette from another cigarette being smoked—one should always use a new match.

This may have had something to do with the World War I superstition about not lighting three cigarettes from one match (the duration of the light making a suitable target for snipers).

The interview was quite brief and informal. The board already had my fitness report from the *Cardiff*. All that I can remember about the questions was that I gave a stupid answer to one of them. Asked to comment on the tidal pattern around the Island of Aran in the Clyde, where the *Cardiff* had operated, I mumbled something about noticing that high tide seemed always to come in the afternoon! My answer provoked audible amusement, and I left the interview feeling sure that I had failed.

Among my classmates at the school was Jack Plant (many years later, when they were both in the Foreign Service, he and my brother John became friends). During a particularly long period of drill on a hot July day, we were ordered to remove our blouses (the blue smocklike outer garment) and continue drilling in our white tunics. Jack seemed very reluctant to do this, but he had no choice in the matter. He was wearing a false front instead of a tunic, that is, a square of white cloth that looked like a tunic when seen above the V neck of the blouse but was actually secured to his chest by a series of strings, something like a corset. As the wearing of improper uniform was frowned on, Jack was sure that something unpleasant would be in store for him. He was right. He was called forth from the ranks and instructed, corseted as he was, to march, salute, present arms, and so forth—an exercise of humiliation. He was approved, however, to go on to the next phase of King Alfred, as were most of us.

At the end of the two weeks, we moved on to Lancing College for the second phase of training, which lasted eight weeks. Lancing was a boarding school some miles west of Brighton that had been requisitioned by the Admiralty. We were housed in dormitories that had been modified into austerity by removing all furniture and replacing it with iron-frame bunk beds and metal lockers. No hammocks were used here.

We were now officially "Officer Cadets," wore a white band around our hats to mark this fact, and were addressed as "Cadet," rather than by our actual rating. We were part of an intake of about 120 cadets, with the entire intake forming a division. Divisions were given the names of famous admirals; we were classed into Rodney Division. Each division was divided into four platoons, A, B, C, and Y. Members of a platoon went through the training curriculum together as a unit or class. The "Y" referred to our youth; on graduation, we would be commissioned with the rank of midshipman, rather than sub-lieutenant. Any graduate age

$19\frac{1}{2}$ years or older was commissioned a sub-lieutenant directly on graduation. At weekly intervals, a new division entered the school. At any one time, there were several divisions in the school, each at various stages of progression through the courses.

Training was intensive, beginning with physical training at 0600 and continuing with classes, drills, and practices until the evening. We marched everywhere. From time to time, instead of standard military commands, such as "left turn" (which meant that everybody should simultaneously turn left) or "left wheel" (which meant that the front of the column should lead around to the left, the whole column following like the tail of a snake), we were given orders as though we were a flotilla of ships. Thus, when a column of ships was to "wheel" left around to another course, the flag that went up on the leading ship's yardarm was a red turn flag (red because each ship would be turning to port) followed by numerical flags indicating the number of degrees of the turn, usually 90. The actual turn began when the flags were hauled down. The cadet leading the platoon had to shout, "Red nine-oh," followed by "Down" at the actual moment of turn. Part of the rules of the game was to obey every order exactly as given, even when it was obvious that the order was mistaken. In fact, we were particularly supposed to obey such orders so that the ensuing chaos would teach the erring cadet who had given the order. Thus, if the cadet happened to make the mistake of saying, "Red three-six-oh," which meant that the column should turn left in a complete circle, the front row would start to do so on the command "Down," with the immediate effect that an ever-increasing spiral of men would end up milling around as a mob.

After we had practiced navigation on chart tables, we concluded that part of the course with a navigation exercise conducted in a large field. The field was dotted with scaled-down buoys, a miniature lighthouse, a church steeple, and a small rock or two. The whole thing looked rather like one of those putting golf courses found in amusement parks. Working in pairs, we were provided with a chart of this "ocean" and an ice cream vendor's tricycle, the top of the freezer box being fitted out as a chart table with a bearing compass, dividers, parallel rule, and binoculars. Each pair was given a task, such as "Plot course from point A to point B," these points being defined by bearings from the lighthouse or steeple. Not much was learned from this otherwise totally enjoyable and ludicrous exercise, given the facts, in addition to our ignorance, that the all-steel frame of the tricycles rendered the compasses nearly totally ineffective and that we were continually trying to avoid colliding with each other in the available space. As the officer in charge had decided to leave us to it, the situation rapidly degenerated into a game of collisions, two sides forming and charging each other with the intention of ramming. In fact, one or two of the tricycles were capsized, but no injuries to crews were reported.

A West Country gunner's mate at Lancing was in charge of small-arms instruction. One of his lectures was a description of the mechanism of the short Lee-Enfield .303 rifle. For the gunner's mate, the events in the interior of the rifle formed a complex chain of thoughts. He began:

> This 'ere's the trigger. You put your finger on the trigger and you squeeze 'er. Finger thinks, "Oi've been squeezed, Oi 'ave," and 'e presses little old trigger. Little old trigger thinks, "Oi've been pulled by little old finger, Oi'd better move." So 'e moves and 'e 'its little old spring. Little old spring says to 'imself, "By God, Oi've been 'it," and 'e 'its little old striker. Strikers says to 'imself, "Spring 'as 'it me. Oi'm going to strike little old detonator there," so 'e strikes 'im.

This conversation went on right up to the point at which "little old bullet" sees "little old target" and hits it. He did not report the subsequent remarks of little old target.

These lectures on the inner consciousness theory of the rifle had become widely known. Word of them was passed on from each class of cadets to succeeding classes. My brother John went through the hands of this gunner's mate when he entered officer training some time later.

Invariably, some cadet raised a hand in the midflight of the lecture and asked in a serious tone, his pencil poised over his notebook, "Chief, I didn't quite get what little old detonator said to little old cartridge. Could you repeat it?"

Without a break in his stride, the gunner's mate responded: "This 'ere's the trigger. You put your finger on the trigger and you squeeze 'er. Finger thinks . . ." and so on through the whole thing from beginning to end.

A background theme in the training was the necessity to deal with unexpected emergencies and, by the same token, to respond quickly to unexpected orders. This theme was put into effect in various ways. Once, for example, a navigation class taking place in a first-floor classroom was interrupted by the instructor's shout, "All cadets jump out of the window." The order was not specific as to which of several windows we were to jump through and whether or not we should bring along our navigational equipment. The result was that some immediately jumped out of the nearest window and landed in a small disorganized group below; others carefully climbed down from the window ledge, parallel ruler in mouth and rolled-up chart clamped between chin and neck. Yet others, concluding that this was really a practice at "abandon ship," dived out of the window to land with swimming motions in the grass that edged the building.

At other times, we were told that we were a marooned group of survivors on a Pacific island and needed to communicate this to an airplane overhead that was looking for us. We managed to guess the solution and create an "SOS" by lining up to form the letters. Emergency bridges were built over local streams with ropes formed by tying together the black scarves from our uniforms, and so forth.

About halfway through the course at Lancing, I had a minor accident during a swimming exercise in the school indoor pool—all officers, but not ratings, had to know how to swim. In the course of lifesaving exercises, we began to indulge in horseplay. During the scuffle, I somehow banged the point of my jaw against the stone edge of the pool side. It cut right through to the bone, and a lot of blood poured into the water. I was sent off to sick bay, where the surgeon-lieutenant cleaned and disinfected the cut, stitched it up, and then ordered me to stay in sick bay for a couple of days until he was sure that it was healing properly. The result was that I was now missing whatever part of the training the rest of Rodney Y was doing (one could not miss a single day of training) and, when I came out of sick bay, I was moved back to the intake group that had followed mine by a week, the Jellicoe Division. My friend Jack Mayne (whom I saw on a number of later occasions) was in Jellicoe, and it was in that division that I was to be commissioned. The chin scar is still faintly visible after fifty years.

We did not get much shore leave at all, maybe two or three evenings off during the whole period. There was not much to do in Lancing except have a couple of beers at the local pub. The shortest route from the school to the village of Lancing lay through the fields, with a pathway passing close to a large pond at one point. The pond was inhabited by a number of swans, some of whom became visibly annoyed when people passed by—much hissing, craning of necks, flapping of wings, and threatening approaches. One evening, one of our number, a person who was alleged to be a veterinarian in civil life, was present at a conversation during which the question of the swan danger was being examined— "they can break your arm or leg with a belt of their wings." The veterinarian assured us that this was true, but that the secret of victory in the man-swan struggle lay in the fact that the attackers were always male (wrong, by the way!) and that the male genitalia were located under the right wing, hence a swift kick under the upraised wing would disable the attacking bird and permit safe passage at leisure.

The inevitable happened. A cadet, muddy and bruised, staggered into the dormitory one evening and sought out the veterinarian for a discussion. Threatened by a swan, the cadet had tried the wing-kick tactic, but this had merely turned an already infuriated bird into an insanely enraged one. Pursued by the audible beating of wings and hisses of vengeance, the cadet had managed to escape without limb fracture, but he was in a mood very like that of the swan's. I was not present at the inevitable reckoning with the veterinarian, but we all took care to avoid the pond in the future.

In due course, we moved from Lancing back to Brighton, where the main component of King Alfred was located. It had been built originally as a seafront resort center, with ballroom, restaurant, meeting rooms, and other amenities. One of these was the basement parking garage, which had been turned into a dormitory. We slept on the usual iron-frame bunks, enclosed by the gray concrete of the garage and the amplified echoes of any sound.

Instruction continued as before. Navigation classes included a session in the "action plot." Action plotting required that the navigator keep a continuous track of the whereabouts of the ship in relation to other ships, friend and foe, during active engagements or other circumstances that involved frequent changes of course and speed. The position of other ships was reported by the radar and sonar operators from moment to moment. In order to provide basic training in this task, a simulator had been built at King Alfred. It consisted of a chart house complete with engine room telegraph repeater, revolution counter, speed log, compass repeater, charts, dividers, parallel rulers, voice pipes, and other items. The chart house was mounted on rollers, and the dark interior had a dim light over the chart table. The cadet was given an initial position to mark on the chart, and then the exercise began. The chart house pitched and rolled; there were loud noises of gunfire accompanied by flashes and glare. Down the voice pipes came a stream of reports and orders, some of them relevant, others simply distracting. The compass needle swung to indicate changes of course, the engine room telegraph repeater went from "Slow" to "Full speed ahead" to "Stop engines" to "Emergency full ahead," while radar reports told of shifting blips on the screens.

All of this was programmed, so that at any point in the exercise and at the end of it all there were correct answers to such questions as "Where are we now?" "Where are the enemy?" and so on. The competence of the cadet navigator was reflected in the size of the error in his answer to these questions. All in all, it was quite a stressful experience. Later experience of the real thing confirmed that the simulation had been reasonably realistic. With the introduction of PPI (position-plotting indicator) radar, action plots became generally unnecessary.

More primitive simulations were employed to teach us the ranging techniques used in naval gunnery. One was a rectangular traylike tabletop device, in which was fixed a metal silhouette model of a target ship. At the side of the tray was a keyboard with typewriter keys. Each key acted to raise a small white metal shape to represent the splash of a falling shell. Depending on the key pressed, the splash appeared short of the target or beyond it. The gunner's mate operating this contraption privately decided on the "true" range of the target from the cadet's observation point. The cadet guessed at a range and called it out. Somewhere near the target, a splash appeared as the gunner's mate pressed one of the keys. The cadet then changed the range up or down, depending on the location of the splash. This process of increasing or decreasing the range followed standard steps, the first being a large correction in the opposite direction from the location of the splash. Thus, if the splash appeared beyond the target, the cadet reduced range by eight hundred yards. If the next splash appeared short of the target, the cadet increased the range by four hundred yards. This series of changes in the range continued by decreasing amounts until the target was hit. At this point, the gunner's mate pressed the target key, whereupon the target sank out of sight.

Early mornings saw us, clad in shorts and T-shirts, running along the seafront parade under the constant heckling of a physical training instructor petty officer. At night, we served watches in the several sandbagged observation posts dotting the seafront. These had been placed there in 1940 for observers to spot German airplanes approaching and, perhaps, German assault vessels.

Other kinds of instruction included lectures from visitors. One, David James, recounted his escape from a German prison camp and concluded with advice about how to escape should we be captured. If I remember correctly, he reported that the escape route through France was best followed by hiding out in bawdy houses, the madams of which were reputed to be very sympathetic to Allied fugitives. Other experienced officers gave us additional tips that did not appear in the *Admiralty*

Manual of Seamanship, such as remembering to go to the head (toilet) before going on watch. Any urgency developing on watch could be relieved only by the quite public use of a bucket kept on the bridge for that purpose, and this was to be avoided if possible. We were advised not to become "popularity Jacks" when we finally went to sea as officers—namely, not to behave in ways intended to curry favor with the crew. It was alleged that this generally led to diminished respect, a condition that was bad for discipline and therefore bad for the safety of the ship.

I was commissioned on 30 September 1943 with the rank of Midshipman RNVR. Each newly commissioned cadet, armed with a uniform allowance, went to one of the many tailors who had set up shop directly opposite King Alfred. Doeskin and blue serge were measured for our uniforms, and brass buttons, gold lace, and purple collar tabs were ordered. In a few days, we were transformed into passable facsimiles of sea officers. Duly uniformed, we returned our rating's gear to the ever-frugal Navy, keeping only the hairy underwear, black boots, money belt, and sailor's jackknife. Bursting with pride covered only thinly by an affected nonchalance, we entered the wardroom mess.

Another month of training followed. By day, we wore our new caps, reefer jackets with white ascot scarves or turtleneck sweaters, gray slacks, and the khaki canvas gaiters that marked us as still in training. Once a week, we appeared at a formal dinner in Number One uniform, complete with wing collar and black bow tie. For some reason, one of these dinners included "entertainment" by a popular music hall comedian, Max M. Some entertainers, and Max was one of them, seemed to believe that what the troops really wanted was a parade of obscene and scatological humor. Freed from the constraints imposed on him when broadcasting on the BBC, he delivered what he thought we were waiting to hear. It was pathetic. At the end, there was perfunctory laughter and applause. He was not invited back again.

At the end of our time at King Alfred, each member of our class was interviewed to inquire our preferences for a seagoing appointment. Like more than 90 percent of my classmates, I wanted to be appointed to a convoy escort vessel—one of the glamorous U-boat hunters, such as a sloop, frigate, corvette, or destroyer. My request received a friendly and encouraging hearing at an interview with two officers, one of them an RNVR lieutenant commander, who was in charge of appointments. His name was Aymeric Straker. In spite of the encouraging attitude of the interviewers, I received orders for minesweeping. (Eleven years later, in 1954, I would return to England from the United States with a Ph.D. in psychology. I applied for a position as a psychologist with the government and was interviewed in London by a selection board of the Commissioners of the Civil Service. At the interview table was a vaguely familiar face. It was Aymeric Straker. He commented, "I have met you before," and of course he had. He had my dossier before him, and it must have contained records of my naval service. He was the chief psychologist of the Prison Service, and it was to that service that I was appointed.)

At the end of our training at King Alfred, we were given a few days' leave. I headed home to Manchester, before going on to what I confidently assumed would be a frigate or some other convoy escort vessel. At the railroad station, there was a woman, quite well dressed, with several bags. Porters were in short supply during the war. She assumed that I was some kind of porter and probably would be reluctant to carry her bags unless assured of a tip. She addressed me, "Oh, Porter! Could you carry these bags for me? There'll be a good tip for you." Feeling resplendent in my new uniform, I was particularly incensed at her failure to recognize the glory of the insignia. Drawing up to my full height, I responded haughtily, "Madam, you are speaking to a naval officer." Her facial expression indicated a convinced skepticism, and she mumbled some comment to the effect that I didn't look much like a naval officer to her.

3

The Minesweeping Trade

With little rest they give their best,
  To keep an open gate.
And every time they sink a mine
  Another victory's won.

—HUGH CAMPBELL, UNTITLED POEM QUOTED IN
GORDON HOLMAN, *STANDBY TO BEACH*, 1944

HMS Lochinvar

At the end of the first week of November 1943, the familiar buff envelope
came from the Admiralty. Opening it eagerly to see what kind of convoy
escort I had been assigned to, I learned that it pleased Their Lordships that
I should take myself to HMS Pembroke, the Royal Naval Barracks,
Chatham, Kent. There I would undergo two weeks of gunnery training
and from there be transferred to HMS Lochinvar, the minesweeping
school of the Royal Navy in Granton, just outside of Edinburgh. On arrival
in Chatham, I discovered that a significant proportion of the Jellicoe
Division had received exactly the same orders, so I was back with a group of
my King Alfred classmates, including Jack Mayne. So much for the
placement interview at King Alfred. Not long before, the Ministry of
Information (the propaganda ministry during the war) had published a
book titled *His Majesty's Minesweepers*, which began with the cheerful
opening assertion that all men engaged in minesweeping were "picked
volunteers"! We were willing and ready to go wherever the Navy wanted us
to go, but the "volunteer" comment was a frequent source of wry humor.

At Chatham, we were trained in antiaircraft gunnery, using 20-mm Oerlikon guns, 0.50-inch heavy machine guns, and small-caliber Lewis guns. Training was conducted partly in a simulator, known as the Dome Teacher, and partly with live firing on a gunnery range at Sheerness, where we fired at sleeve targets towed by aircraft across the range. The Dome Teacher contained a 20-mm Oerlikon gun in the middle of the floor of the large dome. A movie projector on a swivel projected the image of an airplane moving up across the vault of the dome, which was painted with a cinema screen surface. As the image of the airplane came overhead, at a distance in front of the nose of the plane was superimposed a yellow dot. This dot represented the correct point, ahead of the plane, at which to aim in order to hit the plane. In action, a gunner must "lead" the target (i.e., fire ahead of the target plane at a distance at which both bullet and plane will meet). This distance varies with the speed, angle, and altitude of the target and requires experienced estimation by the gunner. In the Dome Teacher, the gunner wore yellow goggles and could not see the dot. When he pressed the trigger, a beam of light was directed at the screen. If the gunner had correctly estimated the position of the yellow dot and hit it with the beam of light, the contact activated the continuous ringing of a bell as long as the gunner stayed on target. Those waiting to take a turn could observe the position of the yellow dot and the accuracy of the gunner's aim. We all became very involved, vying with each other to see who could stay on target the longest, rather like the players of video games decades later.

From Pembroke, our group went by train to Lochinvar to go through the minesweeping course proper. As we were allowed a few hours in London between trains, Mayne suggested that he and I take an earlier train out of King's Cross and get off at Peterborough, where he lived. When the Flying Scotsman stopped at Peterborough, we could join the rest of our fellows on the train and arrive together at Waverley Station, Edinburgh, the following morning.

The plan worked out. Jack and I spent the evening with his parents, and it included a stop at a pub conveniently near the station. The stay was protracted to a point that saw us dashing onto the northbound platform to find the Flying Scotsman already in, steam hissing from the piston valves and the conductor blowing his whistle and waving a green flag to signal departure. Some of our group, who knew that we had gone ahead to Peterborough, were leaning out of the carriage windows and urging us to speed. As the door closed behind us, the train was already moving. We would have encountered some kind of discipline if we had missed the train and reached Edinburgh later; as it turned out, we simply acquired a mild notoriety for having been symbolically insubordinate.

The course at Lochinvar consisted of a mixture of seaborne and classroom instruction. Lochinvar itself was really only a name for a few Nissen huts scattered around the dockyard at Granton, a former dockyard office building, and two rather ancient trawlers tied up to the wharf. We lived on board these vessels and were slinging hammocks again. Our accommodation was in what had been formerly (and unmistakably) the fish hold. The regular crew of skipper, stokers, and seamen occupied the normal living quarters of the trawler.

Granton lies on the south bank of the Forth River, a short distance north of the city of Edinburgh. The tall spans of the Forth Bridge dominated the view, towering over the wintry waters of the river. A few motor minesweepers and trawlers lay at the wharves. There was little of interest in the town; for entertainment, we could take a streetcar into Edinburgh. Oddly enough, I have no recollection of eating while at Lochinvar. We must have done so, but I cannot recall where I ate or what the food was like, which suggests that the food was more than usually unappealing. We were there to learn about mines, however, and that we did.

Mines and How to Sweep Them

German mines came in several different types. Each worked in a different way, and each had to be rendered harmless in a different way. At Lochinvar, the construction and destruction of the various kinds of mines was the core of our instruction. German mines that had washed up on British beaches without exploding had been salvaged and then defused, and these were used for instructional purposes. They and their innards lay exposed for examination, along with samples of the more conventional mines that had been in use by both sides for many decades.

The most basic type of mine, the contact mine, operated quite simply. It was a large metal sphere containing explosives plus some air for buoyancy. Metal horns protruded from the outer surface. Each horn contained a glass tube filled with acid. Should a passing vessel strike the horn, the glass tube fractured and released acid, which then flowed into the components of an internal battery. This instantly completed a detonating circuit and the mine exploded, blowing a hole in the hull of the vessel. She usually sank. Lucky ships were only badly damaged.

Contact mines were anchored to the seabed by a thin wire cable, long enough to keep the mine itself a few feet below the surface where it could not be seen by passing ships. As the depth of water over the mine was least at low tide, that was the most dangerous time to be near a mine field. High tide, necessarily, was the best time to be sweeping a mine field, as there was some possibility that a shallow-draft sweeper could pass over the mines without hitting one.

Minelayers laid these mines by dropping them over the stern into the water. Each mine sat on a small wheeled trolley; the trolleys were lined up on rails along the deck. The trolley contained the mooring weight plus a delay device for the release of just enough length of mooring cable to permit the mine to rise to a point below the water surface. If the cable rusted through or parted for some other reason, the mine floated to the surface. Hypothetically, this would activate a safety lock designed to prevent the mine from exploding on contact, because loose floating mines were dangerous to all ships, not just the enemy's. In practice, the safety locks often rusted solid and failed to work.

The key to sweeping contact mines was to cut the mooring cable and destroy the mine when it bobbed to the surface. Crew members fired machine guns and rifles at the mine; when a bullet happened to hit one of the horn switches on the mine, it exploded with a ship-shaking roar, and a geyser of white water spouted skyward—quite an exciting sight at first. Machine gunners aimed just below the water line of the mine in order to pierce its metal shell so that the mine would slowly fill with water and finally sink to the seabed, where it was no further danger to shipping.

To cut the mine mooring cable, the minesweeper towed a long wire hawser behind it. This was designed to serve as a scythe and was the basic sweep used against contact mines. At the extreme outer end, it was supported by a buoyant metal torpedo-shaped cylinder, known as the Oropesa float. The float carried a small flag that was easily seen from the deck of the minesweeper. Two devices, known as the "kite" and the "otter," were attached to the sweep wire. Similar in construction, they each consisted of a rectangular steel frame, with the inner space containing angled vanes rather like a partially opened venetian blind. The kite was attached to the sweep wire and, by a separate wire, to the ship. The length of this latter wire determined the maximum depth to which the kite could sink. When the minesweeper moved forward, the flow of water over the vanes pushed the kite down to the preset level below the surface. At the outer end of the sweep wire, the flow of water through the otter pulled the Oropesa and the sweep wire out and away from the minesweeper, thereby creating the required scythelike curve. The wire itself was designed to cut through the mooring cables of any anchored contact mine, which would then bob to the surface to be destroyed by gunfire. The entire apparatus of wires, kite, and otter was referred to as the "sweep."

The inner end of the sweep wire was attached to, and reeled in and out by, a powerful winch on the quarterdeck of the minesweeper. The sweep wire itself was a wide-gauge steel hawser constructed so that one strand was twisted in the opposite direction from all of the others. This produced a sawtooth edge designed to cut through the thinner mooring cables of the mines. Dragging this across the mooring cable of a mine was like cutting the cable with a hacksaw. It worked effectively provided that the mooring cable first came into contact near the inner end of the sweep wire, thereby ensuring that the entire length of the sweep wire would be dragged across it. This did not always happen. Therefore, to ensure that the mooring cable would be cut, the sweep wire was also fitted at intervals with metal clamps in the shape of a V; these would snag the mooring cable as the sweep wire dragged across it. Each clamp held a small explosive charge designed to detonate on contact with the mine mooring cable when it was snagged. "Arming" the sweep referred to attaching the clamps at specified intervals—far enough apart to give the sawtooth edge a chance to cut the mine mooring but not so far that the mooring might escape entirely. When the sweep wire was winched back on board, the clamps were removed one by one as they came in; otherwise, they would have exploded on contact with the winch.

There were several dangers intrinsic in this technique of minesweeping. The obvious one, namely that the minesweeper might hit the mine, needs no explanation. It was quite possible that a mine might be cut but become entangled in the sweep wire, and this would not be apparent until the sweep was being winched in. When this happened, the mine would not be visible until it was a few feet from the hull. Quick action in either stopping the winch and/or cutting the sweep wire was necessary to deal with this. Further danger lay in the fact that under the stress imposed on it, the sweep wire might part. Besides making it necessary to stop the ship immediately to repair the sweep, there was a danger that the loose end of the wire might foul the propellers. Worst of all, if the sweep wire were to part at a point on the quarterdeck itself, the backlash from the shipboard end of the wire could be sufficiently violent to kill members of the sweeping crew who were within its range.

For all of these reasons, it was essential that an officer be on the quarterdeck to supervise the continuing operation of the sweep. The main task of the sweep officer, typically the first lieutenant, was to monitor the tension on the hawser by touch and sound to detect any unusual change in the strain. A lookout was posted to watch the Oropesa to make sure that it stayed on the surface of the water. If it disappeared below the surface, it meant that there was unusual strain on the sweep wire, with the risk of its parting. At all times, an ax was stowed on the quarterdeck ready to cut the sweep wire in an emergency. When this was necessary, the cut was made as close to the winch as possible to minimize the length of wire in the backlash. We had occasion to do this some months later.

The tactics of sweeping depended on reducing the danger to the minesweepers as far as possible. If the probable location of an enemy mine field was known, a group of minesweepers would take up a formation in echelon to one side, beginning just outside the edge of the mine field. Much as combine harvesters line up on the prairie, each one overlapping a little into the area just reaped by the machine ahead, the minesweepers followed each other into the rather different kind of field that they were required to reap. This formation, the most common in minesweeping for contact mines, was known as the "G formation."

When ships of a flotilla were sweeping together in G formation, each ship in the line proceeded on a compass course that was intended to keep her inside an area of water that had been swept by the ship immediately ahead, so that a wide swathe (leg) would be swept by the entire group. Ships kept apart a distance of $4\frac{1}{2}$ cables (900 yards). Clearly, the leading minesweeper was at most risk because, unlike the others, she was not moving through swept water on the first leg of the sweep. Unlike the grain or stubble under the prairie harvester, swept water looks no different from unswept water. Hence, when sweeping a suspected mine field, it was necessary to mark the area of water that had been swept. Following the last minesweeper in line were two danlaying vessels. These were usually trawlers. Many trawlers—ships, masters, and men—had been drafted together into the Royal Navy from the peacetime fishing fleets. These men were experienced and hardy seamen, and long experienced in handling trawl gear, which was similar to gear employed in minesweeping. Indeed the principle of the otter had been derived from the otterboard used in trawling. The masters of these trawlers held the formal rank of Skipper, RNR, and wore one or two of the braided stripes that were part of the uniform of that branch of the reserves. Danlayers had the task of marking the two outer edges of the swept swathe with a series of buoys, known as dan buoys, each painted in red and white checkerboard with a pole bearing a red or orange flag for visibility.

At the end of one leg, the entire flotilla turned around in order to sweep in the opposite direction, the lead minesweeper moving just inside the margin of the first swept swathe marked by the dan buoys. One danlayer lifted the dan buoys just in front of the first ship in the advancing flotilla, while the other danlayer began to lay a new row of buoys behind the last minesweeper in the flotilla. This operation continued until the entire mine field was swept. Another major duty of the danlayers was to rescue survivors from any minesweepers sunk in the process. Towing a sweep wire, which was 319 fathoms (636 yards) long, made a minesweeper difficult to maneuver and handicapped her in any attempt to conduct a rescue operation in the middle of a sweep.

Sweeps were streamed out on the side of the ship in which the direction of the tidal flow would tend to pull the sweep away from the ship. This created complications if the direction of the sweep was across the tide. As the minesweeper reversed course to sweep back in the opposite direction, the sweep had to be winched in and then streamed out on the other side of the ship. When five or six ships were doing this fairly close to each other, great care had to be exercised to ensure that sweeps did not become entangled with each other or with the ships' propellers.

The other major category of mines consisted of devices that could be activated without physical contact with a ship. These mines, known as "influence" mines, were designed to detonate in reaction to the sound, the magnetic field, or the pressure field created by the passage of a vessel. Much time at Lochinvar was spent on the technology of magnetic mines and the techniques for sweeping them. A magnetic mine had been tested experimentally by the Admiralty as early as 1917, and further development of it continued during the years between the wars. The first actual use of magnetic mines in wartime, however, was by the Germans, who dropped them from the air in 1939. The operation of the magnetic mine depends on the fact that a metal hull creates a magnetic field around it; hence, a magnet free to swing like a compass needle is deflected whenever a ship passes over it. A magnetic needle is placed inside the mine in such a way that, when deflected, it switches on a detonator. Magnetic mines of this kind have the advantage of being easy to lay. They can be laid from aircraft, which drop them by parachute directly into enemy harbors or coastal waters, or by submarines, which drop them underwater through a mechanism rather like a torpedo tube. Their disadvantage is that they are effective only in relatively shallow water because they lie on the seabed.

Defense against magnetic mines consisted of techniques designed to neutralize the magnetic fields of steel-hulled ships and the use of wooden minesweepers equipped with electrical devices that could create an electromagnetic field at a safe distance behind them. A metal vessel was equipped with a degaussing band (D/G), an electrical circuit installed around the hull to neutralize its magnetic qualities. Each metal vessel had a particular magnetic "signature" or pattern, and the degaussing procedure adjusts the characteristics of the band to the individual signature of the ship. After a major refit, the signature of the ship was likely to change as a consequence of the addition and removal of large metal equipment and of the extended pounding from drills and hammers on the hull. For this reason, it was necessary to check out the degaussing by steaming the ship over a prepared range (D/G range) and pointing her in various compass directions, in which the hull's magnetism could be measured.

Wooden minesweepers came in two types, the 105-foot motor minesweeper (MMS) and the slightly larger British auxiliary minesweeper (BAMS). The latter was a class of minesweepers built in the United States and brought into service during the war in both navies. The U.S. Navy referred to its own version as YMS and to that used by the Royal Navy as BYMS. The YMS stood for yard minesweeper (i.e., built in a private yard). BAMSs and MMSs were designed primarily for sweeping magnetic mines. Although the wooden hull reduced vulnerability to magnetic mines, there was still a great deal of metal onboard, mainly in the engine room. In spite of the advantages of the wooden hull, it was necessary also to degauss the MMSs.

Each minesweeper had a large generator to produce electrical current. Mounted on the stern was a powerful winch with two very thick insulated electrical cables connected together throughout their length. One was 525 yards long, the other about 200 yards long. At the outer end of each cable was a large bare copper electrode. When the sweep began, the generator was switched on to transmit an electrical current down one of the cables to its exposed end; as salt water is a good conductor of electricity, the current was conducted horizontally across the surface of the water, thus creating a magnetic field that could detonate a magnetic mine beneath the water. The short cable pulsed a current opposing that from the longer cable, which created an area of electrically dead water close to the stern of the minesweeper. When a mine detonated at the end of the cables, the cables jumped up from the water in a fountain of spray and the ship vibrated with the shock. The generator alternated the direction of the current from one to the other end of the cables during the sweep so that the change in direction of the flow of electrical current reversed the polarity of the magnetic field. This was essential because any given mine was likely to be sensitive to only one or the other polarity.

It was common for magnetic sweeps to be done by vessels in pairs. Two minesweepers moved parallel to each other, in what was termed the "master and slave" formation, with one of the two ships (the master) controlling the electrical impulses generated by both. This permitted the creation of a magnetic field between and behind the ships, thereby clearing a greater area on each leg of the sweep than could be cleared by two ships operating separately. Additionally, the explosion of mines in the area between the cables of the ships was less likely to damage the cables.

Minesweeping was complicated by the fact that these mines had been designed with a kind of false trigger system, known in the U.S. Navy as a "ship counter." I have a vivid memory of the instructor demonstrating a German device, rather like the mechanism of a telephone dial with twelve notches, one of which was plugged with metal. The act of sweeping an electric current over it served to advance the dial one notch at a time up to a maximum of twelve times. The one that contained the metal plug was connected to the detonator; when that notch was reached, the mine blew up. Therefore, it would be possible to go over the mine up to twelve times before actually exploding it. Which notch was set to produce the explosion was determined by the German minelayers and whatever strategy they were pursuing at the time. The intent was to mislead Allied minesweepers into thinking that an area had been cleared of mines; a few mines were set to go up on the first notch as the field was being swept. Then, convoys might be informed that it was safe for merchant ships to pass through, but the mines sunk a few of the ships. The minesweepers had to return and do the job over again. This cycle was repeated until a combination of sweeping and sinkings had eliminated the mine field. The minesweepers might have to sweep over the same area twelve times to ensure that it was cleared of mines. This could be very monotonous and also quite tense because often there were no mines at all, but the commanding officer had no way to know this until the twelfth sweep was completed. With each successive sweep, there was the growing expectation that the detonating point of the mines would be reached. With completion of the twelfth sweep without incident came a strange mixture of relief and disappointment.

An unavoidable problem with the electrical sweep was that the frequent explosions of mines could crack the heavy insulation of the cable. While the sweep was being winched in, the sweep officer was responsible for scrutinizing every inch of the cable for cracks in the insulation—

cracks that could be very hard to detect. Any cracks noted were repaired immediately with insulating compound and tape. If a crack in the insulation occurred on the inward end of the cable near the ship, the magnetic field would be active all the way back to the crack; this created a serious risk that a mine might be detonated under the minesweeper's own stern. Generally, the stern was blown off, rarely the bow. This is probably what happened when the U.S. minesweeper YMS 350 was sunk off Cherbourg, an incident described in my final diary entry (see chapter 8).

Another type of influence mine was the acoustic mine. This contained a microphone designed to respond to the sound frequencies produced by the beat of the ship's propeller. Minesweepers were then fitted with a countermeasure, a sound-generating apparatus that was lowered into the water at the end of a boom protruding from the ship's bow. The sound replicated that of a ship, and it was hoped that the mine would then detonate well ahead of the minesweeper. Generally speaking, the acoustic mines were not very effective largely because the underwater sounds produced by ships are too complex and differ from vessel to vessel too much to permit a standard tuning of the microphone. During the later years of World War II, it was more common to combine the magnetic and acoustic principles together into magnetic-acoustic mines.

There were other complex devices on both sides. A deadly chess game was played, in which the advantage changed hands as new devices were introduced and changed again as the other side figured them out and developed ways to sweep them. The game included the conduct of dummy sweeps over known mine fields, the purpose of which was to mislead the enemy, whom it was safe to assume was watching, into thinking that a mine field had been removed and that passage through it was now safe.

In the early and perhaps more innocent years of the war, it had been common for minesweepers returning to port, after having completed a successful sweep of a known enemy mine field, to hoist a broom to the masthead to signify a "clean sweep." Objects were hoisted to the masthead for various symbolic purposes. A Christmas tree was tied to the masthead on Christmas day. When the war was over and men of long wartime service were being released back to civilian life, a bowler hat at the masthead of a ship returning to port meant that the commanding officer was celebrating news of his own discharge.

Minesweepers, like other small warships, were organized into flotillas. The most senior officer of a flotilla, invariably the commanding officer of a ship, was known as the S/O of the flotilla. This officer's ship was known as the flotilla leader and marked by a broad black band around the top of the funnel. The half leader, or ship of the second most senior officer (Second S/O) was marked by a narrower band just below the top of the funnel. It was the custom to refer to the senior officer of the flotilla by the number of the flotilla. Thus, the S/O of the First Minesweeping Flotilla was known as MS1, as was the flotilla itself. Ships of a given flotilla might spend considerable time away from the flotilla when they were detached for other duties or assigned to other task forces. It was unusual to see an entire flotilla together in formation at sea.

We wrote all of our technical lecture notes into official notebooks. These were classified as "Secret," and we were not allowed to bring them ashore. When we were individually transferred to active-service mine-sweepers, our notebooks were sent on to us by Admiralty confidential courier mail. My notebook came to me after I joined HMS *Jason*, and it accompanied me on my move to HMS *ML137*. It was not among the possessions sent to me after I was wounded and was presumably destroyed when *ML137* came out of service at the end of the war.

Part of the training at Lochinvar was done in one or the other of two minesweeping trawlers berthed in Granton. Both were coal-fired steam trawlers. Fishing trawlers were uniquely well equipped to sweep mines in all but two respects. Their advantage was that they already possessed the derricks and other gear designed to stream nets away from the ship and to force them down to specified depths—requirements for streaming the cables needed for sweeping mines. Their drawbacks were that they were deep-hulled, hence especially likely to hit mines themselves, and steel-hulled, which made them especially vulnerable to magnetic mines.

In these vessels, steaming up and down the River Forth, we streamed sweeps, set depths, changed depths, swept occasional dummy mines set there for the purpose, gave steering orders, and navigated (not difficult to do when one is in constant sight of the Forth Bridge). We also spent a few hours in the engine room and watched the stokers as they endlessly shoveled coal into the nearly blinding glare and flare of the firebox. They were stripped to the waist, shiny with sweat, and filmed with coal dust. They kept going with constant swigs from a water bottle and occasional breaks on deck to catch the frosty December air on the river.

We rotated duties on these trawlers and gained a little experience at doing each of the things that had to be done—except stoking. Although I am certain that this reflected the unbridgeable gap between engine room and deck in the Navy, I also suspect that the powers that were did not want to see the ships' machinery ruined by the inadequate bumbling of white-handed people who did not know what they were doing.

Minesweeping qualified for a modest payment of "danger money," an allowance given for hazardous duties. On small minesweepers, we also qualified for "hard lying money," an allowance given for service in ships that lacked many of the normal amenities of larger warships. These allowances were not based on rank but applied to the entire ship's company, who shared equally in the danger and the hard lying. My unverified recollection is that my own extra payment of the two allowances combined came to two shillings a day, or about forty cents in U.S. money at the current rate of exchange.

During the period at Lochinvar, we generally had weekend leave on Sundays. There was not much to do in Edinburgh on Sundays. This was mainly a consequence of the pervasive Scottish scrupulousness in observing the Sabbath, but there was even less to do in wartime. Cinemas and most restaurants were closed on Sundays. An officers club on Princess Street had occasional dances or other social events. Most of the time, we went to the free Sunday concerts at the Usher Hall, where very good secular music could be enjoyed provided that you were willing to join in the periodic intervals of hymn singing with which the desecration of the Sabbath was cleansed. The hymn singing, led by a choir, was good, musically speaking, although the selection tended toward lugubrious and despairing themes. "Abide with Me" was popular with the organizers, although the Navy people present remembered it as the song that was sung during the sinking of the *Titanic* and did not share the general enthusiasm for its message. If one had the money, which we mostly didn't, the Café Royal remained open and served Scottish food that could be fairly classed as gourmet.

Food rationing was in full force throughout the war and for some time afterward. The problem of restaurant meals, which could effectively make it possible for the wealthy to avoid rationing by eating their meals in restaurants, had been partly (but only partly) solved by limiting the meal costs at a restaurant to a maximum of five shillings, excluding dessert, hors d'oeuvres, and drinks. The posh restaurants got around this limit by various devices, one of which involved a kind of prix-fixé arrangement wherein, for example, the entrée cost five shillings, the soup three shillings, and coffee two shillings; the whole meal might come to ten shillings but still remain within the letter of the law. An ordinary seaman's pay was two shillings a day, and a midshipman's was six shillings and tenpence a day, so such restaurants tended to be patronized by either wealthy civilians or officers of much higher rank than ours.

At one of the dances, I met a girl whom I dated once or twice afterward during the Sunday shore leaves. Our friendship, however, came to an unexpectedly abrupt end. About the third time I met her, by arrangement, to go to the Usher Hall, she informed me rather tearfully that her father had forbidden her to have anything more to do with me. She quoted him as saying, "I willna have you going oot wi' a Sassenach" (the Gaelic word for a Saxon—an Englishman). Retrospectively, there was a certain irony about this, given the ethnic identity of the Mahers and Powers, but at the time I did not see it that way. My feeling and thinking were nearly entirely as an Englishman born in Lancashire. That was that, however, and we did not meet again.

When the minesweeping course was completed, we were given three days' home leave. I left Edinburgh on New Year's Eve (Hogmanay), 1943. The railway journey from Edinburgh to Manchester was a little complicated. I changed trains at Carlisle, where a southbound train from Glasgow was to carry me the rest of the way. The train, like most wartime trains, was packed well beyond capacity, with no standing room even in the corridors. So, with a small group of kilted Scots soldiers, sailors, and airmen, I sat on a crate in the baggage car and saw the New Year come in as the train rumbled and rattled south through Wordsworth country.

4

North to Scapa Flow

The Northern ocean, in vast whirls
Boils round the naked melancholy isles
Of farthest Thule, and th' Atlantic surge
Pours in among the stormy Hebrides.
—JAMES THOMPSON, "THE SEASONS"

Three days later, I returned to Lochinvar. I was in the usual limbo between completion of one appointment and assignment to another, a limbo occupied by serving as third officer in a minesweeper, HM *MMS84*, based at Granton. This appointment was not due to any desperate need for my services but as a way to keep me occupied and housed until a regular appointment came through. HM *MMS84* was part of a flotilla responsible for sweeping real mines in the Firth of Forth. Because the mines laid in the Forth were generally dropped at night by German aircraft, they were nearly always of the magnetic type and we swept them with electrical sweeps.

I began to keep a diary, which I started on Tuesday, 11 January 1944. Subsequently, when I was assigned to HMS *Jason*, I was required to keep a Midshipman's Journal. The narrative that follows includes the complete entries of that journal, plus the daily entries from the diary, which I continued to keep concurrently and from which I have deleted direct repetition of the journal entries. These diary entries record activities and observations that could not be properly included in the journal, which had the status of an official document. In journal and diary entries, I have

NORTH TO SCAPA FLOW   49

changed some actual names of individuals or used traditional nicknames where this seems appropriate. Rereading these entries years later, I am struck by the way in which each exercise that was conducted during the early months of 1944 provided one component of a sequence that would be put together in the passage to Sword Beach. It was as if we were being given separate pieces of a giant puzzle to study. When we were thoroughly familiar with each piece, we would be told at the right time how and when we were to put the pieces together.

January 11, Tuesday

Diary: [first page missing] . . . and proceeded to A/S [anti-submarine] boom. Met *MMS86*. Sweeping until about 11 A.M. Parted company and recovered missing float by lowering skiff. Returned Granton Roads¹ and anchored. Managed to take two snaps. Shifted anchorage later in the afternoon. Took charge of foc'sle party for anchoring. Argued Russo-Polish question all evening.

January 12, Wednesday

Diary: Weighed anchor 0845 and proceeded Granton harbour entrance. Embarked two training officers (RNR)—one a Belgian. Swept in company with *[MMS]86* from the boom out to the estuary. *[MMS]86* developed defect and dropped astern. Was replaced by HMT [HM Trawler]² *Valmont*. Returned alongside Granton Middle Pier at 2:30 P.M. Went onto *86* and chatted with Spooner. Then went ashore. Met Mayne and Callum. Spooner, Mayne and I went onto the Cavendish for a dance. Aboard 11:30 P.M.

January 13, Thursday

Diary: Rose late (0830) and after good breakfast called on Spooner on the *86*. Both went along to see Mayne on HMT *Pierre Andree* and after a brief chat went in search of a bath at Larkfield Officers quarters. Went into the Royal Forth Yacht Club by mistake, and after a brief confab with a Capt. Tanner, RNR, wended our way. Duly bathed and visited barber. Back on board to find Lt. Kinloch (C.O.) with his br. (a CW candidate). Had lunch and talked shop. C.O. and his br. went ashore for a few hours. No. 1 went out for the afternoon. Spooner came

1. Roads refers to a semiprotected area of water near a harbor that is available for passage or anchorage.
2. Most of the HM trawlers had been requisitioned by the Admiralty into the Royal Navy for the duration of the war.

over for whisky. Had tea with C.O, and br. when they returned. Quiet evening listening radio. Wrote Des.

January 14, Friday

Diary: Quite a busy day. "General Drill" in the morning. The hands dashing from action stations to fire stations[3] and the Commander M/S yelling orders from the jetty. Then along to hear a lecture from him in the Transit shed of the Middle Pier. Later in the morning went along to the Pay Office for the pay of the ship's company. Just after lunch Spooner came dashing over to say Mayne had an appointment. Both went over to the *Pierre Andree*. He is going to Algiers as No. 1 of an MMS or BYMS. He went home on three weeks leave this afternoon. Last I shall see of him, I suppose. Left harbour 5 P.M., anchored at 5:25 in Granton Roads. Couple of flares dropped over Granton—nothing of importance.

January 15, Saturday

Diary: Weighed anchor 0930. Sweeping with *MMS86* until 1230. During the morning did chart corrections. Practised weighing anchor by hand in afternoon. Went into the engine room to have a yarn with Chief Engineman. Lazy day on the whole. Anchored off Granton Roads all afternoon and evening. Note: The Wardroom. Small but cosy. Two cabins adjoining—one for the Captain, one for No. 1. Tiny collapsible table in one corner with right-angled locker seat. Small cupboard and serving-hatch. Capt's desk in other corner. Wireless set on top of safe completes other corner. Two arm-chairs, small electric fire, and book-shelves. Telescope on bulk-head, beneath clock and barometer. This is our home. Capt. (Kinloch) ex-lawyer—from Glasglow. No. 1, (Craigie) ex-accountant—from Alexandria (Glasgow).

The A/S boom referred to when the diary opens was a defense against intrusion by U-boats into the waters of the River Forth. Each major harbor was protected by a boom, which consisted of two long metal nets that hung down to the seabed from a thick wire cable supported by a series of floats. The nets met and overlapped in the middle, like a divided gate. One of the nets was attached to the stern of a boom-net vessel that had the immensely tedious job of towing the boom around to open the

3. The crew were ordered to action stations to deal with any impending attack, to be ready for any combat action, or to deal with any serious emergencies. Each man had an action station at a gun, in the engine room, or elsewhere. My station was at the navigation plot on the chart table in the wheelhouse. Fire stations were the locations assigned to crew members if the ship was on fire.

gate to permit ships to come in and then towing it back into position to close the gate. Boom-net gate vessels had been named (by somebody at the Admiralty with a glimmer of humor) with names such as *Punnet*, *Magnet*, *Planet*, *Plantagenet*, and *Jennet*. The "net" ending presumably compensated for the complete inappropriateness of these names to the activities of a boom vessel.

In *MMS84*, I was really a supernumerary, helping in, or just watching, various tasks while sweeping and sleeping on the wardroom couch at night. Kinloch and Craigie had had some falling out well before I came on board, which took the form of not talking to each other unless absolutely necessary when in the wardroom. Duty made it necessary for them to suspend this war of silence when we were actually at sea or otherwise working. This left me in the uncomfortable and unsolicited position of acting as intermediary between them whenever communication became necessary. Thus, "Would you mind asking Craigie if he has finished with the mustard yet?" and "Please as Kinloch whether or not that is my copy of *The Scotsman* that he is reading." Both read *The Scotsman*, a major Scottish newspaper, and both did the crossword puzzle that was in it each day. This produced a kind of tacit, and taciturn, competition as to who was getting the puzzle completed first, with hints from each to me that perhaps I could report how far the other had gone toward the solution.

Relief came on 16 January with news of a regular appointment. I had orders to report immediately on board HMS *Jason*, a fleet minesweeper of the First Minesweeping Flotilla lying at Portsmouth. The whole Royal Naval Barracks at Portsmouth, in its capacity as a stone frigate, was known as HMS Victory and is now known as HMS Nelson. The original HMS *Victory*, a ship of the line berthed at Portsmouth, had been Nelson's flagship at the Battle of Trafalgar. In peacetime, the *Victory* is open to the general public. In wartime, it was used to house officer cadets who were judged to require further training before receiving a commission. The *Victory* is now permanently maintained as a museum ship by the Navy and always has been the symbolic flagship of Commander-in-Chief, Portsmouth; it continues to be the flagship of Commander-in-Chief, Naval Home Command.

January 16, Sunday

Diary: Weighed anchor at 0900 and proceeded eastwards to No. 22A buoy in company with HM Ts [trawlers] *Wallena*, *Elena* and *Valmont*. Dan buoys laid by yacht *Sylvana*. Swept westwards from 22A buoy to Granton Roads, 1230–1730. Berthed Middle Pier. Lt. Jack waiting for us to tie up. Brought me along to M/S Office where appointment was waiting for me. Proceed Portsmouth immediately to join HMS *Jason* (Fleet-sweeper, *Halcyon* class). Packed bags, caught 2140 train from Waverley.

HMS *Jason*

The commanding officer of HMS *Jason* (Comdr. Trevor George P. Crick, RN) required that I keep a journal in the proper manner. He commanded me to order the regulation Midshipman's Journal, and meanwhile to keep my journal in the standard issue Royal Naval Note-book, S 1295-a, to be copied into a regulation journal when available (thus I have called my Midshipman's Journal "temporary"). When I tried to order the regulation Midshipman's Journal from the supply office in Portsmouth, however, I was informed that this journal was no longer being produced because of the war; therefore, the temporary journal was never recopied. I had no example of what a Midshipman's Journal looked like. When I inquired of Crick, he said it was important to record things that contributed to my training and experience as a sea officer. It was his insistence that keeping the journal include the practice of making appropriate diagrams of maneuvers and sketches of ships and harbor views. I was required to present this journal to Commander Crick from time to time for his inspection; when inspected, he stamped each last entry with an oval stamp recording the date and reading COMMANDING OFFICER HMS *JASON*, which he signed T. G. P. Crick.

The journal opens as follows:

January 17, Monday

MIDSHIPMAN'S JOURNAL
(Temporary)
Midshipman Brendan Arnold Maher, RNVR

1944
JANUARY   H.M.S. *Jason*—PORTSMOUTH

Monday 17th. Joined H.M.Ship *Jason* at Portsmouth Dockyard 1245. Reported to the Officer of the Day (Lt. Rivers, RNVR) and then to the First Lieutenant, Lt. Owen, RNR. The *Jason* is undergoing final stages of refit and is in the hands of dockyard workmen. Later in the day reported to the Captain (Commander T. G. P. Crick, R.N.) and saw to the stowage of my gear in the ship's office. Camp-bed was rigged for me and I turned in early. Note. The *Jason*, now a fleet minesweeper of the *Halcyon* class, was originally built as a surveying vessel by the Ailsa

Shipyard. She is now second Senior Officer's ship of the First Flotilla and was based on and operating in North Russia before refit. Complement approx: 125 men. Main armament: one 4-inch gun. Displacement 1300 tons (approx.)

Ward Room Officers

First-Lt.	Lt. Owen, OBE, RNR
FXLE[4]	Lt. Rivers, RNVR
Gunnery Lt.	Lt. James, RNVR
Asdic and CBs	Lt. Bridges, RNVR
Engineer	Eng.-Lt. Sharp, RNR
Electrical Off.	Elec-Lt. Sandhill, RNVR
M.O. [Medical Officer]	Surg-Lt. Guy, RNVR
Navigator.	Lt. Charter, RNVR

Diary: Traveling overnight. Arrived King's Cross 0945. By tube to Waterloo. Caught 1045 train to Portsmouth. Arr. 1200. After much difficulty managed to get a taxi to the docks, sharing it with Free French ensign. After stooging around the docks, found *Jason* and reported to 1st Lieutenant. Ship undergoing final stages of refit. Dockyard workers swarming all over. Terrific racket from drills, etc. Had lunch. Saw Captain—Commander Crick RN—and settled in. Sleep on camp-bed in ship's office. Turned in early.

Commander Crick was a career officer who had retired just before the war started. He had been immediately called back into the service, as were all retired officers and men in the reserves. He was a stocky, muscular man and was rumored to have been the middleweight champion boxer of the Royal Navy in his time—his pair of the most battered cauliflower ears that I had ever seen convinced me that this might well have been so. He was ruddy of face, not much given to humor, and deliberate of speech and manner except in emergencies. I found him to be a fair-minded man, devoted to the Navy, and somebody in whose seamanship we all had confidence. Truly, like Sir Patrick Spens of the old ballad, he was a "skeely skipper."[5]

The officer in command of a ship of the Royal Navy is always referred to as the commanding officer (CO). A commanding officer does not necessarily hold the actual rank of captain. The CO can be of a lower

4. Abbreviation for forecastle, or fo'c'sle (foc'sle, British spelling). Lieutenant Rivers was in charge of the fo'c'sle (i.e., of anchoring, mooring, etc.) in addition to his watchkeeping and office duties.

5. From the ballad "Sir Patrick Spens," author unknown, circa sixteenth century; the term means skillful seaman.

commissioned rank or higher but is always the highest-ranking executive branch officer on board. The commanding officer's rank could be as low as midshipman in very small craft, such as certain kinds of landing craft. In the Merchant Navy, the correct term for the officer in command of a merchant vessel is the master. The use of the term "captain" to refer to the officer in command of a ship is so ingrained in nautical tradition and popular use that it is often used in ordinary speech within the Royal Navy but never in official documents.

Should the commanding officer be killed or injured too badly to exercise command of the ship, the next highest-ranking executive branch officer assumes command, regardless of the possibly higher rank of any other specialist in the ship. For example, during World War II, a frigate escorting a convoy in the Atlantic was hit by a torpedo. The ship stayed afloat, but the explosion killed or severely wounded all the officers on the bridge except the midshipman who was down aft at the time. He automatically assumed command of the ship; the engineer officer, of much higher rank and senior to the midshipman, nonetheless now became subordinate to him. The second officer in seniority, immediately below the commanding officer of a warship, is referred to as the first lieutenant. Colloquially, fellow officers call that officer "Number One," while the ratings always use the term "Jimmy the One," or "Jimmy" (although not in the officer's hearing). First lieutenant is not a rank—it is a position. Thus, in a very small vessel commanded by a lieutenant, if the second senior officer holds the rank of sub-lieutenant, that officer is still referred to as the first lieutenant.

Lieutenant Owen, RNR, the *Jason's* first lieutenant, was a dark-haired man of middle build, with a plumpish face that almost always wore a wary, somewhat testy expression. He had been a deck officer in the P&O line. Passenger lines, such as the P&O, Cunard, and Royal Mail, required a certain amount of elegance, as well as high competence, in their officers. Lieutenant Owen reflected this. Being, by virtue of his rank, the president of the wardroom mess, he tried hard to maintain some of the rituals of peacetime. A plan to institute Mess Night dinner in the wardroom fizzled after two or three attempts. The conditions of sea service made the black bow tie and wing collar impossible to maintain on a regular basis. Even so, Lieutenant Owen appeared in dinner dress himself—starched shirt and black bow tie, his feet encased in calf half-Wellingtons and black silk hose.

Lieutenant Owen was mildly unpopular with the other members of the wardroom mess, especially with the chief engineer. On one occasion, Owen managed to get some braces of hare. He insisted that these be hung until the hoped-for rotten smell indicated that they were "high," at which time they could be served as jugged hare. To the distress of the stewards, the hare was hung in their pantry. In due course, the ripeness of the smell met Owen's standards, jugged hare was served as a mess dinner. Owen was pleased with the menu, although he criticized the wine and blamed the officer who was "wine secretary" for the choice. Personally, I found the combination of wine and cooked rotten meat quite distasteful and was at a loss to understand why it was considered a delicacy.

Lieutenant Sandhill, the electrical officer, was from Yorkshire. He had graduated from Sheffield University in electrical engineering. Clearly a master of his trade, Sandhill was well liked and respected by everybody. He was particularly kind to me. He felt that the Royal Navy was hard on midshipmen and that, in time of war, perhaps some of the differences in rank might be observed with less vigor. He was outspoken in his objections to Mess Night and to jugged hare in particular.

The chief engineer was Lieutenant (E) Sharp, RNR. Like all chief engineers, he was invariably addressed as "chief." Sharp had spent his life as an engineer, mostly with the P&O Line on freighters in the Far East. As an officer in the Royal Naval Reserve, he was called into the Royal Navy when the war came. Chief was Cornish and had a broad Cornish accent. His understanding of marine engines was apparently excellent, but he had attitudes that years of service in the Merchant Navy tended to generate. One of these had to do with the cost of fuel. Merchant ships always sailed at the speed that was most economical with fuel, mainly because traveling at maximum speed added enormously to fuel consumption per mile without adding more than one or two knots to actual speed. One less day on a two-week voyage added costs that did not justify the small percentage of time gained. Fuel economy was the responsibility of the engineer, and the company would be critical of an engineer whose fuel consumption appeared extravagant.

Another Merchant Navy attitude was that the captain was in command of the rest of the ship, but the chief engineer was in command of the engine room and its crew. This was not legally the case, but the custom had evolved and was rarely challenged. In the Royal Navy, where discipline was much stricter, no such custom existed, although a wise commanding officer dealt respectfully with the chief engineer. Shortly after leaving Portsmouth bound for Scapa Flow, Commander Crick decided that he should test the speed of the *Jason* to make sure that the refit had done whatever it was supposed to do to engine room performance. Accordingly, he ordered "emergency full ahead." This was rung down on the engine room telegraphs. Crick noticed an increase in speed but not what he had expected. He called down the voice pipe and asked if this was really all that could be achieved with the engine flat out. A kind of rumbling came up the voice pipe, and suddenly the ship picked up speed, with clouds of black smoke pouring out of the funnel. Crick appeared satisfied and began to read various instruments to check the speed. At that point, the door to the bridge burst open. Chief stamped onto the bridge, cap on head, clad in blue dungaree overalls spattered with oil.

He shouted at Crick, "You can't do this, we're using too much fuel, and the company won't like it. I'm going back down below to reduce speed."

Crick looked at him with a kind of puzzled compassion. "Chief," he said, "I'm the commanding officer. Do as I say. And try to remember that there is no company."

Yet another hangover from Chief's earlier days arose from the fact that his stokers and firemen on the P&O line had been mainly lascars (Indians recruited in Asia). Discipline was enforced in the engine room of a freighter with fewer regards for the established rights of ratings than was the case in the Royal Navy but also with fewer disciplinary measures officially available. The use of fists and other physical abuse was more common in merchant ships; although verbal abuse was common enough in the Royal Navy, for an officer to strike a man, or vice versa, would result in very serious consequences. Chief chafed under these restrictions. He frequently complained that the Navy, in general, and Crick, in particular, would not let him have "a fair crack of the whip." In spite of his irascibility, Chief was always rather friendly to me. Perhaps matters of rank were less significant to him, and I benefited from that. On one occasion, I proposed to him that his grumbling was an attempt to get "a fair whap at Crick." The bad pun amused him, and it became a current phrase in the wardroom for a while.

All of this contributed to an incident that arose during the censoring of letters sent by the crew. All mail going out from the ship had to be censored to remove anything that might be of use to the enemy— location, actions taken, other ships in the area, and so forth. Censoring was done by officers, mainly the surgeon-lieutenant ("Doc"), but with assistance from any other officer available at the time. Surg.-Lt. Guy was a physician first, second, and third; being a naval officer came a distant fourth. He was respected as a physician and much liked as a member of the wardroom, but he was not always as punctilious in his observance of naval requirements as he might have been. During one censoring session, he laughed aloud and began to read a quote from a letter written by a stoker to his wife. The stoker had written to the effect that he liked the ship but disliked the engineer; he described him as a "bloody awful engineer—not fit to be the chief engineer to a pram," plus more to the same effect. Chief was in the wardroom as this was read aloud, and he was on his feet in an instant, demanding to know who had written the letter. Doc, realizing that he should not have read the contents of a letter aloud anyway, refused to identify the writer.

Chief made for the door and headed in the direction of the stokers' mess. He was muttering angrily, "I know who it is, I know who would write a thing like that, I'll teach him!" Two or three other officers present seized him by the arms and forced him to sit down until he cooled off. The first lieutenant reminded him again that the stokers were not lascars and this wasn't the P&O. Nothing more was heard of the incident, but Doc learned to do his future censoring in silence.

When I joined the *Jason* at Portsmouth, as recorded in my diary, she was just completing a refit. Her last voyage before the refit had been to Murmansk, Russia, as an escort for a convoy carrying weapons, tanks, and other materials of war to the Soviets. The voyage had been made in winter under very harsh conditions. When she arrived at Portsmouth, some of the crew, after being granted leave home, were assigned to other ships, but several of the officers and many of the men remained with the *Jason*. In Murmansk, they had obtained fur hats on which they had sewn their normal cap badges. As these hats were not "proper uniform," they were worn only when the ship was at sea. They appeared when we were bound for Scapa Flow after the refit had been completed. Incidentally, at sea there was little concern for uniform. While it was more or less necessary to wear a uniform cap and badge, any kind of pants, sweaters, or seaboots were acceptable. At action stations, we wore steel helmets, with the stripe of rank painted in miniature on the front.

Parenthetically, I should mention that certain kinds of clothing—woolen caps, woolen gloves, scarves, sweaters, and other items known as "comforts" (presumably to distinguish them from necessities) were not part of the official issue of clothing. These items, mostly made ashore by volunteers or donated by commercial companies, were always under the jurisdiction of the base chaplain, who issued them to ships as circumstances seemed to warrant. Although warm clothing of this kind was always available for service in northern waters during the winter, apparently it was not always adequate for weather conditions during the passage to Murmansk, hence the attraction of the Russian fur caps. Chaplains also issued other comfort items, such as phonographs and records and popular books. Official naval clothing issued for cold-weather watch-keeping was either the ubiquitous beige-colored duffle coat or a long black greatcoat, reaching down to the ankles, that was known as a "watch coat." On small ships, where bridge and watch positions were very exposed, a kind of single-garment coverall insulated with kapok was provided. These were standard issue on motor torpedo boats (MTBs). Watch coats and duffle coats were issued to the ships, rather than to individuals, and were passed from hand to hand when the watch changed. Inevitably, the supply dwindled as enterprising individuals founds ways to take them when they were transferred to another ship or went home on leave.

Reminiscences of the Murmansk convoys were common in the wardroom and mess deck. Ships of the First Minesweeping Flotilla had served as escorts to those convoys for some time and had been attacked by German aircraft and ships more than once. Experiences in Murmansk and the Kola Inlet had not been positive. By Russian order, Allied officers and crews were not allowed any shore liberty. Individuals went ashore only on Royal Navy business. What particularly came up in conversation was the treatment by the Russians of their own citizens. When the *Jason* was surrounded by ice at the dockside, civilians tried to come up to the ship's side to barter or ask for cigarettes or food. In some cases, Soviet soldiers fired on them to drive them away. The net impression that most of the *Jason*'s crew gained was of a suspicious, hostile, and readily brutal attitude toward any interaction between Soviet citizens and Allied forces.

Escorting convoys to the Soviet Union was regarded rightly as one of the hardest duties to which a ship might be assigned. Some members of the *Jason*'s crew had known friends in her sister ship, HMS *Bramble*, also part of the First Minesweeping Flotilla. During the escort of the large convoy JW 51.B to Murmansk, the *Bramble* was sunk in a battle that pitted a German force consisting of the pocket battleship *Hipper*, the cruiser *Lützow*, and six destroyers against five British destroyers and five smaller craft. The last message from the *Bramble* was that she was in contact with the enemy and was going in to attack.[6] One British destroyer and the *Bramble* were sunk before the arrival of the British cruisers *Sheffield* and *Jamaica*. The Germans then withdrew, leaving the convoy undamaged. The German failure to affect the convoy is reported to have led Hitler to replace Adm. Erich Raeder with Adm. Karl Dönitz as commander-in-chief of the German naval forces, with a resulting shift away from surface vessels and toward U-boat warfare.

Convoys consisted of merchant ships carrying troops, military supplies, and other items of war, together with warship escorts to protect them from enemy assault. Each convoy had a letter designation, followed by an identifying number. The most famous (or disastrous) of the convoys was PQ 17, which suffered particularly heavy losses in 1942. Before a convoy proceeded to sea, the captains of all ships involved, both naval and merchant, assembled on board the ship of the convoy commodore to be briefed about the disposition of ships in the convoy at sea, the reported presence of U-boats, signals to be used, and action to be taken should the convoy be attacked.

When time allowed, as was the case during a refit, training continued. Many short training courses were available at large bases, such as Portsmouth. The midshipman was a natural candidate for whatever training there was to be had. My first days in the *Jason* were occupied mostly in these courses.

The *Jason* was a happy ship, although (or perhaps because) discipline was strict. The facilities were good—sick-bay, medical officer, ship's canteen for the crew, good food, and a good atmosphere in the wardroom despite Chief's outbursts and Owen's tendency to fits of surliness. The *Jason* was a "pusser" ship, a slang term for purser, which meant that things were done as the Navy wanted them done. Uniforms and procedures were according to the manuals of instructions and other regulations. This might sound cramping, but it wasn't. We really knew that this was the professional Navy and felt very much a part of it.

---

6. Published accounts of this action vary somewhat. Donald Macintyre, *The Naval War against Hitler*, New York: Charles Scribner's Sons, 1971, reports that the *Bramble*, which had been searching for stragglers from the convoy, came under fire immediately on arrival at the scene of the battle and had time only to send a signal that she was in sight of the enemy before being overwhelmed by German gunfire.

January 18, Tuesday

Midn. Journal: Went MA/STU (No. 16) [Mobile Anti-Submarine Training Unit] with Lt. Bridges and was shown plotting, with navigator's yeoman to assist. "Asdic"[7] appears to be one of the most interesting branch of Naval Science. Refit continues with various difficulties arising from time to time.

Diary: Appeared to have done well [at plotting] and will probably get it as a permanent job. Everyone very short-tempered over refit snags.

January 19, Wednesday

Midn. Journal: Again to MA/STU in morning and continued instruction and practise in plotting. In afternoon went over to the boat-shed and with guidance from Ldg. Seaman Allen brought the motor-boat alongside *Jason*. It was then hoisted inboard. Controls of the boat are quite simple to operate but I would like and need more practise in handling the boat.

Diary: In afternoon went over to boat-shed and collected motor-boat, which, with L/Sea. Allen to guide me, cox'ned it back to the *Jason*. Did two or three high-speed turns before bringing it alongside. Quite good fun. In the evening went to the Royal Naval Junior Officers' Club in Portsmouth with Bridges. Had a good meal and a mild drinking bout.

January 20, Thursday

Midn. Journal: Went again to the MA/STU in the afternoon and continued plotting practise. Also did one or two attacks. The correct technique in attacking will require some study, and Lt. Certes advises that I read CB[8] #4097. During the forenoon was present at "Up Spirits" which was supervised by Lt. Bridges.

Diary: Did nothing except try to keep out of the way all morning— rather dismal. MA/STU in afternoon. "Guns" came along with us, too. Saw "Up Spirits" done correctly in morning. Letter from Peggy and one from Dad. Quiet evening aboard.

The MA/STU was an apparatus designed to simulate the experience of detecting and attacking a U-boat. This one consisted of a double-decker London bus painted battleship gray. The top deck was fitted with

7. Equivalent to U.S. sonar. Asdic was named from the initials of the Allied Submarine Detection Investigation Committee. Under these auspices, asdic was developed at the end of World War I.

8. Confidential book. CBs include code books and certain technical instruction manuals.

bridge instruments, voice pipes, plotting table, compass, and other needed instruments. The lower deck of the bus was manned by a crew who operated simulating devices that produced asdic (sonar) echoes at specified ranges and bearings as would a real U-boat. At sea, a warship maintained continuous operation of the asdic transmitter. This device was suspended in a protective dome just below the hull of the ship; the operator transmitted repeated sound beams around the various points of the compass. If the beam encountered a solid object, a reciprocal echo was heard by the operator. Large hollow metal objects, such as submarines or wrecks, gave a characteristic echo. When such an echo was received, the operator reported the range and bearing to the bridge.

Officers and men being trained in the MA/STU took their stations on the top deck. Here, they performed what would be their actual duties on the bridge at sea, namely listening to sonar echoes, identifying and reporting bearings and distances, giving speed and helm orders, and determining depth charge settings while keeping a plot of the movements of their own hypothetical ship and the hypothetical U-boat. The goal was to get our own vessel right over the U-boat and then drop the depth charges. Getting into this position required calculating the speeds, courses, and distances of the U-boat and the attacking ship and determining the course and speed that would enable the attacker to intercept the U-boat at exactly the right point. The training officer and his crew controlled the simulation of the U-boat's movements and tried to outwit the attacker. All this was primitive simulation but very useful in training.

January 21, Friday

Midn. Journal: Basin trials in the forenoon. Stationed on bridge to watch wires leading to the jetty, during the trials. Worked in the ship's office during the afternoon. In the afternoon about 1700 went with Lt. Bridges to the CB office and thence to the *Aries* to discuss the procuration of a Midshipman's Journal with Midn. Lloyd [a classmate from King Alfred]. Air-raid over Portsmouth in the evening.

Diary: Generally tried to assist on board, mainly by standing on the bridge and watching the wires leading to the jetty, while engines were being tested. Captain spoke to me in the afternoon about Midshipman's Journal, which I have not yet been able to obtain. Went over to the *Aries* to see Midn. Lloyd. Dined there and then went up onto the upper deck to watch an air-raid in progress. Saw several planes caught in searchlight cones. One was hit and came streaming to earth with flames pouring from the fuselage. Flak looked like a fireworks display.

January 22, Saturday

Midn. Journal: Slipped 0840 and proceeded to D/G range. Thence to Cowes, Isle of Wight, to do HF/DF [high-frequency direction finder] trials with *Isle of May.* Weather too bad for trials to be undertaken. Returned to Portsmouth and berthed alongside *Alresford* and *Plover.*

Diary: Slipped 0840 and went out to D/G range. Ship heeling over at angle of 30° due to beam wind. Then on to Cowes to do trials. These were postponed due to weather so we returned to harbour and berthed alongside HMS *Alresford* and *Plover.* Went over to *Aries* and brought Lloyd back to dinner in the evening. Quite a pleasant evening with sherry and cigars.

January 23, Sunday

Midn. Journal: Went to the MA/STU with Lts. Rivers and James. The Captain came later on in the forenoon and all combined in practising attacks.

Diary: Later Lt. Certes the MA/STU officer came along to the ship to drink gins in the wardroom, and the Capt. came in to spin some yarns. In the afternoon read a little, wrote to Peggy and generally lazed around. Turned in early.

January 24, Monday

Midn. Journal: Went by steam pinnace with the Surg-Lieut. to the R.N. Hospital [Royal Naval Hospital], Haslar, Portsmouth in the forenoon. Afternoon proceeded by train to Petersfield Station and thence by wagon to HM Signal School for commencement of a short cypher course. Also with us were Lt. Robertson and Midshipman Lloyd of the *Aries.* Signal School situated in Basing Park. Course lasted from 1330 to 1800 and included cyphering and coding. On return to Portsmouth found that *Jason* was once more berthed at North Corner Jetty having been out on D/G range during the day.

Diary: Went ashore early in morning with "Doc" and caught steam-pinnace over to Haslar hospital. After ordering supplies came back via ferry and went for a hair-cut to Gieves while Doc went to the Post-Office. Then to have a snack in Kimball's café and caught train to Petersfield in company with three officers from the *Aries.* Arrived Petersfield and found truck waiting to take us and a sixth officer to H.M. Signals School. Arrived at Signal School (Basing Park) and after good lunch commenced cypher course. 1400–1830 with a break for tea at 1630. Wren Officers[9] instructing. Quite a pleasant afternoon. Returned

9. Term for WRNS (Women's Royal Naval Service).

to Pompey [Navy slang for Portsmouth] and found that *Jason* after day's trials in Solent was back at her old berth. Turned in very tired.

January 25, Tuesday

Midn. Journal: Landed at 0825 in morning with Surgeon Lieut. and watched *Jason* leave for further trials. Proceeded to RNB, Portsmouth to purchase some clothing. Thence by train to Petersfield for second day of cypher course. Instruction in the use of "frame" and "one-time pad" methods of cyphering up. Returned to Portsmouth and back on board *Jason* at 2010 hours. Did "rounds" with First Lt.

Diary: Left ship just as gangplank was being taken away. Watched ship leave harbour for further trials. Went to RNB to get some slops and then into the wardroom there. Snack at Kimball's again. Train to Petersfield, same routine as yesterday. Sun was shining and the Hampshire countryside looked marvelous. Back on board at 2010 hours.

Both naval clothing and the clothing stores from which it could be obtained were termed "slops." Sailors, unlike soldiers or airmen, were given a periodic allowance for the maintenance of their uniforms. This allowance was entered in the sailor's pay book. When clothing was issued, the cost of the item was deducted from the accumulated allowance. Clothing stores were quite variable in the extent of their inventory, with the largest found in the stores at Royal naval barracks. Because of this, it was common to check the items available at slops whenever the opportunity arose. As the laundering of white shirts and their detachable collars was difficult to manage in a small ship, such as a minesweeper, officers tried to keep a substantial supply of white collars, as these could be washed by hand. To save on washing, collars of disposable white cardboard were popular. Although it was possible to have laundry done ashore, it was likely that the ship would have sailed to another port before the clean laundry could be returned. On one occasion, a packet of my laundry followed the ship through three locations before it finally caught up with me.

In the *Jason*, I was treated in the ambiguous way that midshipmen always have been treated in the Royal Navy. On one hand I was a commissioned officer, but on the other hand I was very inexperienced in the skills of the profession. Hence, I was often assigned to do things intended to extend my practical education. Each evening in harbor or at anchor, there was a ceremony known as "rounds," in which the officer of the day (OOD) did a tour of the mess decks to see that everything was clean and shipshape. The petty officer of the day came to the wardroom and reported to the officer of the day, "Ready for rounds, sir." The officer of the day, preceded by a quartermaster piping his bosun's call and by the petty officer of the day, toured the lower deck. The call shrilled, the petty officer of the day shouted, "Attention for rounds," and everybody got to their feet and stood to attention as the little procession passed from one area to another in a fairly rapid walk. The procedure rarely took more than five minutes. It was intended to be an inspection for general order and cleanliness, which were nearly always in good shape at any time.

I had been required to accompany the OOD on a number of occasions to see how rounds were done. One evening, I was told that I should take the part of the OOD. The procession passed off without incident, but minutes after I had returned to the wardroom, the petty officer came to the door and, with a straight face, reported that "This" had been found pinned to a bulletin board. "This" was a reasonably well-executed pencil drawing, showing a quartermaster with bosun's call, followed by a baby in a pram. The baby wore a naval officer's cap and midshipman's tabs on its collar, and the pram was being pushed by a petty officer. The caption read, "Doing the Rounds on HMS *Jason*." I thanked the petty officer, who permitted himself a suspicion of a smile, endured the great amusement of my elders and betters in the wardroom, and kept the drawing. It came home with me to Swinton on leave and was there for years before it finally disappeared.

The cyphering and coding course, mentioned in my Midshipman's Journal above, included a brief introduction to the Royal Navy version of the Enigma scrambling coder. The device shown to us included a rather large typewriter with a series of disks mounted vertically next to each other, marked with numbers on the rim. The operator set the disks at a sequence of numbers, rather like one does with a suitcase lock, and then typed the message in plain language. With each stroke of the keyboard, the disks revolved and the numerical sequence determined which letter of the alphabet would be actually printed. To decode the message, the receiver had to have the same machine and know the original setting of numbers.

At sea, the radio telegrapher's office received a continuous flow of coded messages. These covered anything to do with the movement of ships, our own or the enemy's; weather reports; technical instructions from the Admiralty; and other information. In the *Jason*, we did not have anything as sophisticated as the Enigma machine. The codes all involved the transmission of groups of digits, which were preceded by a set of digits indicating the page and column of the code book to be used in decyphering them. Decyphering, always done by officers, involved laboriously checking the groups of digits against the code book to turn them into letters. Most of the signals turned out to be reporting some event hundreds of miles away, but every so often one turned out to have immediate importance to us. The atmospheric interference in radio transmissions meant that there was always a steady sprinkling of errors that produced so-called corrupt groups of digits impossible to decode. Sometimes we could guess the intended meaning of the corrupt group (e.g., that "battleshop" really meant "battleship"), but it was a major problem when the missing item referred to a latitude or longitude, bearing, or distance.

There were different levels of code book for varying degrees of security. The maximally sensitive were more complicated and were changed with greater frequency, that is, what was identified as Column 1, Row 1, as the starting point would vary every few hours (the "frame" method). Thus, the same string of digits meant a different letter depending on the time of transmission; by the time the enemy figured out what a particular string meant, the meaning would have changed. In the "one-time pad" method, used for messages requiring a lower degree of security, the transmitter selected a page from a cypher pad to make up the message and indicated the page number when the message was transmitted. The message was decyphered from that page of the pad, but the response was made by selecting a different page to encode the letters; hence, a given set of digits in the response would decode into different letters than the same digits in the original transmission. When not in actual use, code books and cypher pads were kept locked in the ship's safe with other confidential books. At sea, certain confidential books, including the code books, were kept on the bridge in a large bag with perforated sides and weighted with lead. The bag was to be thrown overboard in the even of the ship sinking or being in danger of capture.

After the *Jason*'s refit was completed, several more tasks were necessary before the ship could proceed to sea in a condition fit for active service. New crew members arrived to replace those who had been drafted to other ships at the beginning of the refit. The new arrivals had to be integrated into the working teams of the ship. This meant practice in the operation of the sonar and radar systems, lifeboat drills, boat handling, gunnery, depth charge firing, and other procedures. Much of this could not be done in harbor and therefore had to wait until the ship put to sea.

The arrival of new crew members involved a significant amount of paperwork. Naval paperwork followed arcane principles; to understand it required training. In addition to instruction in cyphering and coding, my own training at this point included naval office procedures. The following journal and diary entries record the unfolding of this process.

January 26, Wednesday

Midn. Journal: Landed 0800. Proceeded with Surg.-Lt. to RNH Haslar. Thence to RNB to pay office to obtain clothing and tropical clothing coupons. Also raised one or two queries which Lt. Rivers was dealing with.

Diary: Ashore again in the morning before 0800. Whiled away an hour in the lounge of the Keppel's Head hotel and then went over with Doc to Haslar Hospital. Later went to RNB for clothing coupons and then on to Petersfield. Did final afternoon on cypher course and then back to ship. Riding from the Signal School to Petersfield Station in the twilight was good. Hampshire lanes and villages look their best at that hour. Letter from Dad on board. Turned in early.

January 27, Thursday

Midn. Journal: Working all day in the ship's office. Appointment arrived for Lt. Rivers to go to Asbury Park N.J. for BYMS. Commenced rudimentary instruction in office routine, given by Lt. Rivers. Relief due to arrive on 31st is Lt. S. T. Fox, RNVR.

Diary: Did nothing in particular except to root around the ship's office to see what there was of interest and acquaint myself with the office routine. Lt. Rivers received a draft chit to go to the USA to pick up a ship and as Assistant Correspondence Officer I am trying to learn rudiments of his job.

January 28, Friday

Midn. Journal: Went with Lt. Rivers to the office of the Dockyard Cashier to draw pay for the Ship's Company (£650 approx.). Assisted with General Payment. In the afternoon went to the Pay Office RNB to draw money for casual payments to newly-joined ratings. Leave given to the Stbd. Watch from P.M. today until A.M. Tuesday. Noticed that one section of the Dockyard is working by night in the construction of LCTs [landing craft tanks], etc.

Diary: Paid the men and in afternoon went over to RNB for money for casual payment to newly-joined members of crew. Leave to Stbd. watch granted from Friday P.M. to Tues. A.M. I go on week-end tomorrow noon. Noticed that one part of the dockyard is working all through the night by the light of arc-lamps to build landing-craft. Second Front can't be very far off.

January 29, Saturday

Midn. Journal: Supervised "Up Spirits" in the morning. 1230 proceeded on leave.

Diary: Supervised "Up Spirits" and got a tot neat from the Cox'n. Drank it and immediately went weak at the knees and was almost incapable for the rest of the morning. Sobered up after lunch and caught train, in company with the Engineer Officer, from the harbour station to Waterloo. Thence from Euston to Manchester (arr. 1045 P.M.). Met Lt. Hall at Greengate bus-stop—he used to teach at Moorside School where Mother is teaching now. Family surprised to see me but very pleased.

I still have the Travel Authority for the weekend leave in my possession; it reads:

The bearer, Mid. B. A. Maher, RNVR, is entitled to travel on leave commencing Saturday, 29th January 1944. Signed B. R., Lt. RNVR. For Security Reasons this travel authority should be handed in to issuing authority or new unit on completion of leave.

LCTs were small vessels capable of carrying up to two tanks or other small vehicles, which were unloaded onto the beach with a ramp that folded down from the front of the bow. Because of the square bow and very shallow draft necessary to their task, LCTs were difficult to maneuver, being subject to crosswinds and waves much more than a vessel with a deeper draft. They were crucial to an invasion because they were designed to land their cargoes directly onto beaches. Construction of large numbers of them was a strong indication that the preparations for a major landing were in hand. There were repeated signs, such as the issue of tropical clothing coupons, that the *Jason* might be bound for tropical waters, along with the *Alresford* and probably other ships. By hindsight, it appears likely this was done to mislead both us and enemy intelligence as to our actual future movements.

January 30, Sunday

Diary: Went to 11:00 Mass at St. Mark's. Long sermon and after lunch went over to Peggy's. She was very surprised to see me but also very pleased. Had a good time.

January 31, Monday

Diary: Rose late. During the day brought my ration card to the CWS [Cooperative Wholesale Society]. Also bought some collars from Long-

worth's, and then met Peggy in evening. Jolly crowd at the Banks
ménage—Mary, Peggy, Agnes, Ernest, Kenneth, Mr. & Mrs. Banks and
I. Played cards all evening and then went into town to catch train.

February 1, Tuesday

Midn. Journal: Arrived back on board *Jason* 1045. Lt. Fox now on
board. Arrangements having been made for us both to proceed to the
Accountant Base—Boscawen at Weymouth. Accordingly, caught 1445
train from Portsmouth station and after traveling via Southampton arrived at Weymouth 2030 hours. Wren guide conducted us to
Weymouth Bay Hotel where we were to stay.

Diary: Caught the 1205 train from London Rd. Station, getting into
Euston at 0800. Caught 0845 from Waterloo to Portsmouth harbour.
On arrival on board *Jason* met Lt. Fox and found that we have to go to
HMS Boscawen this same afternoon for a four-day course in correspon-
dence and Navy accounts. After lunch we caught train from
Portsmouth—arr. Weymouth via Southampton at 8.30 P.M. Wren was
waiting at the station to escort us to the Weymouth Bay Hotel. Went to
Criterion Café for supper, and turned in. My first sleep since Sunday
night.

February 2, Wednesday

Midn. Journal: Proceeded to Boscawen pay office and commenced short
course instruction in (a) rating's pay accounts and (b) ship's office routine. Had introductory talk to Commanding Officer, Paymaster-Capt.
G. E. Maynard RN and also to Lt. Cmdr. A. M. Baker RNR, the assistant Paymaster. Ldg/Writer Innes, in the ship's office department, gave
us a very useful list of pay AFOs [Admiralty Fleet Orders].[10]

Diary: Breakfasted late and meandered along to Boscawen. Pottered
about from one department to another all morning, and later lunch at
the hotel, did the same all afternoon. Very nice bevy of Wrens at Boscawen.

February 3, Thursday

Midn. Journal: Continued instruction at Boscawen throughout the forenoon. After lunch went to Portland Dockyard where we obtained tropical kit necessary by reason of the appointment [to *Jason*].

---

10. Bulletins and memoranda, issued with great frequency, by the Admiralty, of
rules, regulations, and amendments governing every conceivable topic, from how to
pay a rating to what to do if the ship is sinking.

Diary: Boscawen in the morning for a short time, and then after lunch went over to Portland Bill to get slops from the Dockyard there. Went to cinema in the evening.

February 4, Friday

Midn. Journal: Final day of course. Dealt with the victualling side under W. Supply O. Parker. Also had talk re punishment warrants with the Capt's Secretary, Pay-Lieut. C. A. Moore RNVR. Heard that the *Aries* is now destined for the Mediterranean.

Diary: Boscawen all day and cinema in the evening. Had tea at Clinton's Café—very nice, with two fellows who went through King Alfred with Fox. Both are officers on LCTs now.

February 5, Saturday

Midn. Journal: Returned to Portsmouth, and when on board the ship commenced on work in the ship's office. Things are in a very bad state, and there will be plenty of work to do before it is straightened out.

Diary: Heard that *Aries* has now gone to the Mediterranean.

February 6, Sunday

Midn. Journal: Working in the office throughout the forenoon. Went ashore in the afternoon. The refit appears to be drawing near completion at last and I expect that we will shortly be sailing.

Diary: Went with Doc to see *Crazy House* at cinema in the afternoon.

February 7, Monday

Midn. Journal: The main task to be tackled in the ship's office today was the making out of lists for the payment of the ship's company. Apparently no Nominal List of any accuracy exists on board, and in view of the fact that the fortnightly pay lists are not yet in order, casual payment must be made to all of the men. This necessitates collecting the men's pay books and calculating the amount of casual payment which they should receive. A very involved and lengthy business.

Diary: Worked in the ship's office all day with very little rest. Ship's affairs in a state of appalling chaos. Money missing from the safe. Secret documents adrift. Rivers may yet come before a board of inquiry. Spent most of the time working out pay for the ship's company.

After Rivers left to join a BYMS at Asbury Park, New Jersey, it became apparent that the ship's office for which he was responsible was quite disorganized. One instance of this was the fact that he left without handing on the combination of the ship's safe, which, of course, was locked. This meant that we had no idea how much money was in the safe, and it was necessary to send an Admiralty Signal to Rivers to ask him for the combination of the safe. His reply was that it was written in pencil on the board that supported the mattress of his bunk, and there we found it. Rivers had served with competence in the *Jason* in the Murmansk convoy escorts. He was a man of integrity, but he seemed temperamentally more suited to the life of an absent-minded scholar than to the daily practicalities of naval life. No doubt the disruptions of the refit, the departure of some of the ship's company, and the arrival of new members had contributed to the confusion in the office.

February 8, Tuesday

Midn. Journal: Working in the office throughout the day. A mess meeting held in the Wardroom. Question whether Midshipmen allowed to take part and vote was raised. Can find no ruling on the matter in KR and AI [King's Regulations and Admiralty Instructions.][11] Doctor trying to arrange a ship's company dance.

Diary: Went to slops at RNB with "Chief" and "Guns." All I could get was a set of underwear and ½ doz. collars. "Doc" busy arranging a ship's company dance for Thursday. Very heated discussion about the running of the Wardroom Mess. Turned in about 0100.

February 9, Wednesday

Midn. Journal: Working in the office throughout the afternoon. Pay lists now complete. Went with Lt. Bridges to MA/STU (No. 16) again and had further practice in Action Plotting. Captain took part in the afternoon's attack teaching. Lt. Fox proceeded to Boscawen to straighten out some of the more intricate points which have arisen in our investigation of the ship's office.

Diary: Again working in office all morning with only a very short break for lunch. After lunch went to MA/STU. Captain was there too. Fox went to Boscawen in evening to see personally about the missing money. Pleasant evening in the Wardroom, No. 1 being ashore.

February 10, Thursday

Midn. Journal: Worked all day in the office. In the evening went to the ship's company dance, which turned out to be quite enjoyable.

Diary: Very hard day, working until about 4:30, almost non-stop. In the evening went to the Queen's Hotel with Bridges and Doc, where we

---

11. *King's Regulations and Admiralty Instructions*, as the title implies, contains all rules and regulations governing the conduct of officers and ratings in the Royal Navy. This is the basic book of British naval law.

met three pre-arranged partners for the ship's company dance. Went on to the Junior Officer's Club for dinner and then to Kimbel's for the dance. Lost our partners somewhere during the evening, so I walked a Wren "home" to the Wrennery, and then walked back to ship.

February 11, Friday

Midn. Journal: Very little of interest today. In the ship's office throughout the day. Refitting trials are now almost completed. Expect that we will be sailing next week. Office work a bit complicated by the absence of Fox who has gone home on compassionate leave.

Diary: Nothing very much of note except that refitting trials are nearly completed. Usual work in office complicated by absence of Fox gone to his mother-in-law's funeral.

February 12, Saturday

Midn. Journal: Worked in the office in the forenoon.

Diary: Lazy sort of day in the morning. Letter from Sid [Walton] from RNAS [Royal Naval Air Station],[12] Camp 2, Bedhampton, near Havant. Rang him up on the 'phone and arranged to meet tomorrow (Sunday). Turned in rather late.

February 13, Sunday

Midn. Journal: Captain mustered the ship's company by the open list. Divine service held on board, and Cox'n given his Good Conduct Medal. I proceeded to Roman Catholic cathedral near RNB. In the afternoon went around the *Victory* and generally ashore. Ship under sailing orders.

Diary: I went off to Portsmouth Cathedral to Mass, and in the afternoon met Sid at the station. We went to the Theatre Royal and then to the "Continental" for dinner. A waitress brought us drinks "with the compliments of the lower deck from the table next but one." Turned around and saw the Captain's steward smiling at us. We went over to thank him. Returned late.

Now the refit was complete, and we were ready for the next step in the long preparation for the Second Front. For the *Jason*, this meant a passage to northern Scotland, where exercises and maneuvers could be conducted at some distance from possible German observation. The wisdom of distant training was to be demonstrated tragically during the rehearsed invasion at Slapton Sands in Devon on the South Coast of England in

12. Shore bases for the Fleet Air Arm.

April 1944. Here, a rehearsal of a beach assault was disrupted by E-boats[13] that penetrated a protective destroyer screen. Two LSTs (landing ships tank)[14] were sunk in the E-boat attack. More than eight hundred men were killed and many others wounded. Secrecy essential for the assault in Normandy was equally essential for the training exercises that were necessary to reach the pitch of readiness that would be required. Secrecy extended to all but the most immediate event. We sailed from point to point at short notice and were never informed of what the longer-term movements of the ship might be. An important part of the training was the experience of cooperating with the ships and men with whom we would actually sail to Normandy. These were assembled in cumulative fashion as our rehearsals progressed.

February 14, Monday

Midn. Journal: Slipped 1015 and proceeded to D/G range. When this was satisfactorily completed, proceeded to Cowes, I.o.W., where we anchored at 1630. Captain disembarked in harbour drifter [small fishing boat used as a ferry] to go to convoy conference. Motor-boat giving trouble. When engine righted by P/O Motor Mechanic, I took it around the anchorage once or twice and found it running well. Weighed anchor 1800 and proceeded to Yarmouth, I.o.W., where we anchored for the night.

Diary: I took motor-boat away and gave Doc a run around. Smashed starboard windscreen against block when coming alongside [an incident not included in the Midshipman's Journal, presumably in the vain hope that the captain would not hear about it!].

February 15, Tuesday

Midn. Journal: On bridge at 0730 when anchor was weighed and course set down Solent. Course then set Westwards along the Channel to join convoy PW. Sea moderate with cold breeze. Noon: Portland Bill abeam to starboard. Worked in the office and stood First Watch (2000–2400) with the First Lieutenant. At about 2130 ship crossed our bows which, when signaled, identified herself as SS *Olavvs*, and then joined in con-

13. Abbreviation for "enemy-boats," a British term used for German motor torpedo boats, capable of high speeds, that the Germans called "S-boats" (for Schnellboot, or fast boat).

14. Large oceangoing vessels with bow doors, rather like a car ferry, that are capable of being beached at the bow so that their cargoes of tanks can be landed.

voy. Radar rather disorganized pro tem, but no doubt will improve with practise. Correct form of reporting, and difference between true and relative bearings appears to be their main difficulty.

Diary: Turned out at 0700 and up on bridge at 0730, in time for weighing of anchor. Very cold. <u>Noon position:</u> Approximately off Portland Bill (abeam). Not feeling very good during afternoon although not sick. The Maltese cook, Benici D., very sick indeed. Went on watch (the First Watch from 2000 to 0000) with 1st Lieutenant and concentrated mainly on radar reports. Impossible to see convoy, and radar the only way to keep station. More ships joined us off Plymouth, including the SS *Olavvs*, which cut across our bows and nearly rammed us. No. 1 quite blasphemous. Turn in at 0030 Wed. morning.

At sea, the working day was divided into watches. The watches were named and timed as follows:

First watch:	2000–2400	Afternoon watch:	1230–1600
Middle watch:	0000–0400	First dog watch:	1600–1800
Morning watch:	0400–0800	Second dog watch:	1800–2000
Forenoon watch:	0800–1230		

In the Royal Navy, midnight is defined as 2400 when it marks the end of the first watch but as 0000 when it marks the beginning of the middle watch. This usage tends to apply even when a watch is not the point of reference. Thus, in harbor, one person might return to the ship and end the day by turning in at 2400, while another begins the day by getting up at 0000 to catch an early morning train to go on leave.

The reason for the two 2-hour dog watches was to create an odd number of watches in the twenty-four-hour day. This meant that when the ship was at sea and the ship's company was on duty in alternating watches, nobody would end up working the same watch periods every day. The period 1600–2000 was picked for this division into dog watches because it was the time of day when the normal daily routine was over. There was free time to relax, thus everybody was off duty two hours each day.

At sea, all watchkeeping officers, which included me, worked watches on the bridge on this schedule. The officer of the watch (OOW) was in charge on the bridge and in effective command of the ship during the period of the watch. The commanding officer was always in charge on the bridge when the ship was entering or leaving harbor; during action; and in any kind of emergency, such as very bad weather. He did not stand a watch, but his cabin was directly below the bridge and connected to it by voice pipes and telephone. It was the responsibility of the OOW to call the commanding officer if any actual or potential problem arose during a watch. At the point in an officer's career when he was judged capable of assuming responsibility for a watch, he was issued a Watch-keeping Certificate.

The ship's company was organized into divisions, also called watches. At sea, there were two watches; the "starboard" and "port" watches. The use of these terms was simply for identification and had nothing to do with the usual meaning of starboard and port. In port, the ship was commonly divided into three watches, known as red, white, and blue.

In harbor, there was no officer of the watch. Instead, one officer was assigned the duty of officer of the day. He was responsible for the super-vision of the activities of the boats, the inspection of libertymen, the maintenance of security, and the general conduct of daily routines. In peacetime, it had been the custom of the OOD to wear a sword. Wartime conditions led the Admiralty to suspend this requirement but to require, instead, that the OOD wear the sword belt minus sword. This meant that the leather loop to which the sword would ordinarily have been attached hung down below the officer's jacket, which gave the distinct impression that one of the suspenders supporting his trousers had somehow slipped from his shoulder. All in all, the effect was a little silly, and it was difficult to be sure which officer on deck was the OOD without checking the rear view of each one.

Sunday routines in harbor differed from those observed during the rest of the week. Divisions and prayers were generally observed. If the ship carried a chaplain, there was divine service. There were no chaplains in small ships; however, if a small ship were alongside a dock on Sunday, the ship's company was required to attend divine service conducted by the base chaplain. In a small ship at anchor, the substitute for divine service was a service of prayers conducted by the captain. For this service, the ship's company assembled on the quarterdeck by divisions. These con-sisted of the Stoker Division from the engine room; the Dayman Divi-sion, all the ratings who did not stand a watch, which was why they were called daymen, such as ratings who were writers (i.e., clerks), stewards, supply assistants, cooks, sick berth attendants; the Seaman Division, sub-divided into the Foc'sle Division and the Quarterdeck Division or more, depending on the size of the ship; and the Petty Officer Division. Each division was in charge of an officer.

I suspect that I was first assigned to the Petty Officer Division because it was assumed that one of the experienced petty officers would prompt me, a total novice, about the various parts of the ritual in whispers. Everyone was in No. 1 uniform. The officer in charge, with a salute, reported the presence and correctness of attendance of his division (e.g., "Petty Officer Division all present and correct, sir"). The first lieutenant then called the ship's company to attention and reported to the captain, "All divisions present and correct, sir," followed by the orders, "Off caps" and "Stand at ease." Then the captain, depending on his capacity to imitate a vicar, which was generally unimpressive, read some prayers from the *Book of Common Prayer.* They always included the prayer that contains a line asking the Lord to bless the ship's company and all those who "go down to the sea in ships and do their business in great waters." Captains who had a mind to it might command the singing of a hymn, but the only hymn they seemed to know was the one with the opening line, "O God our help in ages past," and the refrain, "O hear us when we cry to thee, for those in peril on the sea."

Ceremonials, such as the award of medals or the formal introduction of the crew to the commanding officer, also were generally conducted at this time, as mentioned in the journal entry for 13 February. Whenever there had been a substantial change in the company of HM ships, as had happened with the *Jason* after the refit, the ship's company was "mustered by the open list"; that is, the entire ship's company was assembled and presented one by one to the commanding officer, each man stating his name, rank, serial number, and special technical rating. The commanding officer typically exchanged a word or two with each man, often about his past service.

When divine service was held, Roman Catholics and Jews were excused from attendance but were required to attend a service in their own religions if possible. As the senior, and only, Roman Catholic officer, I was required to march any other Catholic members of the ship's company to the nearest church for service. If the ship were at anchor, I was ordered to take charge of the Catholic ratings and to conduct some plausible substitute for prayers in another part of the ship. I marched my little squad to the lee of a remote gun turret, led them in "Our Father" and one "Hail Mary," and then permitted them to break for a cigarette. When the final rising chorus of "Hear us when we cry to thee, for those in peril on the sea" from the quarterdeck signaled the end of the prayer service, I reassembled my ratings, and we all marched smartly back to join the others.

February 16, Wednesday

Midn. Journal: Did watch as assistant O.O.W. from 1000–1200 with the gunnery officer. First Lieutenant also wishes me to do a similar period every day in addition to doing the 1st Watch with him every evening. Practised fixing the ship by compass bearings (position lines). Not feeling too well although not sick. Exercise action stations at 1730. Arranged with navigator's yeoman to have all action plot apparatus (viz. Gladstone Protractor, pencils, lined paper) stowed away handy for instant access in the case of action. <u>Noon:</u> off Trevose Hd. Left convoy 0930.

Diary: Awoke feeling rather queasy. Up on bridge with "Guns" as O.O.W. from 1000 to 1230. Fixed position at noon (Trevose Head bearing 062°). Course now 044°. Exercise action stations at 1730, fired 4-inch and Oerlikons. Lundy Island on the port beam. Doc now quite well and back again in the wardroom. Sea abating about 1500 although wind still fresh. Parted company with convoy at 9.00 A.M. In company with *Princess Iris*, a troopship, for the rest of the day. Went on First Watch with No. 1. Nothing much of interest happening. Steering 277° around the coast of Pembrokeshire. Went off watch at midnight.

February 17, Thursday

Midn. Journal: Cyphering during the forenoon with Surg.-Lt. Did daylight watch from 1330 to 1500 with Lt. Bridges as O.O.W. Did First Watch for the third time with the First Lieutenant. Practised fixing ship by compass bearing of lights. Recognition of lights (i.e., period of flashing and no. of flashes) a bit difficult at first, but easier with practise. Wrote up the deck log at the end of the watch as I have been doing every night now since we left the I.o.W. <u>Noon:</u> Due west of Skerries Rock, Isle of Anglesey.

Diary: Breakfasted at 0900 and did cyphers with Doc until 1130. Lunched fairly early. Oropesa sweeps[15] tested for an hour or two this morning. Found that we had left *Princess Iris* at 0900 this morning. <u>Noon position:</u> Due west of Skerries Rock on the Isle of Anglesey. Went on the bridge from 1330 to 1500. Saw peaks of the Isle of Man appearing above the horizon, with clouds around the summit. Weather—roughish sea but fine sun and a breeze from E N E. Did First Watch with the First Lieutenant. Passing Belfast about 2000. Went off watch midnight. Camp bed collapsed in the middle of the night. Very uncomfortable night.

15. This was the basic sweep used against contact mines.

February 18, Friday

Midn. Journal: Worked in the ship's office all forenoon (sea much rougher). Dropped a pattern of 5 D/Cs [depth charges] at 1530. No fish to be had although ship hove to, to pick up any that might have been killed by the explosion. Was present at Captain's Defaulters[16] in cabin flat in the afternoon. First Watch again. Only light visible was Cape Wrath, so position line fixing rather difficult. Tried a running fix without much success. Radar range and bearing of the light very accurate. With more practise should become a very valuable aid to navigating. Radar picked up HMS *Milne* with great accuracy at long range. Operators definitely much improved. <u>Noon</u>: W. of the Isle of Skye.

Diary: Worked in ship's office in the morning. Sea much rougher with long Atlantic swell. <u>Noon position</u>: N W of the Isle of Skye. Dropped pattern of Depth Charges (1530) and stopped to see if any fish could be picked up. Only one fish "caught." Gannets must have had rest of them. Captain passed hand message to officers regarding the secrecy of forthcoming operations. Orders are at the moment secret and not to be discussed. Ship's company are ignorant of our destination beyond Scapa. Now our fifth day out of Portsmouth. Captain's defaulters being held in cabin flat as I write (in Lt. Sandhill's cabin). Just caught words "Off cap" spoken by the Cox'n. As I can't get out of the cabin now until "defaulters" is finished I'll write up some of the odd things I think worth remembering.

First is "Colours" in Portsmouth Dockyard. The sound of Bosun's calls shrilling across the water is very impressive, in strange contrast to the dockyard grime. Another one is the bridge at night. The extraordinary silence & stillness of lookouts and signalman. The glow from binnacles and bearing plotters, faintly red, illuminating the features of the Officer of the Watch. The flashing shore lights and dipping masthead lights of other ships. The hot cocoa during the watch. The incessant ticking of the log, and the faint whiteness of wave tops.

"Defaulters" has ended so I can finish. On watch 8–12 going round Cape Wrath.

February 19, Saturday

Midn. Journal: Entered Cromarty Firth and proceeded to the oiling jetty—Invergordon, and when oiling completed went out to anchor. Motor boat lowered to bring back Captain who had gone ashore to see

---

16. In the U.S. Navy, this procedure is usually known as "Captain's Mast."

NOIC [Naval Officer in Charge].[17] Late in the evening ships of the 15th MSF [Mine Sweeping Flotilla], led by *Fraserburgh* entered Firth and anchored. We are now in Force "S," although what the future movements of this force will be are uncertain.

Diary: Approaching Moray Firth. <u>Noon Position:</u> Just outside Cromarty Firth. Saturday evening, the *Fraserburgh* and other ships of the 15th MSF arrived and anchored.

February 20, Sunday

Midn. Journal: Normal working day during the forenoon. Spent the forenoon working in the office, where things are at last achieving a semblance of order. Main task now is the preparation of a Nominal List of the Ship's Company. "Pipe down"[18] in the afternoon.

Diary: Worked in the morning and made up for lost sleep in the afternoon. Wrote to Peggy. Sent a signal over to Jimmy [Banks] on the *Fraserburgh*. Played Lexicon in the evening.

February 21, Monday

Midn. Journal: Worked in the office throughout the day. "Clearing up" operations retarded by the arrival of mail to be dealt with. Typed orders for forthcoming night sweeping operation. This sweep will be done by the *Jason* and two danlaying trawlers, *Alexander Scott* and *Craftsman*. Commander Lewis from *Fraserburgh*, Capt. Jennings and the two trawler Skippers came aboard for a conference at 1500.

Diary: Worked throughout the day. No shore leave granted yet. No mail for me either. Unable to get over to see Jimmy yet. "Make and mend" in the afternoon.

Night sweeping was, in fact, what we were going to be doing during the invasion of Normandy. It was much more difficult than day sweeping because we could not see the other ships in our formation and lights were not permitted. During the day, station-keeping (maintaining the distance between ships) was ordinarily done with the use of a hand-held range finder—rather like a larger version of a camera range finder—which

---

17. A naval port officer and harbor master of a minor wartime shore base in a port or harbor town that did not normally have a naval base; often, retired naval officers were brought back for the position of NOIC.

18. The order to turn in to hammock or bunk to sleep. Ordinarily, it is the last piped order of the day, but it might be ordered at other times if the crew has been without sleep for a long period.

permitted one to check the distance by eye. This, of course, could not be done at night. There were two strategies. One was to attempt to keep the distance by radar readings of the distance of the ships ahead; the problem was that the distances were so close that the precision of radar was not, at that time, accurate enough to let one read distances in cables (the unit of length known as one cable equaled two hundred yards). The other strategy required much greater emphasis on the exact measurement and maintenance of course and speed. The important task was to keep the prescribed distance, which meant not getting too close or the ship would overrun a sweep wire of the ship ahead, too far apart because then mines could be missed.

Hauling in the sweep at night required more than the usual caution because any mine that had become entangled in the sweep wire would not be visible until it was within a few feet of the hull. At this distance, the sweep cable hung down more or less vertically under the ship's stern, and the danger of contact was considerable.

February 22, Tuesday

Midn. Journal: 0100 Weighed anchor and proceeded on operation "Anchor." I personally had no part in the exercise, and consequently had a normal night's sleep. The exercise however consisted of a double "O" sweep by *Jason* and dans laid by the two trawlers to mark the channel thus swept. Operation was completed successfully, apart from the laying of the starboard dans, and we returned to harbour, anchoring once more in Berth 53 at 0915. In course of amending "Manual of Minesweeping" I found it necessary to have certain amendments which were missing. Under orders from the Captain went over to *Fraserburgh* in our motor-boat, and copied out necessary tables. Returned on board at 2030.

Diary: 0100 Weighed anchor and proceeded to night sweeping exercise. Returned and anchored in Cromarty Firth 0915. In the afternoon, Captain sent me over to the *Fraserburgh* in the motor boat to get some amendments from their No. 1. Had a long chat with Jimmy, and returned to find some mail awaiting me. Quite a good day on the whole.

February 23, Wednesday

Midn. Journal: Weighed anchor 0830, and proceeded unaccompanied on day sweeping exercises including the cutting of dans laid on Tuesday morning. Work in the ship's office prevented me from personally taking part in the exercise. Spent my time in the office answering correspondence and preparing "scheme of complement" forms. Returned and anchored approx 1345. "WMP"[19] from *Fraserburgh* commenced on board 1800 and went on until 2015.

Diary: Felt a bit queasy, but it wore off during the forenoon. *Fraserburgh* crowd came over to have a chat and a beer between 1800 and 2000. South African S/Lt. went through King Alfred two divisions behind me. He was in Effingham and I in Jellicoe. Very nice bloke. Spent a couple of hours bringing my journal up to date.

February 24, Thursday

Midn. Journal: Lay at anchor throughout the day. Most of the time was spent in the ship's office. Main task at the moment is arranging the ship's company into divisions, and collecting the True Copies of service certificates. Vouchers arrived from Boscawen for the payment of tropical kit allowances.

Diary: Routine sort of day. Usual ship's office work.

When I was in the *Jason* in Invergordon, the Admiralty decided to issue wartime service chevrons. They were small and red, one for each six months of service. When this order came out, we had the task of calculating everybody's entitlement. We wound up having to order two thousand chevrons for the crew of the *Jason*. The chevrons were to be worn on the arm, just above the cuff or the gold stripe. The whole idea was unpopular from the start, and after the first issue I never heard of anyone claiming additional ones as his length of service increased. The crew did not like the idea of displaying these chevrons on their uniforms, and very few of them ever did. This attitude was common throughout the Navy, and the Admiralty soon decided that the chevrons should be optional. On one occasion some months later, I was in a pub in Dover with some shipmates when two trawler-sweeper skippers came up to the bar to order drinks. They raised their glasses, and one said, "Show your wartime service." Both flipped up the back flaps of their reefer jackets to reveal the chevrons neatly stitched to the seats of their trousers.

An invitation by the officers of one ship to the officers of another to come over for a social evening was conveyed by hoisting the flags R, P, and C, which meant, "Request the pleasure of your company." Acceptance of the invitation was signaled by hoisting the flags W, M, and P, "Accept with much pleasure." When an invitation had to be refused, the signal was conveyed by the flags M, R, and U, "Much regret unable."

19. Abbreviation for the phrase, "with much pleasure." Here, it refers to a party in the *Jason* that had been accepted by officers from the *Fraserburgh*.

Alternatively, a lamp flashing a short Morse code signal was used to convey these invitations and responses between ships.

The skippers of the two danlaying trawlers, the *Alexander Scott* and *Craftsman*, were invited to a party on board the *Jason*. A big bowl of very alcoholic punch had been mixed up, and I had been given the task of seeing that the stewards took care of the guests. The two skippers, along with nearly everybody else in the wardroom, visited the punch bowl quite frequently. At one point, I noticed that one of the skippers was fishing around the bottom of the punch bowl with his bare hand. I asked him what was the matter and if I could help him. He smiled cheerfully, bared his gums, and explained in very blurred manner that he had accidentally dropped his teeth into the punch bowl some time earlier and now wanted to retrieve them as he was going back to his own ship. The steward got a large soup ladle from the galley, and we managed to find his teeth. Under the circumstances, it seemed wiser not to mention to the other guests that there had been an unexpected ingredient in the punch for most of the evening.

February 25, Friday

Midn. Journal: Not a very eventful day. Again working in the office completing divisional arrangements. Weighed anchor 1830 and proceeded to sea to participate in sweeping exercises with ships of the 15th Flotilla. Exercise consisted of "O" sweep, "G" formation to port. *Jason* was rear ship, following *Bootle*. Weather deteriorated as the evening drew on, and by 2130 rain and sleet were falling steadily. At 2130 messenger came for me to go up to the bridge and relieve Lt. Fox, who was the O.O.W. This I did, and Lt. Fox then proceeded to radar tower. The Captain and Navigating Officer were on the bridge, and station-keeping was done mainly by radar. Visibility was extremely poor and there was difficulty in distinguishing dan buoy lights from float lights. Exercise finally completed. *Jason* returned to Cromarty Firth and anchored 0130, Saturday.

Diary: Nothing of importance during the day. 1830 weighed anchor and proceeded to sea in company with ships of the 15th M/S Flotilla for night sweeping exercise. At 2130 messenger came from the bridge down to the Wardroom to tell me to relieve Lt. Fox as O.O.W. When I went up the weather was foul—snow and sleet pouring down and a freezing wind blowing. Visibility about 100 yards. I was relieved at 2300 and was very glad to get down below to hot cocoa. [Here the diary terminates until 28 April.]

February 26, Saturday

Midn. Journal: Captain's mess-deck rounds. During the morning supervised cleaning of the office. Then assisted Navigating Officer in calibrating radar ranges. Went ashore in the afternoon.

February 27, Sunday

Midn. Journal: Sunday divisions. I was allotted to take over Petty Officer's division. After divisions, divine service was held on the mess-deck and then "Pipe down." Went ashore in the afternoon to watch football match (Inter-ship's company) but very thick snow forced us to return to officer's club. Returned to ship by 1700 drifter.

February 28, Monday

Midn. Journal: Weighed anchor 0600 and set course for Scapa Flow. 1200 were joined by *Hussar, Harrier,* and *Speedwell* of the 1st M/S Flotilla. Continued in company, and arrived Scapa Flow 1500. Secured alongside oiler *Danmark* and 1745 slipped and proceeded to buoy in Gutter Sound. Secured 1900.

February 29, Tuesday (Leap Year Day)

Midn. Journal: Working in the ship's office throughout the morning and in the afternoon went to see the Victualling Stores Office on RFA [Royal Fleet Auxiliary][20] *Demeter.* Returned an hour later and continued working in the office.

March 1, Wednesday

Midn. Journal: Captain went to Hospital Ship *Isle of Jersey* after we had secured alongside the *Tyne*—the destroyer depot ship. Managed to obtain some "slops." Took party over to the Dome Teacher at Ringwall pier. The AVGO [auxiliary vessel gunnery officer] took me around the various gunnery teaching devices. Returned on board 1600. Bitterly cold and snowing.

March 2, Thursday

Midn. Journal: Alongside the *Tyne* all day. Working all day in the ship's office. Nothing of importance occurred except 7 days mail arrived.

March 3, Friday

Midn. Journal: Slipped 0830 and proceeded in line ahead, *Speedwell* leading, to sea. Sweeping exercise all morning with *Halcyon* and *Hussar* as Nos. 3 and 4 and the *Alexander Scott* and *Craftsman* as danlayers. Returned and after great difficulty secured to our allotted buoy in Gutter

20. Supply ships of various kinds permanently operated by the Navy.

Sound. O/S O'Shaughnessy broke his finger being buoy-jumper and Leading Seaman Slykes nearly succumbed to cold and was washed off the buoy. He hung on to the shackle and was picked up and taken inboard. No great harm suffered. Very difficult operation due to weather. No. 1 taking place of Captain. Unable to get ashore to dance at Officer's Club as promised to R.A.D. [Rear Admiral Dockyard].

When a warship moors to a permanently placed mooring buoy, she is secured by attaching her anchor cable to a large ring shackle on top of the buoy. Mooring in this way requires that the ship approach the buoy very slowly until she is close enough for the anchor cable (which has been unshackled from the anchor itself) to hang down directly over the top of the buoy. The end of the dangling cable is a few feet above water level. In advance of this, a seaman, the "buoy-jumper," is taken in one of the ship's boats to the buoy, onto which he jumps to wait for the approach of the ship itself. When the ship has come close enough to the buoy for the jumper to reach the dangling anchor cable, he shackles it onto the ring on the buoy, and he is then taken back to the ship in the small boat that has been waiting nearby. In bad weather, this can be a hazardous operation as the buoy rolls and pitches with the waves, which also wash over the buoy and its occupant. Bad weather can also cause the ship herself to bump against the buoy and hurl the jumper into the water. This is what happened at Scapa Flow. Two luckless jumpers were brought aft to the wardroom and given tots of rum to restore their moral equilibrium.

We were now in Scapa Flow, the major base of the Home Fleet. The anchorage lay in the center of the cluster of the Orkney Islands, protected from most directions by land. Battleships, battle cruisers, and aircraft carriers lay at their moorings, as they awaited the opportunity to engage any heavy warships of the German Navy that might venture out of the Norwegian fjords. Scapa Flow was the graveyard of the surrendered German Grand Fleet, scuttled in 1918. It was here that the *Royal Oak* had been sunk by a U-boat in 1939. Admiral Tovey had departed from Scapa Flow with the battleships *King George V* and *Repulse*, together with the carrier *Victorious*, to destroy the German battleship *Bismarck* in 1941. From here also departed the Allied Arctic convoys to the Soviet Union by the hazardous passage to Murmansk.

Now, we were in place to rehearse our part in the drama that lay ahead.

5

The Rehearsal

Practice yourself, for heaven's sake, in little things,
and thence proceed to greater.—EPICTETUS

Shortly after our arrival at Scapa Flow, a number of ships received a signal from the flag officer (RAD) saying that a dance and reception were being arranged at the wardroom mess ashore, largely, it seemed, for the benefit of the Wren officers, of whom there were apparently a fairly large number on the base. Each ship addressed by the signal was required to provide a specified number of officer escorts for this occasion, and I was one of four detailed for this duty by Owen. To add to the complications, we were to be billed for our own tickets to the dance plus those of our (as yet) unidentified partners. The charge for each of us of one guinea (i.e., three days' pay) would appear on our mess bills. Although the weather made it impossible to attend the dance, we were billed anyway and, in spite of complaints, never did receive a refund. We were given the explanation that the expenses had already been incurred and the costs had to be met. What was particularly annoying was that we impecunious junior officers had not volunteered but had been commanded to go.

March 4, Saturday

Midn. Journal: Slipped 0730 and proceeded in company of rest of MSF (1) to day sweeping exercises in the Pentland Firth. Weather calm. Nothing much of interest.

March 5, Sunday

Midn. Journal: Left buoy 0730 and proceeded to the Flow for radar calibration with Port Radar Officer on board. Anchored in Flow and calibration carried out. 1230 weighed and proceeded to firing exercise area with *Speedwell* and *Hussar. Halcyon* is in floating dry dock having fouled some wire yesterday around her propellers. L/A (Low Angle) shoot at towed target very accurate. Starboard scuttle [porthole] of chart house had glass shattered by blast. Aircraft target did not appear so L/A shoot with Oerlikons [20-mm rapid fire antiaircraft guns] at pellet floats towed by *Speedwell* was arranged. Night sweep commencing 2130 and continued until 2400.

March 6, Monday

Midn. Journal: *Hussar, Speedwell,* and *Jason* commenced A/S work-up[1] with submarine in the exercise area. I kept action plot with assistance of navigator's yeoman. Plot turned out very well and was pleased to find that with regular ranges and bearings coming down we could supply bridge with reasonably accurate courses and speeds of the submarine. Chief difficulty arises in connection with use of Gladstone Plotter as speed in revs. [revolutions] given by bridge is only approximate and rough estimating of distance run has to be used. Night sweeping exercises again in the evening—*Halcyon* having rejoined the Flotilla. *Britomart* arrived in Scapa in afternoon.

March 7, Tuesday

Midn. Journal: Alongside oiler at 0800. Launch from *Tyne* alongside 0845. Boarded launch and proceeded to *Tyne,* passing overturned hulk of German battleship on way. Arrived *Tyne* and caught duty launch over to Lyness. Proceeded to C.B. office to collect envelopes. Returned with bag of C.B. documents to Lyness pier and after making unsuccessful effort to obtain drifter back to *Jason* managed to be picked up by *Halcyon's* motorboat and eventually boarded *Jason*—now in Mill Bay at 1300. "Make and Mend" in afternoon. Slipped buoy 1900 and proceeded from

1. Practice exercise in which surface vessels seek to detect a submarine that, in turn, tries to avoid detection.

Scapa in Order 1[2]: *Britomart—Hussar—Halcyon—Speedwell—Jason—Alexander Scott—Craftsman.* Calm sea, full moon, and light breeze.

March 8, Wednesday

Midn. Journal: 0000 hrs. commenced Middle Watch with Lt. Bridges. Flotilla now in Order 2: *Britomart—Hussar—Halcyon* in line ahead and *Speedwell—Jason*—and trawlers abeam in line ahead. Very quiet watch. Speed 8 knots. Turned out 0745. *Halcyon* and trawlers nowhere in sight. Sea and swell rougher and longer than last night. Light breeze. Sunshine. Speed 16 knots. Proceeded south and entered Loch Alsh 1500. Moored to a buoy. Very pretty place and well sheltered anchorage. Village is very small.

March 9, Thursday

Midn. Journal: Still moored to buoy. Rest of flotilla—headed by *Harrier* (S/O) who today arrived in anchorage. Lieut. Charter returned from Inverness. Worked in ship's office most of day.

March 10, Friday

Midn. Journal: Moored to the buoy through the day. Did O.O.D. in lieu of Lieut. Charter who was attending conference in *Harrier.* On return of Lt. Charter, reverted to normal routine. Stayed on board.

March 11, Saturday

Midn. Journal: Slipped 0800 and proceeded on day sweep in "G" formation. Assisted Lieut. Bridges on quarterdeck. Saw to adjustment of sweep wire indicator—measuring sweep for arming purposes. Returned and moored to buoy 1800.

March 12, Sunday

Midn. Journal: Slipped 0800 and proceeded in repetition of yesterday's exercises. same Quarterdeck procedure as before. Returned to harbour and moored to buoy. *Salamander* moored alongside (Lt.Cmdr. Dawson RNR).

March 13, Monday

Midn. Journal: In harbour all day. Mustered Confidential Books with Lieutenant Bridges. Signal regarding return of Captain received, due to arrive on Wed. evening.

2. Warships sailing in company did so in a specified formation or order. The Order flag was a specific signal flag that was followed by a numeral flag indicating the formation to be used in passage. The Order flag was first hoisted by the senior officer and then by each ship in the line. The actual order was executed when the signal was hauled down. Order 1, the most usual order, required ships to be ranked in order of seniority of the commanding officers.

March 14, Tuesday

Midn. Journal: Slipped 0800 and proceeded out of harbour in line ahead, *Jason* being last astern. Day of sweeping exercises. Took my usual position on bridge leaving harbour and then assisted Lieut. Bridges on sweep deck by checking off distances between cutters for arming of the sweep. Returned to harbour 1700.

March 15, Wednesday

Midn. Journal: 0200 slipped and proceeded to sea as before in line ahead for night sweeping exercises. After arming and streaming sweep at 0400, kept alternate watch on the Q. with Lt. Bridges. In sweep (Stbd.) 0800. Out Port sweep 0930. "G" formation to port all the way back to harbour. Secured to buoy 1300 alongside *Salamander.* Did O.O.D. under Lt. Charter. Weather rather rough in loch. "Pipe down" 1300. Captain not arrived Loch Alsh 2130.

March 16, Thursday

Midn. Journal: 0200 slipped and proceeded to sea. Sweep armed and streamed by 0400. Repeated last night's procedure—keeping watch on Q. deck. At about 0900, the *Harrier* with *Speedwell, Salamander,* and *Halcyon* proceeded to Loch Ewe for refueling. Worked in office in the afternoon, when we had returned to buoy—about 1200. Captain came aboard. Cyphering in the evening 10–11 P.M. with Lt. Sandhill and the Surg.Lt.

March 17, Friday

Midn. Journal: Slipped 0500. On the bridge at 0530, having been sent for by bridge messenger. Had forgotten to arrange with quarter master to be shaken in time to be on the bridge for leaving harbour. Left bridge 0800. Entered Loch Ewe 0900 and secured alongside oiler at 0930. Left Loch Ewe at about 1400 and returned to Loch Alsh. Worked in the office and did cyphering throughout the day. Secured to the buoy on arrival.

Upon my arrival on the bridge, Commander Crick's response to my negligence in failing to arrange to be wakened in time to be on the bridge as we left harbor was to inform me that I was to stay on the bridge until such time as he saw fit to let me leave it, as a lesson in the need to avoid mistakes. I stood in the wing of the bridge in disgrace. In the old days, I would have been sent up to the masthead, as was the practice with midshipmen who had been derelict in duty in any way, where I would have perched in the crow's nest until summoned down. Owen respectfully pointed out to the captain that unless I were allowed off the bridge to eat breakfast in the wardroom, I would end up going without food for a long period; I was therefore permitted to leave for that purpose.

Entering and leaving harbor had certain ceremonial aspects that are worth description. All members of the ship's company, officers and ratings, wore the uniform specified each morning as the "rig of the day." At sea, in fine weather, the rig of the day for ratings was usually the uniform cap and dungaree overalls. On more formal occasions, such as entering or leaving harbor, the uniform might be No. 3, the traditional bell-bottom trousers and jumper, with insignia in red braid. No. 1 uniform (I never came across any reference to a No. 2) was the best uniform, with all insignia in gold braid. At sea, when ratings wore dungarees, officers were expected to wear the uniform cap and jacket but could complete the uniform with gray flannel slacks and either a roll top sweater or a white ascot. Technically, it was acceptable to wear collar and tie, but these were regarded as "wet" (too conforming). In heavy weather or cold weather, a duffle coat or oilskins was the normal wear for both ratings and officers on the upper deck or bridge.

When entering a major naval harbor, such as Scapa Flow, Portsmouth, or Plymouth, where there was a flag officer (i.e., some kind of admiral), it was customary to require officers and men on the upper deck or bridge to wear regular full uniform (No. 3 for ratings, full uniform for officers). As the ship approached the harbor, the order was piped: "All men not in the rig of day for entering harbor, clear off the upper deck." This did not apply going into small harbors, particularly under combat conditions. As a ship proceeded to her appointed anchorage or mooring, there was an exchange of salutes between her and every other naval vessel that she met or passed on the way. The rule was that the ship whose commanding officer was junior in rank or seniority saluted a ship commanded by a more senior officer. The salute consisted of the shrilling of the bosun's calls on the junior ship and the crew on deck being called to attention. An identical response was made from the senior ship, followed almost immediately by another bosun's call and the standing of ease of that crew, which was the signal for the crew of the junior ship to be stood at ease. This could occur several times on the way to the mooring, depending on the number of ships present. The ceremony required that a copy of the *Navy List* be kept on the bridge. It gave the rank and seniority of the commanding officer of every ship in the Royal Navy, thereby permitting the commanding officer of each ship to figure out who had to salute whom. Large warships, such as aircraft carriers and heavy cruisers with Royal Marines on board, used a Marine bugler to salute with a bugle call. We had this experience several times in Scapa Flow. The sound of the bugle echoing from the hills of the Orkneys all the way around the harbor was very stirring. At a mooring, when a large ship was coming in, we could hear the exchange of shrill bosun's calls and the echo of the bugle faintly in the far distance and becoming louder and louder as she passed every ship on the way in. Echoes from the surrounding hills gave a melancholy, unworldly atmosphere to the moment.

The exercise of 15 March, in which we went through the procedure for winching in one sweep and veering out the sweep on the other side of the ship, proved to be an exact rehearsal for the night of 5/6 June. On that occasion (see below), we improved our performance and completed the maneuver in a little over an hour, compared with the one and a half hours that it had taken during the rehearsal. These exercises, no doubt, were not only an occasion for practice of maneuvers but also an opportunity for the planners to learn something about the time likely to be needed for them when D-Day came.

March 18, Saturday

Midn. Journal: Captain's rounds in forenoon. Worked in office until 1230.

March 19, Sunday

Midn. Journal: Divisions and prayers in the forenoon. Visited escort carrier *Archer* in evening.

The *Archer* was a small aircraft carrier designed to escort convoys. These carriers, mainly converted from merchant ships, consisted of a flight deck mounted on a merchant hull. The *Archer* was converted from a U.S. merchant ship built by the Sun Ship Building Company, Chester, Pennsylvania. These ships were a wartime expedient that proved extremely successful, and their presence in convoys contributed greatly to the Allied victory over the U-boats. On 3 July 1943, the Admiralty announced that the *Archer* and a surface escort, probably a destroyer or frigate, had joined with aircraft of the Coastal Command and successfully beaten off a powerful force of U-boats attacking a valuable Atlantic convoy over a period of more than two days. Movies were sometimes shown in the hangar deck of the *Archer*, and that was why were invited over.

March 20, Monday

Midn. Journal: Slipped 0730 and proceeded out of harbour on day sweeping exercise. Worked in office during the day. Prepared forms S-1034 for ship's company payment. On the bridge as usual on return to harbour at 1945.

Payment of a ship's company was conducted in a ceremonial manner. A table was set up on the quarterdeck. Facing the table, the ship's company was drawn up in ranks. At the table sat the paying officer with an assistant, usually a writer. A chalk circle was drawn on the top of the table. As each man's name was called, he approached the table, saluted, removed his cap, and laid it right side up on the chalk circle. The writer called out the amount of money due, which was counted out onto the top of the cap. If no money was due, which might occur because of the imposition of fines for various misdemeanors or recent overpayment of advances, the writer called out, "Not entitled." Whatever the amount of pay might be, including nothing, it was not announced until the cap was already on the table. The rating removed his pay from the top of his cap, replaced the cap on his head, saluted, turned around, and marched back to his place in the ranks. To be not entitled was known colloquially as a "North Easter," invariably preceded by an obscene adjective when spoken by the unfortunate rating.

March 21, Tuesday

Midn. Journal: Day in harbour. Worked in office most of the day. Arranged with the Shipwright to paste table of revolutions on bridge. Slipped about 2000 and proceeded on night sweeping exercises. After leaving harbour, I went from the bridge to the quarterdeck to assist in getting out sweeps. Did watch alone from 2400–0400 (Wednesday).

The staff of the engine room of the ship could not regulate speed by knots. What they did was to control exactly the number of revolutions (revs) of the propeller shaft—counted by gauges. In any given ship, the number of revolutions that would produce a given speed in the water differed somewhat from that of other ships, even of the same design. This meant that each ship had to be calibrated for the speed through the water produced by a given number of revolutions of her propeller. The record of this process produced the table of revolutions. If one knew what revs that ship ahead was doing and the speed they produced for that ship, then one could select the correct number of revs for one's own ship to produce the speed that would maintain the proper distance. There was still error, of course, because the weather could affect the ship's speed and could do so a little differently for each ship. Speed commands passed down the voice pipe were given in terms of revolutions, not speed in knots. On the bridge was a revolution counter—a glass-covered device that displayed the current number of revolutions. It had a crank handle, one full turn of which moved the revolutions up or down by three. As a consequence, the normal unit of change was ordered in "turns." For example, an order of "Up three turns" meant an increase of nine revolutions.

In the engine room below was a complex system of firebox, boilers, steam pipes, condensers, valves, and other components. This engine system eventuated in the turning of the propeller shaft. Hence, the control of the number of revolutions ultimately depended on the engineer's skill in making the precise adjustment of the appropriate valve necessary to produce just the amount of pressure needed for the desired change in the number of revolutions. He did this by touch and inspection of the gauges; there was no mechanical control. In diesel firing, unlike electrical propulsion, it was necessary to maintain the appropriate steam pressure. If speed was increased, the increased demand for pressure had to be compensated for by an increase in the heat, or fuel being burned. A number of engine room officers and ratings coordinated the tasks of making adaptations in their parts of the system that resulted in the desired changes in other parts of the system. All of this taking place in a very hot compartment of a ship rolling and pitching in a rough sea required considerable skill and stamina.

March 22, Wednesday

Midn. Journal: 0000-0400 watch on the quarterdeck—sweeps have been streamed. 0400 "in sweeps" so I remained on quarterdeck to assist 1st Lieut. who took charge of getting in of sweeps. Turned in 0500. Turned out 0700 to go on bridge for entering harbour. Secured to buoy about 0800. Did normal work in office during forenoon. "Pipe down" in afternoon. Ashore in the evening.

March 23, Thursday

Midn. Journal: On bridge 1000 for leaving harbour. Then worked in office throughout day until 1700. First Watch with 1st Lieutenant. Some confusion caused in the line by the activities of a fishing trawler which crossed our bows. Cape Wrath abeam approximately 2300. Altered course to due east. Note—during afternoon exercised "Man Overboard" with life buoys and both whalers. 1915 exercised A/S action stations.

The "man overboard" drill was always conducted without warning. The officer of the watch ordered a floating object, such as a life jacket or a wooden box, to be thrown into the water. This was followed by the shrill of the bosun's call accompanied by the announcement over the loudspeaker system, "Man overboard!" and on which side of the ship, port or starboard, this had happened. Immediately, anyone—officer or rating—near the ship's lifeboat made for it, got in, and waited until there was sufficient crew to row it. Everybody else seized the lowering ropes and lowered the boat to a point just above the water surface; on command of the officer of the watch, the boat was released and dropped into the water. The cox'n of the lifeboat put the tiller hard over to turn the boat away from the ship. The tow line attached to the bow of the boat to give it forward momentum was released, and the crew rowed in the direction of the floating object. In the meantime, the duty of the lookout on the bridge was to keep the floating object in view through his binoculars at all times. The officer of the watch hove to (stopped the ship) and ordered "Stop engines," to keep the propeller shaft from turning. A crew member in the lifeboat picked up the floating object, and the cox'n of the lifeboat raised his hand and shouted, "Man aboard." The lifeboat then returned to the ship.

The entire exercise was time from the second that the order was given to the time that the object was in the lifeboat. Because rescuing a man overboard demanded the utmost speed, the Navy required all officers and men, including cooks, writers, stewards, and stokers, to know how to row and steer a boat. In a rescue operation the lifeboat was rowed, rather than motored, because in such an emergency one could not afford to take the risk that the motor would fail to start. In this situation, the lifeboat needed only to travel a short distance in a great hurry. At sea, one of the boats was always swung out, that is, hung over the side on davits, ready for instant lowering. On a large ship, one boat was in readiness on each side.

"Away the lifeboat" meant something quite different from "Away the sea boat." The latter was a signal for a particular crew assigned to that duty and did not imply an emergency. A number of ratings who were good oarsmen and the petty officer cox'n were allocated to the sea-boat crew; this crew rowed or handled the boat at sea, as necessary, in situations where no life emergency was at stake.

March 24, Friday

Midn. Journal: Arrived Invergordon 1400. Anchored off Cromarty. Remainder of First MSF there, including *Seagull* and *Gleaner.* Now eight ships of the 1st Flotilla here. Worked in the office during the afternoon.

March 25, Saturday

Midn. Journal: Assistant O.O.D. Worked in the office in afternoon. During forenoon worked in office after Captain's rounds. In evening went to *Harrier* to collect documents for forthcoming exercise.

March 26, Sunday

Midn. Journal: No divisions due to bad weather. Prayers on the mess deck in forenoon. Shore leave in the afternoon.

March 27, Monday

Midn. Journal: Captain cleared Lower Deck in the forenoon to give talk about forthcoming exercise. Normal day's work in the office.

"Clear lower deck" was an order that required everybody not engaged in absolutely essential duty to assemble, usually on the upper deck when the weather was fine or otherwise on the mess deck, for the purpose of receiving some general instruction or performing some task that required all available hands. This had been the case when hoisting boats in the *Cardiff*. We had had many exercises in the *Jason*, but up to this time the lower deck had never been cleared to discuss them. Retrospectively, this should have hinted the extent to which the exercise was a rehearsal of what we would be doing during the invasion itself. In fact, the sequence of actions during the exercise of 30 March—sweeping ahead of bombarding forces, laying smoke screens at dusk, preparing for E-boat attacks, responding to repeated calls to action stations, and forming a perimeter defense line—was precisely what happened on D-Day. By an uncanny coincidence, the cancellation of the exercise of 29 March and its resumption on 30 March paralleled the sequence on 4 and 5 June.

March 28, Tuesday

Midn. Journal: Usual forenoon's work in the office. 1430 weighed anchor and proceeded out of harbour astern of *Harrier*—whole flotilla in Order 1. Commenced sweeping pre-arranged area at 1730 (approx). From 1500 onwards Lieut. Sandhill and I worked alternate four hour watches in chart house—fixing, writing up log, etc.

March 29, Wednesday

Midn. Journal: Working watches as above. During forenoon watch signal came—"Exercise cancelled—return to harbour." Several floating dummy mines were seen during the morning's operations. Returned to harbour and anchored at about 1800. "Make & mend" given to all hands in afternoon.

March 30, Thursday

Midn. Journal: Left harbour 0230 to recommence exercises. Swept pre-arranged area but owing to parting of sweeps were unable to sweep ahead of bombarding force. Anchored in exercise anchorage at 1800 and ceased alternate watches in chart-house. Anchor watch commenced. "Make Smoke" exercise at dusk. Did evening watch with Lt. Fox. Throughout the night "Exercise action stations" was ordered three times. Went to usual action station in the Action Plot.

Star-shell[3] was fired at "enemy" E-Boats[4] which were picked up by Radar contacts. Ships were anchored on perimeter of anchorage for defensive purposes.

March 31, Friday

Midn. Journal: Morning watch referred to above ended 0630. 0745 weighed anchor and proceeded to recover mines. Proceeded astern of 15th MSF who made clearance sweep. Returned to Cromarty 1700.

April 1, Saturday

Midn. Journal: 0640 proceeded to oiling jetty at Invergordon. Berthed alongside *Harrier*. Returned to anchorage 1010. Shore leave in the afternoon.

April 2, Sunday

Midn. Journal: Normal routine in the forenoon. Weighed anchor 1600 in the afternoon and proceeded in line ahead out of the Firth. Sea very rough. Spray breaking over the bridge. Did the First Watch with 1st Lieutenant.

April 3, Monday

Midn. Journal: Thick fog in Firth on Forth. Action Plot closed up[5] to plot radar bearings of other ships under way. Fog lifted about noon. *Harrier* & *Britomart* proceeded to Leith. *Jason* and others passed under Forth Bridge and moored to buoys outside Rosyth dockyard.

---

3. A shell fired from a 4-inch gun that explodes in the air and releases a large parachute flare (or series of parachute flares); the flare (or flares) hangs in an arc and then begins to drift slowly down. The light is so bright that it illuminates a potential enemy target.

4. In this instance, of course, the "enemy" E-boats were our own motor torpedo boats acting the part.

5. "Close up" was a naval order to go to one's station. Hence, the report, "Action Plot closed up," confirmed the fact that the action plot was now manned and plotting could begin.

April 4, Tuesday

Midn. Journal: Entered dockyard basin at noon. Secured alongside. Proceeded on leave 1500.

April 10, Monday

Midn. Journal: Returned off leave 1200. Commenced work in the office in afternoon. Ship having minor details of refitting completed.

April 11, Tuesday

Midn. Journal: Proceeded out of dock and secured to buoy outside the dockyard. Worked in office all day. Mainly on amendments to standing orders.

April 12, Wednesday

Midn. Journal: 0810 Slipped and proceeded to D/G range at Burnt Island. Completed ranging and returned to buoy. Secured about 1300. 1615 Slipped and proceeded eastwards down Forth in line ahead. Calibrated kites and otters which had been supplied at Rosyth. Air raid alerts from 2000 to 2400. Did First Watch with Lt. James, and later 1st Lieutenant.

April 13, Thursday

Midn. Journal: 0810 On the bridge for entering harbour. Pilot came on board at North Shields breakwater. Proceeded up Tyne river and moored alongside "Oslo" quay—Albert Edward Dock. Assistant O.O.D. under Lt. Charter. Inspected libertymen,[6] and supervised embarking of ammunition.

While in port at North Shields, Commander Crick invited the mayor and other dignitaries to a reception on board the *Jason*. I was assigned the task of welcoming the guests over the gangway and showing them to the wardroom where the reception was to be held. One of the first groups to arrive included a young woman who, in an outburst of enthusiasm, kissed me on the cheek as I was ushering the group along the passageway to the wardroom. I returned to my post at the gangway to greet the next arrivals. I repeated this a few times until all had been checked in and I could join the reception myself. Lieutenant Owen immediately drew me aside and suggested that I look in the mirror and remove the large visible lipstick stain on my cheek—it had been there throughout all of my gangway greetings.

6. Libertymen referred to any group of sailors going to or coming from leave.

April 14, Friday

Midn. Journal: Left harbour in forenoon, approx 0800 and proceeded
out of N. Shields in line ahead. Sweeping throughout the day. The
whole of the flotilla together with *Alexander Scott*, *Craftsman* and *Colsay*
(danlayers) was engaged. Anchored off Tynemouth in the evening.

April 15, Saturday

Midn. Journal: Weighed anchor 0700 and proceeded to continue previous day's operation. Kept alternate watches in chart-house with Lt.
Sandhill. Watch 1230–1600 in chart-house. 1600–1800 on bridge—
keeping station on Oropesa float of HMS *Harrier*. Thick fog came
down about 1800. Proceeded very slowly to last night's anchorage.

April 16, Sunday

Midn. Journal: Anchor watch on the bridge in the morning. Sailing cancelled due to thick fog. Anchor watch in the afternoon by myself on the
bridge. Nothing of note occurred.

April 17, Monday

Midn. Journal: Proceeded at 0700 to the area to re-commence the operation as the fog had lifted. The method used to sweep the area is as follows. The first flotilla in Formation 1 (i.e., ships in order of seniority of
Commanding Officers) sweeps on two courses—345° and 165°. On the
345° course, Oropesa sweeps are streamed and "G" formation to Starboard taken up. At the end of each lap, sweeps are taken in, the reciprocal course of 165° is set, and "G" Formation to Port is taken up.
Following the last sweeper is a danlayer who dans the limit of the lap
swept and then points[7] the last dan laid so that the S.O. of the flotilla
can make straight for the starting point of the next lap. Double flagged
dans are laid at each extremity of the line of dans.

April 18, Tuesday

Midn. Journal: The same procedure as detailed above was adopted.
Took the first dog watch on the bridge so as to relieve Lt. Fox for Radar duties. The distance apart of ships in "G" formation is $4\frac{1}{2}$ cables,
and at this distance the float of ship ahead should be 16° off the sweeping course. Thus when sweeping "G" to Starboard, course 345°, the
float of the ship ahead should bear 001°, the distance apart of ships be-
ing $4\frac{1}{2}$ cables. By this method the correct overlap is maintained ($\frac{1}{2}$ cable)
throughout the sweep. As the distance may vary, a series of alternative

---

7. A maneuver in which the danlayer stops engines, turns, and points her bow close
to the dan, thus making its location more visible to the approaching minesweeper.

bearings for other distances apart is given. These bearings can be ascertained from Higson's Diagrams. Returned to anchorage 2000.

April 19, Wednesday

Midn. Journal: Sailed at 0700 for the area and continued sweeping as before. Through keeping watch in the chart-room was shown how plot is kept of the extent of each lap. By getting dan buoy of lap in transit of lap being swept and simultaneously getting radar range of the farthest dan (preferably checked with range finder), the position of the dan of the lap being swept can be plotted. The reading of the log can confirm the plot when due allowance for tide is made. An example of the information required to plot the second dan of the lap of "B" lap, would be: (i) A_2–B_2 in transit 270°. (ii) Radar range of A_2—1100 yds. (iii) Log between B_1 and B_2 = 1.2 miles. (iv) Co. 345°. When sweep completed returned to Anchorage. Did usual watch from 0600. Sailed 0700. Was allowed to take over watch from 0730 to 0830, no other officer being on the bridge. Giving wheel orders for turns at the right time is the most difficult thing, as it is very easy to turn inside or outside the wake of the ship ahead and thus throw the whole of the line out. Practise required. Usual day's sweeping until 1600. Then in company with *Halcyon* and *Salamander* proceeded to T.I.C. jetty at North Shields to re-fuel. Secured ahead of a Fighting French cruiser. Was interested to note their bugle calls and pipes and tried to translate their "pipes" without a great deal of success. Evening ashore.

April 20, Thursday

Midn. Journal: Lt. Charter fell ill. Lt. Knowles taken on board (Navigator of *Harrier*) for today and tomorrow. I was given duties of Assistant Nav. Officer. Proceeded to anchorage in the evening. Usual state of readiness assumed throughout the night, viz.—an officer of the watch on the bridge. Radar or A/S watch—radar if anchored landward—A/S if seaward. Guns crew standing by.

April 21, Friday

Midn. Journal: Proceeded to sweeping area. *Jason* now leading ship. Assisted Lt. Knowles in plotting as described under "Wednesday 19th." Sweep almost completed. On return to anchorage, Lt. Knowles returned to *Harrier.*

April 22, Saturday

Midn. Journal: Proceeded to sweeping area. Prepared all data regarding tide and courses and on arrival commenced the plot with Lt. Sandhill. Used the range finder for the first time. Radar unable to pick up dans during forenoon as surface of sea hid echoes in ground-wave.[8] Original intention of the S.O. was to sweep four laps. Instead six laps were completed and area finally cleared.

Proceeded back to anchorage as leading ship—*Harrier* having gone back to Tynemouth—and anchored in darkness. Tide set ship one or two cables to the north more than I had anticipated. By means of bearings from breakwater light was able to anchor reasonably close to intended position.

April 23, Sunday

Midn. Journal: Proceeded at 0800 to swept area to calibrate kites and otters. Steaming on reciprocal courses of 165° & 345°. When calibration completed, practised a close range 4-inch shoot. Received instruction in use of the sextant from Lt. Charter, but as I was at action station (during shoot) at noon, was unable to take a sun-sight.

Rendezvous with M/S 1 at 20 D buoy and proceeded down main channel on passage to Harwich. Did First Watch with 1st Lieutenant. Search lights were in operation over Flamborough Head and Scarborough. Particularly alert on watch as E-Boats were anticipated. Passed *Savage* north-bound. One of the destroyers in the *Scharnhorst* action.

April 24, Monday

Midn. Journal: Arrived Harwich at approx. 1600 hours. During the forenoon was permitted to take over as O.O.W. from 1100–1230. Ships in order 1. Passed convoy northbound but otherwise the watch was uneventful. On arrival at Harwich secured to a buoy off Parkestone Quay. Some trouble with a drunken stoker, and was interested to learn how such cases should be handled.

Britomart secured alongside. Working on the preparation of a defect list and leave documents for the watch going on leave. All leave has been cancelled here and also all relatives of naval personnel have been sent out of the port. Very fortunate that leave has been obtained.

---

8. A ground wave occurred when surface radar, scanning very close to the surface of the water, created a layer of radar reflections off the sea itself; this produced a horizontal flickering green band across the radar screen that obscured the reflection of specific objects on the water surface. German radar was particularly handicapped by this phenomenon and could not detect objects lower than forty or fifty feet above the surface of the water. During the RAF raid on Gestapo headquarters in Copenhagen, for example, a squadron of RAF planes flew at a very low altitude across the North Sea and was able to reach the Danish coast undetected by the Germans.

April 25, Tuesday

Midn. Journal: One watch and all officers—except 1st Lieut., Lt. Bridges and myself—went on leave. Captain remained on board. Stoker dealt with and punishment warrant required. Spent some time working on the warrant. Captain took the warrant ashore for approval of F.O.I.C. (Rear-Admiral Baillie-Grohmann). Tugs came alongside 1700 and took us alongside Parkestone Quay. Lt. Bridges supervised Foc's'le—I supervised quarterdeck. Prepared committal warrant.

April 26, Wednesday

Midn. Journal: Captain went on leave 0900. At 1030 lower deck was cleared and as 1st Lieutenant still being ill in his cabin, Lt. Bridges read punishment warrant—I acting as 1st Lt. reporting the ship's company to Lt. Bridges, etc. Went to the C.B. office in the afternoon, and dealt with mail in the office.

The fact that this stoker appeared on the upper deck of the *Jason* while drunk could have happened only by his having smuggled liquor on board earlier or having managed to accumulate his daily tots of grog. Either of these was a serious offense and being drunk on board a further offense. The Royal Navy required that the officers and/or petty officers dealing with a drunken rating should attempt to avoid a situation in which the drunken man might strike them, as this would be an extremely serious offense, one that would warrant a court-martial. Hence, whenever possible, the drunken sailor was to be restrained physically by the master at arms or by other ratings of the man's own rank. We had in the ship's company a regulating petty office (RPO), which was the equivalent of a master at arms but one rank below that. The RPO was always known as the "Crusher"—a derisive reference to the alleged large size of his feet and boots. The master-at-arms, a chief petty officer, was known as the "Jaunty"—apparently a sailors' corruption of gendarme.

Because the combination of the stoker's offenses was too serious to be dealt with by an officer of the rank of commander, the punishment had to be confirmed by the flag officer in charge of the base. The stoker in question was sentenced to jail for a period of months—the committal warrant was the legal authority to send him to jail. Major punishments were reported to the entire ship's company assembled for that purpose on the quarterdeck. The stoker, who had been locked in a cabin, was led out onto the deck by the Crusher, with two ratings standing on either side of him. He was wearing his No. 1 uniform with no collar; the collar had been removed as a mark of his disgrace. I brought the ship's company to attention, marched across the deck to Lieutenant Bridges, and reported, "All present and correct, sir." Lieutenant Bridges then commanded, "Prisoner—off cap." Because the stoker was handcuffed, the Crusher stepped forward and knocked the stoker's cap off his head to the deck, where it rolled on its rim for a few feet, wobbled for a second or so, and then fell flat.

Lieutenant Bridges read the punishment warrant to the prisoner and the assembled ship's company. In this case, the punishment was six months in jail. When the reading of the warrant was complete, the Crusher and the escort of two ratings marched the prisoner down the gangway to take him off the ship and thence to Maidstone Jail in Kent. Two days later, the Crusher and the escort returned to the ship with the prisoner who had been refused admission to the jail because it was full. The punishment was then commuted to six months' loss of all leave, including shore leave. Although the final outcome might have seemed humane and the initial discipline of the Navy harsh, to be drunk on duty in a warship was an extremely serious matter. A drunken sailor at an action station could be very dangerous to the survival of the ship and her company. At a time when the impending invasion made it essential that everybody concerned be tuned to the peak of efficiency, the risk of disaster was even greater.

April 27, Thursday

Midn. Journal: Busy day. Worked in office, supervised loading of Oerlikon ammunition on board, and generally assisting Lt. Bridges as O.O.D. Met an ex-classmate from King Alfred—S/Lt. Jackson of the *Pickle*—one of the 7th MSF (Algerines) and went on board in evening.

This is the last of the entries in my Midshipman's Journal. I was about to be promoted to sub-lieutenant and to leave the *Jason*.

The diary resumes:

April 28, Friday—April 29, Saturday

Diary: Uneventful—people still on leave. Made one or two trips ashore. S/Lt. Jackson left in *Pickle* on Sat.

April 30, Sunday

Diary: Signal arrived from Admiralty "Md. B. A. Maher RNVR appointed HM *ML137* to join forthwith (at Harwich)." Found out from Base Office that *ML137* was at Felixstowe. Arranged to join her from *Harrier* on Monday morning.

6

Moving into Place

If it be now, 'tis not to come; if it be not to come,
It will be now; if it be not now, yet it will come:
the readiness is all.—WILLIAM SHAKESPEARE

On 1 May 1944, I was promoted to sub-lieutenant and transferred to HM *Motor Launch 137 (ML137)* to serve as navigator. *ML137* was a Fairmile B–class motor launch (ML). These MLs were the "maids-of-all-work" of the coastal forces. Among the duties they carried out were anti-submarine, convoy escort, minelaying, minesweeping, air-sea rescue, and ambulance service; they were among the navigational leaders for the D-Day landings. They were excellent sea-boats capable of long voyages under their own power. One flotilla had crossed the North Atlantic to Trinidad via Iceland, Greenland, and North America.

ML137 was equipped for minesweeping and was of shallow enough draft (1.75 meters) to permit close approach to the beach. The ship was 65 tons displacement; 112 feet long; 18 feet in the beam; and powered by two Packard gasoline engines, which could move her at 20 knots, maximum speed, and 17 knots, steady cruising speed. Armament consisted of two twin Oerlikon 20-mm machine guns, one 3-pounder gun, and two twin Vickers machine guns. The ship's company was composed of three officers and seventeen ratings. In addition to myself, the other officers were Lt. Leslie J. Hutchins, RNVR, and Sub-Lt. P. I. ("Mac")

McDowell, RNVR. The oldest member of the crew was age twenty-five, and the youngest seventeen. Most of us were in the age range of nineteen to twenty-two.

When first put in commission, *ML137* was commanded by an American, a lieutenant in the RNVR (referred to as "Hank" in the retellings that I heard), with Hutchins as his first lieutenant. The ship was once badly damaged in an air attack, which wounded several of the crew. Hutchins distinguished himself by giving quick and effective tourniquet first aid to the wounded and directing the return of fire. For these actions, he was awarded the Distinguished Service Cross (DSC). When the United States entered the war, Hank returned home and entered the U.S. Navy. Hutchins replaced him as commanding officer of *ML137*.

An ML was a much smaller ship than a fleet minesweeper, such as the *Jason*. The wardroom was a small cabin below decks, right aft. There were four bunks, two on each side. By day, the upper bunk could be lowered to combine with the lower bunk to form a kind of couch. The galley was in the crew's quarters in the fo'c'sle. We all ate the same food, cooked by a gunnery rating who had been sent to a two-day cooking school to master the craft. No ship of this size ever had a trained cook, sick-berth attendant, or any dayman ratings.

Relations between officers and men in *ML137* were much less formal than in the *Jason*. We knew each other quite well after some months at sea. Forms of address were still used, "sir" and "aye-aye," and interactions were suitably respectful. But we all had the same kind of living on board, everybody was expected to be able to turn his hand to any ship's task, and the basic camaraderie was closer than that in the *Jason*.

ML137 was a unit of the Fifth ML Flotilla. The Fifth Flotilla had spent almost all of its time operating along the English Channel, particularly in eastern waters between Dover and Calais. Dover had been the permanent base of its operations. Dover was the headquarters of a mixed force of minesweeping flotillas, known collectively as Dover Minesweepers. It was also an operational base for high-speed motor torpedo boats attacking German shipping along the coasts of France and Belgium.

Because Dover was exclusively a base for small ships, the informality of small-ship life also pervaded the attitudes of its senior officers. Many had been there for some years and had endured the bombing and long-distance shelling that pounded Dover during the early years of the war. The White Cliffs rising up behind the town long had been a nostalgic symbol of England. Here, indeed, we were at the closest point to the enemy, only twenty miles away in Calais. The relentless roll of events was leading us closer to D-day; our operations in the Channel were a reminder of this.

The main purpose of the next phase of the training exercises for the liberation of France was to start putting some of the pieces together. The Fifth ML Flotilla was to train with the First Minesweeping Flotilla. There was little doubt that this indicated the composition of the minesweeping group in which we would sail in the invasion of Normandy. The joint exercises were now to take place in the waters in which the assault itself would be launched.

The following includes the full entries from the diary that I continued to keep:

May 1, Monday

Diary: Joined *ML137* after going across to *Harrier*. Made Navigating Officer. 1st May—am now due for promotion to Act. S/Lt. Calibrating all afternoon. Captain—Lieut. L. J. Hutchins D.S.C., RNVR, 1st Lieut. S/Lt. P. I. McDowell, RNVR and I complete the wardroom. Left in company with 1st MSF for Portsmouth at 1900. Ankle swollen from insect bites—plus new shoes. Sea rough. 2 hours sleep. Could not stand up because of ankle—rather an unpleasant trip down.

May 2, Tuesday

Diary: Arrived Portsmouth (have now done round trip of British Isles) 0800. Fuelled and secured alongside *Harrier*—anchored off Spithead— 0900. Reported to Surg.-Lt. Scott, showing him my ankle. Apparently had high temperature also. Ordered straight away to turn in. Kit transferred from *ML137*.

May 3, Wednesday–May 5, Friday

Diary: In Sick Bay—sleeping, eating and reading throughout an invasion exercise. Friday morning allowed up and idled in *Harrier*'s wardroom.

May 5, Friday

Diary: In afternoon *ML 237* called alongside. Transferred self & kit on board with great difficulty—heavy sea. Capt. Jennings, RN on board going round all M/S flotillas in the Solent. Eventually entered Portsmouth harbour and secured at Vernon pier. Skiff "manned" by Wren took me over to *ML137* which was moored near Dolphin jetty. Turned in very tired.

May 8, Monday

Diary: 1200. After coaling[1] in forenoon, slipped at noon and set course for Dover. My first complete passage in charge of Navigation. Uneventful. Saw Coast of France from Folkestone. Formations of American "Marauder" aircraft going over on a raid. Saw odd-looking silver torpedo-float-shaped object floating on water. Could not identify it. Arrived Dover 2000. Secured alongside jetty in Submarine basin.

May 9, Tuesday–May 13, Saturday

Diary: This period was, with one exception (namely Thursday 11th) spent alongside the Eastern Arm of the Submarine Basin. Dover as a base is very much in contact with the enemy, as witness the shell-battered houses, the sunken destroyers in the harbour and the nightly minelaying excursions of the MTBs. These latter go out every evening at dusk with eight or ten mines each on the upper deck and return at dawn minus the mines.

The "Pens" (or "Submarine Pens")[2] are used as shelters and docks for the MTBs. When walking along the ramps above the pens, the whole place gives an H. G. Wellsian impression. Every office is completely shell & bomb proof, and all day long the silence is shattered by the roar of engines.

On Thursday (May 11th) in company with *ML141*, 3 MMSs and 3 MTBs, we set course for the French coast. Sweeping took place 4 miles from Étaples—fortunately a thick haze hid us from the eyes of the enemy, and long & heavy day bombing by RAF & U.S. AAF planes of the coast was engaging their attention. One MTB was detached to pick up an airman who had parachuted into the water. On the whole quite an interesting day, although no mines were swept.

In Dover, the senior officer in charge of minesweeping operations was Comdr. Joseph G. Boxhall, RNR; he was known affectionately as "Boxey." He lived in a large requisitioned motor-yacht berthed at a wharf in Dover harbor. From his office in this vessel, he directed the planning of

1. Coaling here refers to the loading of coal needed for the galley stoves and other heating stoves in the ship.

2. Concrete structures with very thick roofs designed to protect ships, such as submarines, MTBs, and MLs, from enemy attack. Pens of this kind were built at Dover, which was vulnerable to German shelling from Calais. The Germans constructed huge U-boat pens in Brest and other Atlantic ports to protect the submarines from the heavy repeated air raids conducted by the Allies.

minesweeping activities. Every once in a while, the yacht put to sea for the minimum time necessary to qualify for the duty-free spirits privilege. Commander Boxhall appeared to have some unexplained fame among officers who had been operating out of Dover for long periods, a fame that I attributed to his undoubted professional competence.

I forgot all about him until many years later when I opened the book *A Night to Remember*, Lord's story of the loss of the *Titanic*.[3] The British luxury passenger liner, on her maiden voyage to New York from Southampton, struck an iceberg and sank on the night of 14/15 April 1912. At the time of the sinking, Boxhall was the fourth officer of the *Titanic* and one of the youngest officers on board. The captain ordered Boxhall into a lifeboat to take charge of it. All but three of the other officers went down with the ship. Young Boxhall survived to follow the sea for the rest of his career. I met him once, when I had to visit the yacht for some official purpose. He was a man of medium height with a wrinkled weather-beaten face, friendly but tinged with a fleeting melancholy. When I met him, he must have been in his fifties. He looked rather older than that. I heard that, when he died, he wanted to be buried at sea where the *Titanic* had gone down.

May 14, Sunday

Diary: Left Dover harbour at 1100 hours with the gramophone relaying nautical marches over the loud hailer, and the base staff & WRNSs waving cheerios on the jetty. This somewhat mollified my annoyance at having a hat-badge stolen at the Wren's dance at Wasp on Friday night. Arrived HMS Hornet (Portsmouth) at 2100 hours and piped down.

May 15, Monday–May 17, Wednesday

Diary: From Monday to Wednesday was spent running on odd jobs for *Harrier* and laying at the buoy in harbour.

May 18, Thursday

Diary: Proceeded out of harbour to Spithead where *Harrier* & 1st MSF (including old *Jason*) were lying. Slipped from *Harrier* at noon and proceeded, by way of swept channel, down eastern Solent, around Selsey Bill and set course for C. 3. Buoy (off Shoreham-on-Sea). Then on arrival at buoy, swept inshore astern of 1st MSF & 15th MSF and on completion of lap returned to anchor 5 miles north of C. 3. Buoy. When dusk came on slipped from *Harrier* and patrolled around anchor-

3. Walter Lord, *A Night to Remember*, New York: Henry Holt, 1955.

age laying smoke screen. Returned alongside *Harrier* at 2400 hours (midnight). Turned in until 0300 and then took over watch from the 1st Lieutenant who then went below to get some rest.

At 0530 an E-boat was seen on *Harrier*'s starboard side. "Action Stations" and we slipped and re-commenced the smoke screen routine until 0615, E-boat vanished. 0630 Set course for home and arrived at buoys in Portsmouth harbour 1000 hours.

May 19, Friday–May 23, Tuesday

Diary: Alongside the jetty all this period. Engine defect requires overhaul. Did nothing very much. On the night of May 22nd (Monday) a terrific racket caused by enemy air-raid. Familiarity with the sound of falling bombs does not breed contempt, as I am quickly learning. Quite a hectic night. Six planes down. Still it was only a skylark in comparison to the RAF efforts over Calais. The hotels and houses on the front at Dover were literally being shaken to pieces by the reverberations of the cliffs behind them of the noise from the German side of the Channel. I could hardly believe this myself until I saw it one night last week when we were there.

May 24, Wednesday

Diary: Proceeded to join MS1 in Solent. Secured alongside *Harrier* at 0930 and embarked Commander T. E. Nichols RN—Commanding Officer (of *Harrier*) and proceeded to HMS *Largs*. Here Commander Nichols disembarked. *Largs* is H.Q. ship for the Second Front. Rear-Admiral's flag flies at her mizzen. We then secured astern of S.S. *Normanville* (A Fleet collier). All hands and officers into full uniform and lined the deck facing *Largs* to await the arrival of the Royal Barge. This appeared from the direction of Cowes, traveling at high speed, preceded by two MGBs [motor gun boats] and followed by one ML. Fighter planes circled overhead. There was complete silence as the barge—beautiful in the bright sunlight, brass work shining, green painted and glistening—drew up alongside the gangway of the *Largs*. From our distant observation point we could see King George VI slowly mounting the steps, followed at a distance by his staff of officers. Then the faint wail of the Bosun's pipes in chorus; the Royal Standard being struck on the Barge; the orders of the Officer of the Guard, faint but clear—and the show was over.

When the Royal Barge departed in a cloud of spray we returned to *Largs* and re-embarked Commander Nichols. The superfluity of braid and buttons among the many Captains and Flag-Lieutenants made a Commander seem very small indeed.

On returning to *Harrier* we boarded and invaded their wardroom for some welcome beer. *ML237*, which had ferried me over to Portsmouth after my sick bay period in *Harrier* was also there. Renewed acquaintance with their First Lieutenant.

1700 Slipped and proceeded to sea astern *Harrier*. Arrived at position 50.35° N and 00.02° E about 2200 and proceeded to night sweeping exercises. Got lost—to put it bluntly—at about 0100 and found ourselves sweeping in perfect formation with the wrong flotilla, and also about ten miles east of our estimated position. Not a very creditable reflection on my navigation. After much use of the loud-hailer rejoined 1st MSF at 0400 to find that the exercise was completed. Set course for home. Turned in at last at 0500 and slept until 0730. Did day's duty with *Harrier*, ending up by bringing an officer into Cowes (I.o.W.) and returning to Hornet at 2000. Turned in at 2100, thus ending May 25th and a weary 36 hours.

7

The Passage

Must I not serve a long apprenticehood
To foreign passages, and in the end,
Having my freedom, boast of nothing else.
—WILLIAM SHAKESPEARE

The invasion of Normandy was now almost upon us. We still did not know exactly when or where it would take place. We did not yet know its name, Operation Overlord, nor that of our own part, the naval part, Operation Neptune. Major assaults, such as the one looming ahead, were planned in a way that permitted the precise timing of different phases without revealing the actual dates and times involved. The first day of an assault was termed *D day* and the actual hour of the assault *H hour*. Days preceding D day were identified as D minus 1, minus 2, and so on. Days following D day were D plus 1, plus 2, and so on. The same system applied to H hour. If an assault had to be postponed, as happened in the Normandy invasion, the date of D day changed accordingly, as did all of the other relative dates and times. Had the precise days and hours been identified in advance, any change would have made it necessary to communicate the new days and hours for specific phases, with a significant risk of dangerous confusion. Other operations, such as the invasions of North Africa and Sicily, had their D days. The historical impact of the invasion of Normandy, however, has resulted in the general use of the term "D-Day" in referring to this assault.

The Eve of D-Day

The diary entries describe the growing feeling of expectation and apprehension at this time:

May 25, Thursday–June 2, Friday

Diary: The nature of Coastal Forces service being such that regular writing of this log is almost impossible, I have decided to write it in "lumps" when circumstances permit me the leisure to do so. This period (25th May–2nd June) was marked by a certain feeling of tenseness aggravated by our comparative inactivity. The deadly monotony of routine at Hornet was broken only by three days calibrating sweeps at EA2 Buoy, roughly S S W of Selsey Bill. The large number of ships rapidly accumulating at Spithead was evidence enough that the Second Front was not very far off, but during those placid three days in the Channel, under a blazing May sun, the thought seemed remote and unreal.

June 3, Saturday

Diary: Last evening a signal came from *Harrier* to the effect that *ML137* was to collect the Commanding Officers and Navigators of all ships of the First Minesweeping Flotilla and convey them to the theatre at HMS Vernon. This we duly did—and a very trying job—and rather irksome to the Captain who does not relish being "bum-boat" to larger ships. The opportunity of watering and fuelling was taken, and the usual daily routine was adopted—deck-scrubbing, splicing and (for me) chart correcting. At 1400 the Captains returned, apparently in good spirits, and we returned to the Solent, distributing the Commanding Officers and Navigators to their respective vessels. Mac and I proceeded ashore in the evening as the Captain was "sealed" (i.e., banned from shore leave) subsequent to this morning's conference.

June 4, Sunday

Diary: Last night was apparently our last night ashore, for this morning Mac and I were "sealed." The information given to us which warranted this action was as follows. D Day is Monday, June 5th, and the point of invasion—Le Havre to Isigny on the coast of Normandy. My feelings on realising the nearness of the great day were surprising to me. Excitement, anticipation and a desire to be off, coupled with a prayer that the weather might abate. Fear that my navigation might not prove equal to the demands upon it, and a feeling of "wait till they hear about this at home" are all that I can recall.

Our programme was to be roughly this. At 1300 Sunday 4th proceed

Operational waters for HMS *Jason* and HM *ML137*, 1944–45.

ahead of 1st MSF down Eastern Solent and set course for France. Roughly 25 miles south of Selsey Bill we would stream sweeps and, formed ahead of the Fleet Sweepers, proceed to sweep a forty mile approach channel to the Baie de la Seine, to be finished due North of Ouistreham. Sweeps would be veered at 2030 on Sunday 4th and taken in at 0600 on D Day. A few miles astern would come the assault ships, and at 0725 would commence the biggest assault in history.

At 1230 our disappointment was intense on receiving a signal, "Operation postponed twenty-four hours." We had already left harbour to take our station ahead of the line, and had a first look at the immense fleet of vessels beginning to assemble outside Portsmouth, and at the worsening weather in the Channel. The signal meant that we had to turn back. We spent the night in Hornet Creek in Portsmouth harbour.

Under Gen. Dwight Eisenhower, Adm. Sir Bertram Ramsay was in charge of the final organization of the naval operation for the invasion of France. The Allied Expeditionary Force consisted of the Western and the Eastern task forces, each of which included minesweeping flotillas, a bombarding force, an assault force, and a follow-up force. The Western Task Force, mainly U.S. ships, was commanded by Rear Adm. Alan G. Kirk of the U.S. Navy, and the Eastern Task Force, mainly British and Canadian ships, was commanded by Rear Adm. Sir Philip Vian of the Royal Navy. Other Allied vessels in these invasion forces included Free French, Norwegian, Dutch, and Polish warships. More than four thousand vessels were involved, not including hundreds of small craft carried to the assault beaches in other landing ships. Approximately 60 percent of the naval forces were British, and the rest were American and Canadian. More than eighty ships with more than six hundred guns made up the bombarding force. At the time of the assault, it was estimated that in ten minutes the naval guns would fire more than two thousand tons of high explosives. *ML137* was one of approximately two hundred minesweepers manned by ten thousand officers and men. The minesweeping gear weighed nearly three thousand tons, and the sweep wires, joined end to end, would have reached from London to the Isle of Wight, a distance of more than eighty miles.

D-Day

Our destination was Sword Beach. The coastline of the invasion area had been divided into five beaches. From east to west, they were named Sword, Juno, Gold, Omaha, and Utah. Sword Beach lay a few miles west of Le Havre. It was approximately six nautical miles from east to west, being bounded on the east by the small port of Ouistreham at the confluence of the River Orne and the Caen Canal and on the west by the village of Saint-Aubin. Farther east, on the other side of the waterways, lay substantial German forces. They were in a position to launch an attack against the eastern flank of Sword Beach. It was therefore crucial that their attack be prevented or delayed as long as possible if the Allied assault troops were to be built up to the strength necessary to defeat them.

The German approach to Sword Beach lay along a highway that crossed the two waterways. Two bridges provided the crossing, and these

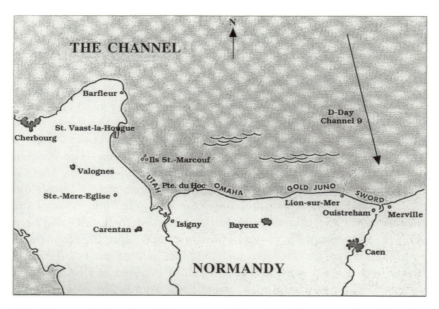

The Normandy beaches, 6 June 1944. Channel 9, the approach to Sword Beach, was cleared by the First Minesweeping Flotilla and the Fifth Motor Launch Flotilla.

were defended by the Germans. Just past midnight on 6 June, airborne troops of a British regiment, the Oxford and Buckinghamshire Light Infantry under the command of Maj. John Howard, landed by glider and captured the bridges. Here occurred the first fighting of the invasion. The airborne troops held the bridges against counterattack until relieved. The flank of Sword Beach was secured. The bridge over the Orne has been renamed Pegasus Bridge, a tribute to the Flying Horse shoulder patch worn by British airborne troops.

The general invasion area had been described, 133 years earlier, in terms that suggested difficulty in finding any significant harbors, an essential requirement for the buildup of forces after the first assault. In the 1811 edition of *The New Seaman's Guide and Coaster's Companion*, we find the discouraging comment:

> From Cape La Heve to Cape Barfleur, on which is a high lighthouse, the course is N W by W about 17 leagues. . . . The shore all along between Cape La Heve and Cape Barfleur is rocky and full of sands. The bay formed by Cape de Caux and Cape Barfleur is about 7 leagues

deep: on the south and west part of it are several small harbours, of which description is unnecessary.[1]

Shortly before we left Portsmouth to take up the position assigned us, a courier delivered a large canvas bag of secret documents. These documents were amazing to me. One of the items was a long, concertina-folded, sea-level panorama photograph of the Normandy coastline over the entire invasion area. It had been made as a composite of a systematic series of photographs taken at very low level from aircraft flying directly toward the beach and was intended as an aid to navigators in identifying landmarks on approaching the beach. The panorama photograph showed us exactly what we should see if we reached our correct position off the beach. When we got there, it was just so. I frequently used it in the subsequent days when operating off the coast of Normandy.

Also in the bag were intelligence reports of the numbers and dispositions of German troops at all points along the line. These reports were impressive; they included such details as the fact that a specific German unit in one of the beach areas had been sent on leave just three days before and had been replaced by inexperienced troops, who might therefore put up less resistance.

I remain impressed by the immensity and thoroughness of the planning that went into this whole operation. Only nine of the twelve MLs in the 5th Flotilla had been assigned to take part in the assault. We learned later that the other three took part in an elaborate mock-attack diversion off Calais, where it appeared that the Germans were expecting the main attack to occur. Selection of the MLs to take part in the real assault in Normandy was made by the most junior of the commanding officers tossing coins. The losers went to the diversion, and the winners went to the real thing. We were obviously a winner.

This large-scale deception was carried out by a substantial number of ships and aircraft maneuvering in the Calais area. Aircraft dropped quantities of metal streamers that had the effect of appearing to be parachute troops when seen on radar. The ships steered courses that directly approached the German positions. Some small ships were fitted with screens to increase the size of their radar reflections and thereby create the impression that they were cruisers or battleships. There was much

1. John Diston, M. Downie, and Alexander Ingram, *The New Seaman's Guide and Coaster's Companion. A New and Correct Edition*, Leith, Scotland: Coke and Reid, 1811, 178. Downie was a master in the Royal Navy, and Ingram was a teacher of navigation and mathematics.

firing of guns and simulation of sounds that would be made by an invading force. Our flotilla mates described this to us during a subsequent reunion. They seemed to have enjoyed it somewhat, although they were deeply disappointed that they missed the opportunity to get into the "real thing" on 6 June. As they soon joined the flotilla, they quickly got into the real thing at Cherbourg and in other sweeping operations.

Admiral Ramsay issued an Order of the Day to all naval men taking part in the invasion. It read in part:

> It is to be our privilege to take part in the greatest amphibious operation in history. . . . This is the opportunity which we have long awaited and which must be seized and pursued with relentless determination; the hopes and prayers of the free world and of the enslaved people of Europe will be with us, and we cannot fail them. Our task, in conjunction with the Merchant Navies of the United Nations and supported by the Allied Air Forces, is to carry the Allied Expeditionary Force to the Continent, to establish there a secure bridgehead, and to build it up and maintain it at a rate which will outmatch that of the enemy. . . . Good luck to you all and God-speed.

The Supreme Headquarters of the Allied Expeditionary Force issued the following communiqué at 0930 on 6 June 1944:

> Under the command General Eisenhower, Allied naval forces, supported by strong air forces, began landing Allied armies this morning on the northern coast of France.

Many years later my wife and I came across a photograph of her father, James Alexander Brown, taken on 12 July 1918 at Camp Colt near Gettysburg, Pennsylvania, where he was then a corporal in the U.S. Army. His commanding officer was Capt. Dwight Eisenhower. It has given us both much pleasure to know that my much loved father-in-law and I had served at different times under the same commander.

June 5, Monday–June 6, Tuesday

Diary: Returned to the Solent and secured alongside *Harrier*. Sea choppy even in a comparatively sheltered anchorage such as this. HMS *Largs* came out from Portsmouth harbour flying the following signal "Good luck. Drive on." The hour was approaching.

From here I give an extract from the ship's log:

1300.   Slipped with 1st MSF, Trawlers, MS1 & *Scorpion*.
1328.   Spithead Boom. Took station ahead of *Harrier*. Course S. 40 E, Speed 4 knots.

1345.   B. Buoy. Altered course S. 60 E

1404.   C. Buoy. Altered course S. 35 E

1415.   D. Buoy. Altered course S. 5 E

1429.   E. Buoy. Altered course S. 20 W

1440.   X. Buoy.

1455.   F. Buoy. Altered course S. 60 E.

1600.   "EA2 Buoy." Took station on *Harrier*'s port beam. Speed 5 knots.

1735.   Altered course S. 25 E. Speed 8 knots

1940.   Passed lettered position "PB"

1952.   Out Port Sweep

1957.   Altered course S. 5 W

2039.   Sweep foul. Cut sweep

2040.   Speed 14 knots

2043.   Speed 10 knots

2115.   Took station ahead of *Harrier*. Speed 10 knots

2150.   Emergency Port Sweep streamed. Course S. Speed 7 knots

2235.   Stopped

2340.   Heavy Flak bearing S. 85 W—Cherbourg Peninsula

JUNE 6, TUESDAY. D-DAY

0026.   In Sweeps. MS 1 turned 180 degrees back up the swept channel to stream the Starboard Sweeps.

0028.   Heavy air-raid on Ouistreham bearing due south.

0100.   Sweeps in. Altered course N. Speed 14 knots.

0125.   Arrived datum dan pointed by *Colsay*. Altered course S.

0134.   Stopped. Out Sweeps—Starboard.² MS1 astern

0155.   Speed 7 knots, Course due S.

0211.   MS 15 sighted to port

0230.   Speed 5 knots

0243.   Channels 9 and 10 converged

0325.   Reached the Lowering Position³

0345.   Altered course due W. *ML141* fell out of formation. Flares over Cherbourg. Ouistreham still under bombing

0430.   In Sweeps. Shells from coastal guns dropping near. Cut Sweep. Full (speed) ahead

2. We had rehearsed the maneuver of changing the side from which sweeps were to be streamed in an exercise on 15 March (above). Then, it had taken one hour and thirty minutes. This time, it took one hour and eight minutes. We had improved with practice.

3. The position at which the small landing craft were to be lowered from the large infantry landing ships to carry the assault to the beaches. At this point, we were directly opposite Sword Beach.

0532.   Altered course E. Action Stations. Speed 16 (knots)

0541.   Speed 6. Heavy bombardment of beaches by HM ships *Warspite, Scylla, Orion, Argonaut, Belfast* and others

0600.   Large vessel on Starboard beam sinking. Bows and stern only visible. Action Stations secure

0630.   Took Station astern *Harrier.*

0700.   Stopped near Lowering Position. Landing craft commenced assault.

0725.   H-hour. Assault force on the beaches.

Here I will break off and describe more fully the period covered by the rather laconic entries in the log. The scene when passing Spithead Gate was absolutely incredible. Ahead of us the modern destroyer *Scorpion* zig-zagged to reduce speed, while we slowly overhauled the great series of Landing Ships and Craft. As far as the eye could see were row after row of LCTs, and towering above them the impressive bulk of the *Empire*[4] ships (*Empire Broadsword, Empire Halberd, Empire Battleaxe*, etc.) with LCAs [landing craft assault] slung at the davits and troops massing their upperworks. The LCTs—ungainly and slow moving vessels—were packed to capacity with tanks and armoured vehicles of all kinds. One LCI [Landing Craft Infantry] I observed had rows of bicycles stacked and lashed neatly on the upper deck.

The weather was uncompromisingly grim. The sky leaden and the sea rough. A long and heavy swell was also adding to our discomfort. Much to my annoyance I was violently sea-sick for the first time in my life, but was quite OK afterwards. Of the long hours of darkness in the wheelhouse, hearing nothing but occasional orders on the bridge, and navigating by verbatim reports from the C.O.—my steel helmet weighing a ton and the rolling and pitching becoming even more violent—of these only a blurred memory remains although it was only a fortnight ago.

The "flak" over Ouistreham was an amazing sight. The peculiarly leisurely way in which the red and yellow and green tracer mounted upwards seemed quite divorced from the mission of destruction. The roar of bomb and gun could be heard at a distance of twenty miles. Eventually

---

4. The *Empire* ships (*Empire Broadsword* and others) were LSIs (landing ships infantry) or LSLs (landing ships large). These large vessels were designed to carry infantry to a point near the beach during an invasion. Each of these ships had a large number of small infantry landing craft swung out at the davits. When the ship reached her assigned position off the beach (lowering position), these craft were lowered into the water. The troops climbed down into the landing craft by large rope nettings hung over the ship's side. Once loaded, the landing craft took up formation and were ready to speed to the beach when the signal was given. This method was used to land the bulk of the troops in most beach assaults.

dawn came and with it H-hour. I shall never forget that vast concourse of ships in the Bay. The flash and roar of the battlers' guns and the clouds of dust and smoke rising from the cliffs; the faint rattle of machine guns, and the unswerving manner in which the little craft made straight for the shore, as if on an exercise; the *Scylla* going so near the shore that she had to leave stern first, still bombarding, as there was no depth of water to turn; the dismal spectacle of a fine ship going for ever, bows and stern sticking out of the water, and the ships passing her unheeded—these fragments come to mind as souvenirs of H-hour. Then the whine and splash of shells ahead of us and the order, "Cut sweeps for Christ's sake!" and away into the less dangerous waters of the minefield. Exhausted by a sleepless night we yet had a gruelling day ahead of us.

Immediately following our escape from the coastal batteries, a day of sweeping commenced. I revert to the ship's log again. 6th June:

JUNE 6, TUESDAY. D DAY (CONTINUED)

1010.   MS 1 proceeded to sweep Channel 56.[5] Took station astern with *ML141* as mine destruction vessels. Course N. 10 E. Beaches hidden in smoke.

1110.   2 mines detonated

1116.   1 mine detonated

1120.   1 mine detonated

1125.   1 mine detonated

1126.   1 mine detonated

1130.   2 mines detonated

1155.   Mines all around the ship. Commenced destruction.

1247.   7 mines sunk (5 by *ML137*, 2 by *ML141*)

1305.   Speed 14 knots

1512.   Reached north end of channel. Altered course, S. 10 W.

2007.   In Sweeps at south end of lap.

2038.   Ordered to Portsmouth

2115.   Took station astern *Colsay*. Set course for Portsmouth. Speed 9 knots. Course N. 65 W.

This was a long & monotonous day—although an intense feeling of satisfaction was caused by sinking the enemy mines. The order to re-turn to Portsmouth was very welcome and—the weather unabated—we

---

5. After the original ten numbered channels had been swept and the assault on the beaches had begun, the minesweepers began to sweep the mine fields between the channels that already had been swept. These areas were identified by the numbers of the channels previously swept. Thus, Channel 56 referred to the area between Channels 5 and 6, which were to the west of Channel 9—our own original swept channel.

turned for home. During the return voyage I snatched four hours sleep, the first since Sunday night.

We commenced destruction by shooting at the mines that had come to the surface when the sweep cut their mooring lines. This target shooting was done by our machine gunners and anybody else who was available; members of the ship's company not otherwise engaged lined the upper deck and fired at the mines with rifles. I took a position on the edge of the bridge and rested a rifle there to take aim at the bobbing and swinging mines.

Our role in the invasion had placed us as the first ship in Channel 9, one of the ten channels that were to be swept. Channel 10 was the most easterly channel; Channel 1 was at the extreme western edge of the American landing zone. Our task was to sweep mines to leave a safe depth for the larger fleet sweepers of the 1st Flotilla, led by the *Harrier*. They, in turn, swept at an even greater depth and width to clear the water necessary for the larger invasion vessels coming in behind them. Channel 9 was one of the approach channels for Canadian troops, who were in the landing ships behind the minesweepers. It led straight to Sword Beach, its direction being due south (magnetic) on a line directly terminating at Ouistreham. During the night sweep across the English Channel toward France, the tide turned shortly after midnight. This necessitated hauling in the minesweeping gear from one side and streaming the gear from the other. In order to do this, it was necessary to proceed slowly or stop altogether while performing the maneuver. The plan called for us to turn around and head back north slowly to permit the change of sweeps and then, once the sweeps had been changed, to turn around southward and resume the approach. It was necessary for all ships in the sweeping group to do this at the same time; as no signals were permitted on the radio, the signal to make the turns was given by the brief exposure of a small light on the masthead of the *Harrier*. It was crucial that this signal be seen by every ship so that all would turn together. A clear recollection is of the intense strain of watching from our stern to where the *Harrier* was following somewhere in the total darkness and very stormy sea. The *Harrier*'s light flashed briefly at 0026, and the entire maneuver was completed by 0155, at which point we were once more headed toward France.

As we reached the last few hundred yards of our sweep, the German defenses were clearly visible through binoculars. My initial thought was to wonder why they were not already firing at us. The approaches to the beach were packed with thousands of ships, stretching back to the horizon as far as the eye could see. The Germans had no lack of targets, and the smoke clouds and thunder of our own bombardment had been in evidence for quite a while. It was as if the whole thing had taken this particular part of the defenses by surprise. Right ahead of us was an artillery bunker built into the dunes that bordered the back of the beach. Through the slit in the bunker, I could see the broad outlines of a face, officer's tabs, German helmet, and binoculars. He was looking directly at us. Perhaps he simply could not believe his eyes and was immobilized by disbelief. This was the first time I had seen the enemy so close.

The plan also called for us to remove ourselves into the unswept water outside Channel 9 when the time came for the assault craft to make their run for the beach. Strictly speaking, we were expendable at that point and the crucial thing was to get out of the way of the minesweepers behind us and the landing craft behind them. We did so by turning westward into the mined waters between Channels 9 and 8. Here, we began to haul in the sweeping gear, but a German artillery bunker seemed to have selected us as a target; shells began to drop around us. To get out of the range of the German guns, we were compelled to cut the sweep wire that we were hauling in. We then replaced the missing sweep from our spares. Later, in clear daylight, I could see the bunkers on the beach through binoculars, but they had already been overrun by the Canadians and were no longer firing.

As we moved out of the way into the mine field, we watched the endless panorama of landing craft and ships of all kinds heading toward the beach, bombarding the German positions further inland, moving this way and that, and turning sharply to avoid mines and other obstacles. We were passed by a Canadian landing craft full of soldiers, each carrying a bicycle. I have tried to figure out which unit this might have been. In *D-Day, June 6, 1944*, Ambrose gives an account of the landing of the 10th Commando on Sword Beach, one troop of which was equipped with bicycles,[6] and it might have been this unit that we saw.

We also passed an LBK (landing barge kitchen), perhaps the one described by Lt. Comdr. C. Anthony Law (see next section). I remember being surprised to see this ungainly craft so close to the assault stage of the operation. At another point, we were close to a trawler hove to next to a Jeep that had been underwater, presumably part of the cargo of a sunken landing craft. The trawler skipper had swung the cargo boom of

6. Stephen Ambrose, *D-Day, June 6, 1944: The Climactic Battle of World War II*, New York: Simon and Schuster, 1994.

his mast out over the side and hooked the Jeep to the end of the wire hawser. Slowly winching the Jeep out of the water, he had it hanging precariously from the hook, with water dripping from the wheels and bumpers. Every item of equipment that had gone to the invasion had been defined as "expendable," that is, its loss would not have to be reported.

Hutchins hailed the trawler skipper, "You don't have to rescue that, you know."

"I'm not rescuing it," shouted the skipper. "I've never had a car in my life, and now I've got one. This is coming home with me."

Once the main assault had been launched from the lowering areas, the minesweepers were to proceed to clear the still unswept areas between the swept approach channels. The goal was to clear the entire coastal area of mines from east to west. At the end of the day, we were ordered back to Portsmouth.

We returned to Normandy on 9 June. The diary records:

June 7, Wednesday. D-Day + 1

Diary: On arrival we fueled instantly, victualled and watered and then proceeded to the buoy at Hornet. Then some welcome sleep after a glance at the newspapers to see exactly what we had been doing the past two days.

June 8, Thursday. D-Day + 2

Diary: In harbour mainly, repairing defects, collecting mail and becoming human again. The Captain went ashore—then urgent signal: "Join MS1 in Solent before darkness." A hurried rush to recall the Captain, a 8dash in the dusk to the Solent and orders to slip at 0230 in the morning. A few hours sleep.

June 9, Friday. D-Day + 3

Diary: Slipped at 0230 and proceeded to sea. At 0520 took station as Mine destructor astern Flotilla, with *ML293* and trawlers *Craftsman* and *Lord Ashfield*. Sweeping continued for fifteen hours—no mines being swept—just a round of navigation, watchkeeping and a few hours sleep.

The endless convoys to France presented a fine sight—ship after ship of guns & tanks, troops and trucks. Aircraft flew unceasingly overhead. A grim reminder of the realities—four floating Carley rafts[7] drifting in the tide in various places along the convoy route; once a flotsam life-belt.

---

7. A Carley raft is a flat, oval-shaped life raft made of flotation material; a number were kept lashed to the upperworks of a ship—ready to be cut loose if a ship were sinking.

At 2055 sweeping being finished we set course for the beaches of
Port-en-Bessin for the night's anchorage. From here the ship's log:

2055.   Beach bombed—Action Stations

2137.   Actions Stations secured

2140.   Heavy flak over the anchorage. Action Stations. Seven Focke-
Wulfe aircraft flew overhead at 1000 feet. Opened fire with all
guns.

2141.   Cease fire

2215.   Secured alongside *Harrier.* Action Stations secure. HMS *Hussar*
carrying out depth-charge attack on U-boat 2 cables to the
south of our position.

2255.   Action Stations. Heavy air raid on the anchorage

2320.   Dropped astern of *Harrier*—secured. Action stations secure.

The thrill of opening up at enemy aircraft was unbelievable. I found
myself jumping and shouting with excitement and cursing the gunner
for not bringing one down. The all-night action stations were exhaust-
ing and my assistant in the wheelhouse, Ordinary Signalman Gordon
Wyld, was dropping asleep. By continually blasting the unfortunate lad
I managed to keep awake myself.

All of us had firsthand experience of being on the receiving end of air
raids, and the wish to fight back in a direct way was intense. Incidentally,
the "unfortunate lad" mentioned was seventeen years old, apparently a
mere "lad" to a nineteen-year-old, such as I was then.

June 10, Saturday. D-Day + 4

Diary: The log continues:

0200.   Action Stations—E-Boats illuminated by star-shell bearing east

0210.   Actions Stations secure

0415.   Action Stations. Bombs dropped. Heavy flak

0520.   Action Stations secure

0600.   *Harrier* weighed (anchor)

0900.   Co. N. 20 E Speed 7 knots, took up K-formation sweep.

1021.   1 mine detonated

1025.   1 mine detonated

1145.   Altered course N 10 W

1225.   Altered course N 45 W

1248.   Altered course N 10 E

1300.   Speed 10. Altered course N 30 W

1303.   Speed 7

1315.   Mine dead ahead. Stop engines

1401.   Mine sunk. Altered course N 50 W. Speed 14
1520.   Altered course S.
2020.   In Sweeps
2155.   Secured alongside *Harrier*

Thus another 15 hours at sea non-stop—15 hours of work for everyone. The night watch (I had the Middle Watch) was comparatively
quiet. The usual multicoloured tracer and deafening explosions. The
earth tremors and fires on the coast were still there. A quiet night—
comparatively.

Getting some sleep seems to have been a continual concern during this
period—and during any extended period at sea. I suppose that, given our
ages at the time, getting sleep was important. We took any opportunity
to snatch a short nap.

Three or four days after D-Day, *ML137* was ordered to go alongside
the U.S. cargo ship *Eleazer H. Wheelock*, anchored some distance from
the beach, to replenish our food supplies that were getting low. I went on
board with two ratings and was taken down into the hold. It was chilly
and cavernous. Row after row of meat carcasses hung on overhead racks,
and cases of packaged food were stacked high everywhere. We didn't
qualify for a carcass (being too few in number to justify it), but we did get
some chickens, plus several cases of prepackaged rations. Each ration was
packed in a brown cardboard box wrapped in wax paper and bearing the
printed title "Breakfast" or "Dinner." Typically, a box contained small pet
food–sized cans of preserved meat (Spam, Prem, or corned beef); a bar
of compressed dried fruit; a packet of fruit-flavored crystals to make a
kind of juice-oid drink; a water-purifying tablet; a pack of five cigarettes
(such as Old Gold "toasted with apple-honey," Camels, or Chesterfields);
and five sheets of toilet paper. Naturally, everything was dried or powdered, and we never did discover a conceptual difference between the
contents of "Breakfast" and "Dinner." They were all welcome and had
the advantage of readily being made edible without heating or cooking—
a distinct benefit under the conditions at the time.

I remember being mildly puzzled by the ship's name, although many
ships involved in the invasion had names of people who were not familiar to Britishers. Not until many years later, when I was giving an invited speech at Dartmouth College in Hanover, New Hampshire, did I
discover that Eleazer H. Wheelock had been the founder and first
president of that institution. He was a preacher and much involved in
trying to provide free education for native Americans. I can imagine his

spirit might have been pleased to be represented in another kind of liberation.

One of the many great wartime shipbuilding achievements in the United States was the design and construction of the Liberty ships. These cargo vessels were originally built in the shipyards of the Kaiser Shipbuilding Company. Each had a displacement of 10,000 tons and was built in three separate sections that were welded together to form the finished ship. The entire process took only ten days, which resulted in a production rate of cargo ships much greater than their rate of loss to U-boats. The major weakness of the Liberty ship was at the point of the main welds. I saw one that had gone aground on the Goodwin Sands (a particularly dangerous shifting set of sand banks off the southeast coast of England). As the tide fell, the ship became gradually high and dry. When completely dry, the unsupported weight of the hull became too heavy for the welded seams to bear and caused her to break neatly into the original three pieces, each of which was stuck in the sand slightly apart from the others. Something of the same problem tended to occur in many of the large flat-bottomed landing craft designed to land their cargoes over the ramp in the bow directly onto the beach. If the beach was tidal and the unloading delayed, the larger and longer of these craft might be partially stranded as the tide fell, which caused some of them to break in the middle. The strategy of the invasion was such that it was not critically essential for these vessels to be used more than once. Their breakup was more of a nuisance, as a result of the obstacles they created, than a serious loss of future transport capacity.

June 11, Sunday. D-Day + 5

Diary: Proceeded to flagship HMS *Scylla* with MS1. Convoys still arriving. A careful study of the beaches through binoculars reveals an orderly unloading and despatch organisation and now no sign of the enemy. A pall of smoke hangs over the land further inland but the beachheads are now secure. Saw one or two War Correspondents on *Scylla*. At 1200 we set course for Portsmouth with *ML293*, after collecting the Fleet Sweepers mail. Arrived 1900, watered and fuelled and thankfully piped down.

By this time, the invasion was already proceeding well. The uncertainties of the naval operations were behind us. Ahead lay the enormous task of securing and clearing one or more major ports to permit the landing of the mass of supplies that would be required during the coming months. That effort was about to begin. Now, however, we could contemplate the extraordinary events in which we had participated. They have been described by many writers. Those that follow seem to reflect my own experiences most closely.

Additional Observations of the Invasion

The extract that follows is from a description by Lt. Comdr. C. Anthony Law, RCNVR, who was commanding officer of the Canadian 29th Motor Torpedo Boat Flotilla. During the invasion of Normandy, the task of the 29th Flotilla, in company with the 55th Flotilla, was to protect the eastern flank of the British assault area and to attack and destroy enemy shipping working from Le Havre. Law's flotilla, operating just east of Channel 10, directly protected our flank during the approach to Sword Beach.

The 5th of June arrived, a dull and miserable day. The wind blew very hard and the sky was overcast with formidable dark clouds. I received a top secret signal; Operation Neptune was on. The knowledge that the long-awaited time had come at last filled me with a strange emotion. As the day wore on the weather deteriorated. An almost incredible variety of ships moved out in an orderly fashion past the Portsmouth gate vessel. Minesweepers appeared off the Normandy coast, and by nightfall the swept channel stretched right across, making the beach-head approaches safe for the hundreds of vessels that were to come. Once the minesweepers had completed their work, destroyers, cruisers, and battleships moved into a position to bombard the Normandy coast. . . .

[We] were to protect the minesweepers sailing to Normandy against E-boats and we empathized with them as they set out through the raging seas, winding through the endless landing craft before finally slipping out into the angry channel. Choppy seas were very hard on the crews of the little boats. At 1400 sharp the colourful pennants went up and the boats moved slowly out in to the middle of the harbour, taking up their positions in line-ahead formation. The Number Ones and crews, dressed in their sea-going gear, including the RCN life-jackets with their high collars, lined the fo'c'sle as the Admiral's flag was piped, a ceremony which could under no circumstances be omitted. Then the ships' companies fell out and hastened to action stations, closing up their guns. . . .

During the voyage we passed a most peculiar vessel, which was tossing and bouncing even more than any of the other craft. Closing it we discovered that it was a self-propelled floating kitchen, and it was having an extremely tough time. The kitchen craft closely resembled an overgrown caboose set on a barge, and its many smoking stove-pipes made this unseaworthy Noah's Ark look most out of place battling it out in the mean sea toward Normandy, where it was badly needed. This boat, unique in our experience, quickly faded into the background as our unit moved on, passing in our course other craft far superior to the gallant kitchen ark. . . . I have always believed they [the Merchant Navy] were truly the Silent Service of the war. Throughout the war merchant ships took part in every major operation, and few people realize the heroic sacrifices made by the seamen who manned them.[8]

I, too, salute the officers and men of the Merchant Navy. I am privileged to have as a friend Robert Wentzell of Indian Point, Lunenberg County, Nova Scotia, who served in the U.S. Merchant Marine and was on board a merchant ship during the invasion. Lying about his age, Wentzell was only sixteen when he enlisted in the Merchant Marine. It was as a boy that he experienced the challenge and horror of the Normandy invasion. After reading my journal, he told me that he was in a merchant ship behind us. "We must have crossed bows," he said. I was moved when he added, "You swept for me."

The following is from the pen of naval historian Correlli Barnett:

In early evening the minesweepers began sweeping the ten two-mile wide approach channels through the German mine barrier, marking the boundaries with Dan buoys as they went. Despite the west-south-west wind and a 2½-knot tidal stream running dead abeam, which compelled some vessels to make as much as 40° allowance in order to keep a true course, the assault forces followed the minesweepers on through the night hours with few errors of navigation.

And still the enemy had not stirred. The only Allied casualties had been the minesweeper USS *Osprey* sunk and the destroyer HMS *Wrestler* and a landing craft damaged by mines, and some 50 smaller craft swamped by the rough seas. That long day of mass movement had passed without attack by German aircraft or U-boat or E-boat. Ramsay, waiting in his headquarters at Southwick House for news, could hardly believe their luck.

"There was an air of unreality [he wrote in his report] during that passage of the assault force across the Channel curiously similar to that on D − 1 in *Husky* as our forces approached Sicily. The achievement of

8. C. Anthony Law, "The Day of Judgment," *The Chronicle-Herald—The Mail Star*, 2 September 1989. Reprinted by permission of C. Anthony Law.

strategical surprise was always hoped for in *Neptune* but was by no means certain, whereas that of tactical surprise had always seemed extremely unlikely. As our forces approached the French coast without a murmur from the enemy or from their own radio the realisation that once again almost complete tactical surprise had been achieved slowly dawned."[9]

As other historians have established, the German command had been blinkered. The first problem was the weakness of the Luftwaffe, which was unable to maintain adequate surveillance of Allied shipping concentrations and movements during the weeks preceding the invasion. A second critical problem was caused by the Allied elimination of the German weather ships in the Atlantic. German weather forecasting was inaccurate, particularly its attempts to predict the weather for days ahead. The unfavorable state of the weather on 4 June led the Germans to conclude that the invasion was not imminent. In *The Longest Day*, Ryan reports that the Germans believed that the extremely bad weather in the Channel ruled out any possibility of an invasion during that night.[10] Normally, the German Navy operated a continuous E-boat patrol across the Bay of the Seine to watch for a possible invasion but, on this occasion, had canceled it because of the weather. The Germans did not know that the Allies had predicted a window of improvement in the weather for 6 June and a few days thereafter.

Reassured that there was little risk of invasion, Field Marshal Rommel, commander of the German forces between the Seine and Loire rivers, had departed to Germany for his wife's birthday. He was five hundred miles from Normandy when the invasion began, and there were decisions to be made. German radar did not detect the advancing invasion fleet; several German radar stations had been put out of action by Allied air attacks. As a result, German coastal defense troops and the crews of gun batteries were asleep in their emplacements as the invasion fleet approached. Those on watch saw nothing as they scanned the horizon of the dark sea.

Finally, from British war correspondent Gordon Holman, who was on board HMS *Enterprise*, a summing up:

9. Correlli Barnett, *Engage the Enemy More Closely: The Royal Navy in the Second World War*, New York: W. W. Norton; London: David Higham Associates, 1991, 811. Reprinted by permission of W. W. Norton Co., and David Higham Associates. Copyright © Correlli Barnett.

10. Cornelius Ryan, *The Longest Day: June 6, 1944*, London: Victor Gollancz, 1960; New Orchard Editions, 1994.

It was on the day that the Prime Minister passed safely to and from France that the Admiralty stated that a message congratulating all officers and men of H.M. Minesweeping forces for their continued success in destroying enemy mines had been conveyed by the First Lord of the Admiralty on behalf of the War Cabinet: ". . . the War Cabinet fully appreciates that, but for the courage, skill and devotion of H.M. Minesweeping forces, the success of the recent amphibious operations, and especially of the landings in Normandy, could not have been achieved. . . ." Never was commendation better earned than by these men of the sweeper flotillas. With more and more ports to sweep, in addition to their daily task on the supply routes, their responsibilities increased as the weeks went by, but they carried on with a determination and cheerfulness which was an example to all who came in contact with them.[11]

Securing the Beaches

I return to my diary for a record of our own movements during the days that followed D-Day:

June 12, Monday

Diary: Went ashore to get much-needed hair-cut (first since Dover), a new battery for the radio, and one or two necessary luxuries. Returned at 1300 to find that the ship had sailed to Poole. Went to Hornet and unburdened my woes—was issued with travel warrant and returned for tea to *ML141*. Caught 8:30 P.M. train from Pompey (Portsmouth) to Poole and arrived Bournemouth at 11 P.M. There being no means of getting beyond there, and as population seems mainly American forces who had never heard of Poole, I finally spent the night at the Meyrick Mansions Hotel, starting at 1 A.M. in the morning.

June 13, Tuesday

Diary: Arrived Poole by bus at 1030 and, amid smiles of crew, resumed normal work. Poole seems a fine place. Old-fashioned streets, wide marshes, fishing quay and general Dorset charm of its own. I will like it here. Met Sub-Lieutenant Inayat Khan and Sub-Lieutenant Ellington who were at Lochinvar with me—both now on MLs off Fleet Sweepers. Rather chokker[12] too, as in truth I am now. Still life is fine at Poole.

11. Gordon Holman, *Stand By to Beach*, London: Hodder & Stoughton, 1944, 142–43. Reprinted by permission of Hodder Headline PLC.

12. Slang for "fed up," bored, frustrated; from the term "chock-a-block," which refers to the position of two pulleys hauled so close together that there is no further room for movement.

Strawberries and cream for tea—fresh milk and a daily newspaper. Laundry and shoe repairs. Just step off the ship and walk 20 yds. across the quay to the street. It's like a rest cure. Tadpole, as the base is called, is new and the base wallahs[13] seem quite good. However, time will tell.

June 15, Thursday

Diary: Did chart corrections in the forenoon. Went ashore in the afternoon, bought cakes for tea—(what a life)—saw the town and came back on board. Trouble over theft of 30 shillings from Able Seaman Monksfield's belt. Searched kit with no results.

Able Seaman Monksfield held a gunnery rating. He was stocky, cheery, and eternally optimistic; he had, in a word, just the right temperament for small-ship life. I am not sure where he came from, I think from London. At sea, he was gunner, watchkeeper, and helmsman in turn, as circumstances required. As was the case in all small ships, however, he did other things. Specifically, he acted as a part-time wardroom steward to the three officers. This consisted mainly of bringing down the meals from the galley, making up the bunks, and some general cleaning. He also took our laundry to local laundries in such places as Portland and Dover when we were there.

The galley was in the crew's quarters in the fo'c'sle, and the wardroom was aft. Because there was no longitudinal passage through the ship, Monksfield had to carry our meals on a tray along the upper deck. In heavy weather, the rolling and pitching of the ship turned this into an exercise in balance and dexterity, with Monksfield leaning this way and that as the ship rolled. His transit rarely ended in complete disaster but almost always added a strong flavor of seawater and salt to the already unattractive dishes. Baked beans, partially fried bacon, and Channel water comprised a particular favorite, followed closely by canned cold spaghetti on sea-soaked toast. By the time Monksfield arrived, the food inevitably was cold.

Monksfield was one of the sweeping crew when I was wounded later in Holland. He had no injury himself but appeared as a witness to describe the events at the inquiry that followed.

June 16, Friday

Diary: Went to Bournemouth in the evening. Dined at the Norfolk Hotel and went on to the Odeon cinema. Quite a pleasant evening, in an

13. Term that originated in India and passed into general British usage; can be roughly translated as "chaps" or "guys."

atmosphere of civilization rather remote from the war. Population appears to be 90% American forces.

June 17, Saturday—June 19, Monday

Diary: Slipped at 0900 with *ML138* and set course for Portland Bay. Passed close south of Anvil Point and thence to Weymouth Bay. Secured in ML pens at noon. During afternoon received orders to join escort for convoy leaving for Isigny area (base of the Cherbourg Peninsula) at 2100 same evening.

Slipped at 2100 with *ML138* and joined escort consisting of sloop *Londonderry*, and corvette *Clarkia*. Convoy consisted of 16 U.S. LST's. Proceeded along S. Coast to a point south of the I.o.W. and then set course for Isigny. Arrived at the area at 1200. LSTs proceeded to the beach. Secured alongside *Londonderry* for the afternoon. At about 1500, June 18th—i.e., 3 hours later, a launch with a U.S. Ensign and two ratings came alongside and told us to prepare to join convoy sailing for Portland at 1530.

1535 slipped and took up position on Starboard quarter of convoy. On our Port beam was U.S. LST 133 in tow to a British tug, having had her stern blown off. The rest of the convoy rapidly drew ahead and the Captain decided to remain with the tug. At 2330 exactly, as I was checking our position on the chart, seven German aircraft (Junkers 88) came out of a cloud and, splitting formation, commenced their run in to bomb the tug and LST. All guns opened fire instantly and we turned 180 degrees to come up near the tug and give covering fire. Bombs dropped harmlessly in the water, and the combined fire of all three ships proving unpleasant the enemy rapidly vanished. Half an hour later aircraft returned to the attack, but with no more success than before. We remained at Action Stations until 0300 expecting E-boats to be hot on the trail. The rest of the passage was uneventful, we leaving the tug and LST at St. Catherine's Point and making our way to Portland—then to Southampton. Arriving at Portland at 0630 (June 19th) we secured to the jetty and turned in.

The same afternoon went ashore to Weymouth, passing a Prisoner of War cage on the way. About 500 German prisoners were being searched here, and a very dispirited crowd they seemed. Average age appeared to be about 19. Lots of blond Aryans amongst them!

The description above is much more matter of fact than the actual bombing experience. There was something very ominous about the systematic way in which the German planes took up position for the bombing run—their firepower seemed (and was) much more impressive than ours at that point. They came in very low, low enough for us to see the markings on the their fuselages. My own task in this action was to direct the gunners from one target to the next, depending on the most immediate danger that they presented. I don't know why the Germans missed us, but perhaps our combined flak looked worse coming at them than it did to us because we saw it directed at so many targets. When we were approaching Portland harbor, now quite safe from attack, the gunners began to pick up the scores of empty brass shell cases lying around the 20-mm guns—the brass to be recycled by the Admiralty arsenals. Only then did I really begin to realize what a near miss the attack had been and actually to feel my knees go weak. During the action itself, somehow, the concentration that was required damped down the conscious feeling of fear.

From 19 to 22 June, we remained in Portland—refueling, replenishing stores, and taking a break. The diary resumes:

June 22, Thursday—June 26, Monday

Diary: We left at 0345 on the morning of June 22nd in company with *ML143*, HM ships *Londonderry* and *Clarkia* with a convoy of U.S. LSTs. The trip was uneventful and we arrived at the Kansas Light Vessel (6 miles N N E of Isigny) at 1700. Two and a half hours later we set course for Portland. At midnight we were proceeding in line ahead, *ML137* in the rear, when three Junkers 88 aircraft came in out of a cloud and flying at masthead height commenced to attack. Vicious AA fire from all four ships upset them, and the nearest bomb was fifty yards away. Our Oerlikon guns ripped into the belly of the rear plane and it is supposed that damage was caused. The aircraft then turned tail and disappeared into the clouds. The trip from then on was uneventful and we secured in the pens at Portland at 0530 on the morning of Friday, June 23rd.

Another two days in harbour—a trip to the cinema at Weymouth to see *Wuthering Heights*, and orders to sail on Sunday, June 25th with *ML454*, HM ships *Rochester* and *Petunia*. Waited at Portland breakwater until 2300 during which time USS *Texas* and *Arkansas* joined the convoy. On the morning of Monday, June 26th at a position 15 miles S S E of the I.o.W. we left the convoy and set course for the Kansas Light Vessel, speed 15 knots, arriving at 1000. We were then routed to the USS *Augusta*, thence to the USS *Raven* (minesweeper). Here we were told that we were needed for the minesweeping of Cherbourg harbour. For this purpose a large fleet of minesweepers—about 60 in number—mainly British, was anchored two miles east of the Isles of St. Marcouf.

Agnes Power Maher in
the uniform of Civil
Defense ambulance
driver, Manchester,
England, 1944.
(Navana Studios, Ltd.,
Manchester)

Midshipman Brendan
Maher, RNVR,
December 1943.
(Navana Studios, Ltd.,
Manchester)

Ordinary Seaman
Brendan Maher, RN,
May 1943. (Navana
Studios, Ltd.,
Manchester)

Below left: John
Desmond Maher,
leading supply assis-
tant in the Royal
Navy, 1942. *Below
right:* Ciaran Patrick
("Kerry") Maher.
(Navana Studios, Ltd.,
Manchester)

HMS King Alfred, Brighton, Sussex, December 1943. The author is at the extreme right in the second row. (Royal Navy photo)

HMS *Jason*, First Minesweeping Flotilla. Commanding officer, Comdr. T. G. P. Crick, RN. (Royal Navy photo)

Ship of Fifth Motor Launch Flotilla, viewed from fo'c'sle.

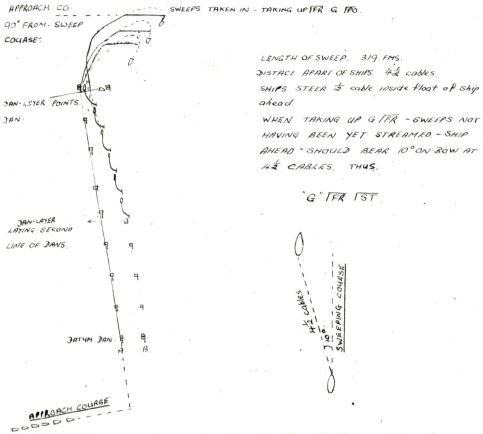

METHOD OF SWEEPING IN "G" FORMATION.

APPROACH CO.
90° FROM. SWEEP
COURSE.

SWEEPS TAKEN IN - TAKING UP √FR G √PO.

DAN-LAYER POINTS.
DAN.

DAN-LAYER
LAYING SECOND
LINE OF DANS.

DATUM DAN

APPROACH COURSE

LENGTH OF SWEEP. 319. FMS.
DISTACE APART OF SHIPS. 4½ cables.
SHIPS STEER ⅝ cable inside float of ship
ahead.
WHEN TAKING UP G √FR - SWEEPS NOT
HAVING BEEN YET STREAMED. - SHIP
AHEAD " SHOULD BEAR 10° ON BOW AT
4½ CABLES. THUS.

"G" √FR √ST.

4½ cables
10°
SWEEPING COURSE

Technical notes on minesweeping formation, from Midshipman's Journal.

EVE OF THE ATTACK ON EUROPE

flying the following signal. "GOOD LUCK
DRIVE ON". The hour was approaching.
From here I give an extract from the ship's
Log.

EXTRACT.

1300 Slipped with 1st M.S.F. Trawler, M.S.1. &
      "Scorpion"

1328 Spithead Boom. Took Station ahead Harrier
      Co. S.40°E. Speed 4 knots.

1345 "B" Buoy. A/C S.60°E.

1404 "C" Buoy. A/C S.35°E.

1415 "D" Buoy. A/C S.5°E.

1429 "E" Buoy. A/C S.20°W.

1440 "X" Buoy

1455 "F" Buoy. A/C S.60°E

1600 "E.A.J. Buoy" Took Station on Harrier's Port Beam
      Speed 5 knots.

1735 A/C S.25°E. Speed 8 knots.

1940 Passed lettered position P.B.

"D - DAY"

1952. Out Port Sweep.

1957. A/C S.5°W.

2039. Sweep Foul - Cut Sweep

2040. Speed 14 knots

2043. Speed 10 knots

2103. Stopped Engines

2115. Took Station Ahead of Harrier. Speed. 10 knots.

2150. Emergency Port Sweep Streamed. Co. S.
      Speed 7 knots

2235. Stopped.

2340. Heavy Flak Bearing S.85°W. Cherbourg
      Peninsula.

6th June 1944

0026. In Sweeps. M.S.1 turned 180° back up
      swept channel to stream Stbd. sweep.

0028. Heavy air-raid on Ouistreham bearing due S.

0100 Sweeps in. A/C N. Speed 14 knots

0125. Arrived datum dan pointed by "Colsay".
      A/C. S.

SWEEPING THE CHANNELS TO BEACHES

0134. Stopped. Out Sweeps - Starboard. M.S.1. astern.

0155. Speed 7 knots. Co. Due. S.

0211. M.S. 15 sighted to port.

0230. Speed 5 knots

0243. Channels 9 & 10 converged

0325. Reached lowering Position

0345. A/C due. W. N.u. 14. fell out of formation
      Flares over Cherbourg. Ouistreham still under
      bombing.

0430. In Sweeps. Shells from coastal guns
      dropping near. Cut Sweep. Full Ahead.

0532. A/C. E. Action Stations. Speed 16.

0541. Speed. 6. Heavy bombardment of beaches by
      H.M. Ships. "Warspite", "Scylla", "Orion", "Argonaut"
      "Belfast" and others.

0600. Large vessel on STBD Beam sinking. Bows &
      stern only visible. Action Stations secure.

0630. Took Station astern Harrier

0700. Stopped near lowering Position. Landing

H-HOUR

craft commenced assault.

0725. H-Hour. Assault force on beaches.

Here I will break off and describe more fully
the period covered by the rather laconic
entries in the log.

The scene when passing Spithead Gate was
absolutely incredible. Ahead of us the
modern destroyer Scorpion 219 zig-zagged to
reduce his speed, while we slowly overhauled
the great series of Landing Ships & Craft.
As far as the eye could see were row after
row of L.C.T's and towering above them the
impressive bulk of the "Empire" ships
(E. Broadsword, E. Halberd, E. Balltrace etc)
with L.C.A's slung at their davits and troops
massing their upperdecks.
The L.C.T's (Landing Craft Tank) - ungainly
and slow moving vessels were packed to

D-Day deck log, 5–6 June 1944, from diary kept by author.

Aerial view of Cherbourg, France, 21 June 1944. (National Archives, Washington, D.C.)

German mine detonated in waters off Cherbourg, 2 July 1944. (National Archives, Washington, D.C.)

German explosive mine obstructor swept by *ML137*, Brest harbor, December 1944. Shown with the device are Sub-Lt. P. I. McDowell, RNVR *(front row)*, A/B Monksfield *(second row, extreme right)*, A/B Varney *(top row, left)*, A/B McLaughlin *(top row, center)*, and other crew members.

ML189 coming alongside *ML137* during minesweeping operations in Cherbourg harbor, July 1944.

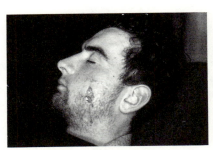

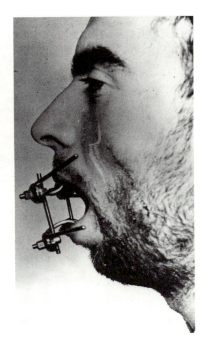

Above: Photograph of author, with wound received while minesweeping in Holland, June 1945. *Right:* Author with device to keep his fractured jaw in place, June–August 1945. (Courtesy of RAF surgeon, Wroughton Hospital, Wiltshire)

Kitchener Barracks soccer team, HMS Pembroke, Chatham, Kent, 1947.
Author is third from right, back row.

Identity photograph of
author after his promo-
tion to lieutenant, 1947.

8

Clearing the Ports

Never trust her at any time,
When the calm sea shows her false alluring smile.
—LUCRETIUS

With the invasion beachhead secured, it was imperative that permanent ports be obtained to permit the off-loading of the enormous numbers of troops and quantities of material that were required to supply the continuing assault on the enemy. Of the two Mulberry artificial harbors that had been towed across the Channel and settled in the shallow water off the edge of the beaches, one had been destroyed by severe weather a few days after D-Day. The other was vulnerable to the same fate and, in any case, could not handle the job. The nearest suitable port was Cherbourg, still occupied by strong enemy forces, and it was crucial that this be taken as soon as possible. Other, smaller harbors also might be of some service, and these had to be surveyed for usability.

Cherbourg

The assault on Cherbourg consisted of two components. By far, the most important was the main attack by ground forces advancing northward up the Cotentin Peninsula. This attack was developed and carried out by the U.S. Army VII Corps under the command of Lt. Gen. J. Lawton Collins. When the VII Corps had pushed the German defenders back into Cherbourg itself, there came a point at which assistance was needed from Allied naval forces. The big guns of the battleships could bombard the German defenders from the north, while the army pushed on in from the south. In effect, the defenders, under fire from both directions, would be caught in a nutcracker.

From approximately 18 through 29 June, Allied naval forces engaged the German defenders in various ways. The first major requirement was that naval forces assist in the reduction of the German forces defending Cherbourg against the land attacks of the VII Corps. In order to get within range of the German defenders, it was necessary for a task force of battleships and cruisers to approach as closely as possible to the northern edge of Cherbourg harbor. Two obstacles stood in the way: the mine field blocking the approach from the sea and the array of gun batteries and forts defending the port from the land. Many of the batteries were installed on the outer breakwater or on the points of land that controlled the approaches to the breakwater. As minesweepers could not effectively clear the mine field all the way up to the breakwater while under fire from the shore batteries, the battleships had the task of eliminating the shore batteries first.

On the breakwater and in the nearby forts, the large concrete casemates and bunkers were equipped with heavy guns capable of firing twenty nautical miles. The Allied naval forces possessed guns of larger caliber, but these guns had a range of only sixteen miles. In order to come close enough to engage the German defenses, the ships would have to endure enemy fire for at least four miles before being in a position to respond. A dilemma existed in the fact that this exposed area would have to be cleared of mines, without the benefit of covering fire from the Allied forces, before the heavy warships could approach close enough to engage the enemy. The minesweepers would be at risk for some considerable time before they could expect supporting fire from the naval task force.

This operation was to begin on Sunday, 25 June, shortly after midday. The Allied task force, under the command of Rear Admiral Kirk, USN, consisted of the U.S. battleships *Arkansas*, *Nevada*, and *Texas*; the U.S. cruisers *Quincy* and *Tuscaloosa*; the British cruisers *Glasgow* and *Enterprise*; and eleven destroyers, including the U.S. destroyers *O'Brien*, *Barton*, and *Laffey*. This force was divided into two units. Group 1 included the *Nevada*, *Tuscaloosa*, *Quincy*, *Glasgow*, and *Enterprise*. Group 2 included the *Texas* and *Arkansas*. It was not clear that the German guns would open fire on the Allied vessels, as the German commander in Cherbourg was already sending signals to his high command that he could no longer hold out. Surrender was imminent and with it, presumably, evacuation of the German gun batteries. The minesweepers' instructions were to proceed with the sweeping of the harbor approaches until they came under fire, at which time they would follow specific orders as received from Admiral Kirk.

German gunfire was heavy. At 1500, it was decided to break off the bombardment. This engagement is described by observers:

> The naval force intended to avoid engaging the shore batteries as long as possible in order to close the shore and provide the support requested by the troops. The Germans waited until the vessels came well within range and then opened fire. The destroyers laid smoke screens, but enemy fire became more intense and the minesweepers which accompanied the Allied force were obliged to withdraw.
>
> Having approached shortly before noon, the force found the German fire so heavy and accurate by 12:30 that they were directed to maneuver independently, while the large ships fired at targets inland designated by Shore Fire Control Parties and spotting planes and the destroyers tried to silence the shore batteries. However, this latter mission could not be carried out completely and the force was under fire until it withdrew shortly before 3 P.M. The Army reported that of twenty-one firings requested on inland targets, nineteen were successful. Of the seven battleships and cruisers engaged, six were damaged in some degree, the destroyer *O'Brien* was seriously damaged and the *Barton* and *Laffey* were slightly damaged.[1]

War correspondent Holman describes the scene on 25 June as follows:

> The situation around Cherbourg had been developing rapidly, and we knew that the Americans had entered the outskirts of the town and that the Germans only held the thinnest of strips along the top of the peninsula. . . . When we sailed at dawn on the 25th the impression was that the bombardment was not all-important. The big ships were going to cover the little minesweepers, whose task it was to clear a channel to within a few miles of the French port. They would be well within range of the big coastal batteries still in German hands.
>
> The sun rose into a cloudless sky as the *Tuscaloosa* led the combined British and American squadron across the Channel. The big guns of our

---

1. Roger Kafka and Roy L. Pepperburg, *Warships of the World—Victory Edition*, Centreville, Md.: Cornell Maritime Press, 1946, 42–43.

force were in the U.S. battleship *Nevada*. The other ships with Rear-Admiral [Donald P.] Moon were the *Quincy*, a lovely new cruiser with fine lines and sharp bows as beautifully proportioned as those of a yacht, the *Glasgow*, not quite so elegant, but extremely workmanlike and looking particularly powerful from the bridge forward, and the *Enterprise*, prepared to show that a good "old 'un" could keep company with the best of the youngsters.

Two other powerful U.S. ships, the *Texas* and *Arkansas*, had been detached and formed a strong supporting unit under Rear-Admiral [C.H.F.] Bryant [USN]. The big ships were swept across the Channel by the Fleet sweepers and other vessels who were to do their main work under the noses of the enemy shore batteries. Out in front were the two smallest vessels of all—two motor launches, making a double sweep to offer protection to the first of the Fleet sweepers. They, too, had work to do on the other side. They would lay the smoke screens between the land and the Allied ships if it became necessary to give them cover.

The channel that we followed was marked at regular intervals with buoys, which meant that some other hand-maidens of the Fleet, the Dan buoylayers, were in attendance. . . .

When we were still fifteen miles from the French coast a curious thing happened. The horizon ahead of us lost its sharpness as though a mist had risen. At first it was taken for mist caused by the heat and coming from the land. In a short time, however, there came a strong smell of burning and it was realised that the smudged horizon was due to a great belt of thin smoke blowing out to sea from the terrific fires raging along the battle front around Cherbourg. The smoke was thick enough to hide the coast at a distance and there was no point in straining one's eyes. It was to our ears that the first real indication came that we were rapidly closing the land. A low thunder which could be heard above the noises of the ship and the slight swish of the water, and which was added to occasionally by larger and more distinct "thumps," gradually became evident. It was the noise of battle on the mainland and the "thumps" were heavy bombs going down from our aircraft on to the German-held fortifications. . . .

None of these evolutions disturbed the sweepers in the slightest. They, too, had turned but they kept on sweeping at the same steady speed, and continued to do so all through the exciting hours that followed. . . .

An officer found time to point out to me our position on a large scale chart. "We are well within range of the 11 in. guns in the shore batteries," he said. "We shall be turning presently to go in on the last leg," he added. "When we are about five to six miles off Cherbourg we shall turn and run on a parallel course again, while the minesweepers finish their task. If the Germans do not open fire on the minesweepers, or us, I doubt if there will be any battle, because our first aim is to cover the sweepers while they finish their job."

A fair impression of what was to take place had been given to the ship's company earlier in the morning, when Captain [H.] Grant [RCN] made a short and to-the-point broadcast over the loud-speaker system. It had given considerable satisfaction because the sailors felt that they were going to be [of] direct assistance to the American soldiers fighting so well ashore.

While I was still on the bridge, an officer said, "The minesweepers have turned on to the new course for the run in towards Cherbourg," and, with a thrill, I realised that the moment had come when a direct challenge would be delivered by the Anglo-American naval force to the Germans in the Cherbourg fortresses.

The sweepers—at least one little trawler was amongst them—went in under the enemy guns with a nonchalant air of "do not bother us, we have some work to do." The even smaller MLs went with them, still dutifully sweeping for the sweepers, and the big ships followed after.

No sight could have been more stirring. From the *J.65*, the *J.27*, the *J.00*, the *T.350* and many other little vessels, there fluttered battle en-signs almost as big as those flown from the cruisers. No ships, I felt, were more entitled to them. And in company with the White Ensign there went the Stars and Stripes. The two flags which symbolise the freedom of the seas were to wave together in battle. . . .

The signal came after the little ships had turned on to their final sweeping area, less than five miles from the outer breakwater of Cher-bourg harbour. It came from a German battery which opened fire on the minesweepers. At once the big ships replied. One of the first salvoes roared out of the *Enterprise*'s forward turret, the flame from the guns sending a gust of warm air back over the signal-bridge. Fore and aft, great bursts of flame from the *Glasgow* and the American cruisers were followed by the thunder of the guns. Thus challenged, the Germans promptly transferred their fire to the fighting ships. Their first shells, splashing in the water, made it clear that they had a very good idea of the range. The 14-inch guns of the *Nevada* sent huge projectiles screaming back towards the shore. More shells from the enemy burst around the bombarding vessels and the MLs raced in to lay a smoke screen between the ships and the shore. Shells from both sides went high over them as they did so. Also between the ships and the shore were some of the minesweepers, still imperturbably going about their business.[2]

The battleships and cruisers returned to Portland and prepared to resume the attack the next day. At this point, we were ordered to take part in the minesweeping element of the second attack. Departing from Portland at about midnight on 25 June, we crossed the Channel in convoy with the battleships *Texas* and *Arkansas* as they returned to renew the attack on Cherbourg. Because it was pointless to send minesweepers into action until the defenses had been eliminated, we were to wait in readiness to proceed to Cherbourg when that had been achieved.

The reduction of the German defenses took longer than had been expected. We took part in one of the unsuccessful attempts on 29 June, described in the diary entry below. Dwindling fuel had compelled us to leave the convoy to refuel at a tanker close to the Normandy beachhead. This took us some miles distant from the fleet minesweepers, which had already proceeded to the breakwater area. With fueling completed, we made maximum speed to catch up with our flotilla, which was already preparing to sweep. The coastline of the Cherbourg peninsula lay on the horizon, and the dull thuds of falling bombs and heavy guns could be heard from far away. A pall of dark gray smoke hung over the horizon in the direction of the harbor. Some minesweepers were already leaving the area before the breakwater, but we proceeded as ordered. When we reached the breakwater area, it was evident that the German guns had not been silenced and that the task force of battleships and cruisers was under heavy fire. The order "Make smoke" had already been given, and the destroyers were doing that. MLs made smoke artificially from an apparatus on the stern, known as the CSA gear (from whatever chemical was used to create the white smoke that issued from it when a valve was opened). We turned on our valve and added our share to the white fog that was being laid between the heavy ships and the shore batteries.

Shortly afterward, the order came through to cease making smoke, abandon the operation, and return to anchorage. One of our flotilla, however, known to be somewhat careless about maintenance, was having difficulty in opening the valve on her CSA gear. From the near distance, we could see two men banging away with a wrench and hammer as they tried to loosen the obviously rusted valve. Just as the order arrived to cease making smoke, their valve came unstuck and white smoke poured

2. Holman, *Stand By to Beach*, 180–86.

out from it. Meantime, the other ships had ceased making smoke and were beginning to withdraw. As the wind blew the smoke screen away, the bombarding warships once again came under heavy fire, until, providentially, the smoke from our tardy fellow ML rolled in to cover the gap again and continued for some time—the same two men with wrench and hammer were finding it equally difficult to close the valve. Some time later, the commanding officer of the ML received a medal for his "alert recognition of the continuing danger of enemy gunfire and prompt action in 'resuming' smoke-laying to protect the targets." This was one of the rare occasions when poor maintenance was handsomely rewarded.

The Germans had held their fire until the ships were well within range, and their accuracy compelled the task force to take avoiding action. One step was the order to make smoke. The German fire was sufficiently heavy, however, that we minesweepers were ordered to withdraw immediately and the heavier warships ordered to operate independently in firing at the inshore targets in support of General Collins's troops.

The German garrison surrendered on 26 June, but some die-hard groups held out in the forts and snipers remained active in the city for some time after the surrender.

June 27, Tuesday

Diary: We proceeded eastwards keeping inshore calling at Vierville and Arromanches-les-Bains, and finally at a position N E of Bernieres where we fueled to capacity from RFA *Chant 67*.[3] Landing operations were in full swing with a steady stream of DUKWs[4] piloted by Negro soldiers plying between ship and shore. Desultory shelling of our ship off St. Aubin's from long range enemy guns continued.

June 28, Wednesday

Diary: Today was uneventful except for a trip to the USS *Augusta* where I went on board for a quarter of an hour. When I descended to the ML again I was amazed to find Admiral Kirk USN in matey conversation with Hutchins (our C.O.). The Admiral gave a friendly wave of the hand as we departed.

---

3. A channel tanker; the Royal Fleet Auxiliary Chants were usually oilers, although one or two were freshwater tankers.

4. Amphibious vehicles, equipped with wheels and propellers, that were used in shallow water and on land. They were universally known as "Ducks." The origin of the name is a U.S. Army code: D for the year of design (1942); U, amphibious vehicle; K, all-wheel drive; and W, dual rear axles.

During the course of the various movements and maneuverings that were involved in all of this, *ML137* was required to carry dispatches to Admiral Kirk in his flagship, the USS *Augusta*. Once, when we were alongside the *Augusta*, I went on board to deliver a sealed envelope to the signals officer. Coming out of that office to get back on board, I saw that Admiral Kirk was leaning over the wing of a lower level of the bridge and inspecting *ML137* with some interest. He called down to Hutchins to ask about our speed, armament, and previous service. He turned to me and asked why I had come on board the *Augusta*. What impressed me was his lack of formality, beginning with his addressing me as "son"—something that no RN flag officer would ever do. It was by his insignia that I knew his rank, and I learned his name only when I asked a crew member of the *Augusta*. He was a likable and genial man, it seemed to me. At his side was a rating carrying a microphone attached to a very long line. I learned that he was the "talker," who relayed orders and information throughout the loudspeaker system of the ship and stayed close to the admiral for that purpose. The scene on the *Augusta* was one of organized chaos—people scurrying here and there and a constant sequence of orders over the loudspeaker, always beginning with "Now hear this. Now hear this." (British usage was to begin with "Do you hear there? Do you hear there?"—a question format that didn't permit an answer, however!)

Cherbourg itself was in U.S. hands by 27 June, and most of the garrison had surrendered. We could not begin minesweeping until the few German diehards, fighting from the gun batteries on the breakwater, had been destroyed. The diary tells the story:

June 29, Thursday

Diary: 1300 we slipped and leading three other MLs set course for Cherbourg. At 1430 we rounded Cape Barfleur and to our amazement saw the flotillas of Fleet minesweepers in retreat with two U.S. destroyers laying heavy smoke screens. A big cloud of oily smoke was pouring from the upper deck of HMS *Blackpool*. Two Aldis lamps worked rapidly and with bitter disappointment we read "Operation abandoned. Return to anchorage." Returning to anchorage we lay alongside HMS *Blackpool*. A shell from the German coastal batteries had pierced her side just forrard [forward] of the bridge and landed in the Gunner's Store. One man was injured but otherwise there were no casualties. A certain amount of bitterness evident amongst the British at the failure of the two American destroyers to even return the fire of the German guns. Cherbourg will have to wait.

A late night in the Wardroom of *Blackpool* drinking sherry and playing cards. Crept on to my wheelhouse bunk feeling rather groggy.

Given the discrepancy between the caliber and range of the German artillery and that of a destroyer's guns, the Americans, of course, were quite right to put the protection of the minesweepers ahead of what would have been a futile response to the shelling.

During some part of the evening in the *Blackpool*'s wardroom, discussion turned to the possibility of claiming reimbursement for various personal items that had been stored in the gunner's store, where the shell had struck. Some personal luggage, items of uniform, and the like had been placed there; this was not uncommon in warships at that time, as the allocation of personal space was based upon the relatively small peacetime size of the ship's company. In wartime, ship's people ate, slept, and stored possessions wherever a niche might be found. On a later encounter with the *Blackpool*, we learned that the Admiralty had disallowed all personal claims on the grounds that they had been improperly stored.

The delay in initiating the clearance of Cherbourg harbor led to renewed interest in the possibility of using some of the smaller harbors on the same coastline. To this end, we were ordered to survey the little fishing harbor of Saint-Vaast-la-Hougue, an indentation on the northeast corner of the Cotentin peninsula, not far from the Ile de Saint-Marcouf.

June 30, Friday

Diary: On the afternoon of June 30th we slipped from the *Blackpool* and proceeded to the USS *Chimo* to pick up Lieutenant-Commander Gresham, RNVR and set course for St. Vaast. When about half a mile from the breakwater Lt.Cmdr. Gresham and a signalman boarded a small U.S. landing craft and, taking our signalman, Signalman A. T. Batten, with them, cautiously proceeded to the entrance, signaling the depth to us continuously. A few minutes later they signaled "Enter," and at slow speed, the first British ship entered St. Vaast. The entire population had by now gathered on the jetty and were talking to each other excitedly. We went onto the jetty, whilst the Captain and Lt.Cmdr. Gresham went into the town to see what the conditions were.

When I climbed up on to the jetty a man detached himself from the crowd—whose excitement was intense at the gifts of cigarettes and chocolate which the crew were giving out—and addressed himself to me, with the remark that his daughter could speak English. His daughter—Ginette—lovely dark-haired girl of about twenty years then appeared and we commenced a tête-a-tête in a mixture of my French and her English. Shortly afterwards the Captain returned and told me to take one watch (one half of the crew) ashore. We walked across the village square to an Estaminet, where we drank cognac (really Calvados) with some local fishermen. All too soon our stay came to an end, and amidst the "Au revoirs" of the populace we left the harbour.

One or two points which struck me about the place & people. Firstly, they did not appear to be ill-clad, but rather similar to people of similar station in England. Secondly, there did not appear to be a great deal of amity between the U.S. forces and the French. Thirdly, the British Navy carries a great deal of prestige with the French. Almost as much as the RAF. Fourthly, although there was quite a deal of work to do in cleaning the harbour, no assistance was being given by the locals to the U.S. forces engaged on it, although there were many vigorous fishermen watching.

That it was not really the "entire" population is evident from the fact that there were many more people at the jetty when we returned the next day. An old pocket address book that I have from that time notes Ginette as "Mlle. Ginette Bordier, Villa Madeleine, St. Vaast-la-Hougue, Departement de la Manche."

The point of this approach to the harbor had been to see if it was suitable for landing troops and heavy vehicles so that the resistance of the Germans at Cherbourg harbor would not cause further delay. The harbor of Saint-Vaast was not very suitable, as the rise and fall of the tide meant that for some part of the day there was very little water at the jetty. I do not know whether it was ever used much for unloading. I doubt it, as the fall of the Cherbourg forts took place soon afterward and there was no real need for any other harbor then. Other than our second visit on the following day, we never returned to Saint-Vaast. Our first visit there was one of those occasions photographed so often during the liberation of France. People put chains of flowers around the necks of the crew members, some brought out wine, and there was a happy, festive air to the whole thing.

One surprise to me, however, was the occasional person who came along to point out somebody else as a "collaborateur." This happened often enough to leave the impression that there had been some division of loyalties in the village and that the liberation was going to bring a settlement of accounts. I suppose that I was surprised because I had always assumed that hatred of the Germans was universal among the

French, as that was the way it always appeared in war movies. I had no conception of what living under German occupation was actually like.

I was also surprised by the extent to which the local people stood aside from the actual work of the invasion. American forces were trying to clear wreckage from the harbor, a task that would eventually make it usable by the fishermen again, but the local fishermen showed no interest in lending a hand. Looking back on this, it is more striking in contrast to our experience, months later, when we were minesweeping the harbor of Brest. The Bretons we met then were quite different in attitude, and the local Maquis actively hunted down the occasional last-ditch German snipers who harassed us spasmodically as we swept the area.

Further recollections of these events were written much later, on 14 April 1945, and dated with the aid of the ship's log:

> Diary: Many months have now elapsed since the last entry in the diary, but as at the present moment there are no other means of passing the time it seems an ideal opportunity to go back and fill in the big blanks.
>
> At this minute we are secured alongside *ML293* at Parkeston Quay, Harwich. The flotilla is based here, and has been since February this year. Legally we are based at HMS Beehive (the shore base at Felixstowe) which is just across the River Stour from here. As all minesweeping forces are operated by Harwich, we berth either at Parkeston Quay or at Pin Mill on the River Orwell.
>
> The current routine is singularly depressing—defensive escort patrols and a rather deadening rota of duty at Pin Mill. However, of that, more anon. To return to the episode at St. Vaast-la-Hougue:
>
> We returned the following day (July 1) to the harbour, with *MLs 143, 140, & 257*, after sweeping an approach channel, and then anchoring until the tide permitted us to enter with safety. Mac took one watch ashore and I was left to guard the ship with the other watch. A crowd bigger even than that of the previous day had accumulated—amongst them being Ginette. We had an earnest if somewhat incoherent conversation in which I tried to explain that duty prevented me from coming ashore for the time being, but she was apparently unimpressed and departed the jetty rather frigidly.
>
> Came my turn to go ashore, and I dashed madly to the shoreward end of the jetty and bumped into "M. le Maire" complete with bicycle, black beret and overall suit. He directed me to his house—"Villa Madeleine." I hastily proceeded there and knocked rather diffidently at the front door. A blond female of rather imposing proportions suddenly appeared at the window, her hands covered with flour and clutching a

bread knife. "Etes-vous Boche ou Americain?" she demanded fiercely, I hurriedly explained that I was English and she relaxed, and opened the door leading me to the drawing-room.

Perched uncomfortably on a horse-hair chair and surrounded by china dogs, faded photographs, I explained that Ginette was practically an old friend of mine and asked where she might be found. "Maman's"[5] puzzled expression quickly vanished and she exclaimed that I must be the "so-charming" officer of the Royal Navy who had spoken to Ginette. This caused me to blush, but the intention seemed friendly. Ginette was apparently drawing rations from the Franco-American civil administration, and as my leave was on the verge of expiring I had to go with her valedictions following me down the street. I ran through the rain and a few minutes later we were steaming out of harbour and the crowd, somewhat thinned out by the rain, grew smaller and smaller, as our tiny column approached the Ile de St. Marcouf.

On Sunday, 2nd July, at 1025 we arrived outside the main breakwater of Cherbourg harbour with MLs *143* and *257*. Recollection is of necessity hazy after the long interval which has elapsed since the days of which I now write, and only a general impression of the scene can now be given.

At 1040 we anchored, or to be precise *ML143* anchored and we secured, one ML on either side, about 3 cables north of the Fort de L'Ouest. Hands piped down, and we dozed in somnolence in the Wardroom after a midday meal of the usual indigestible nature. At Two Bells[6] in the Afternoon watch—or 1 p.m. shore time (or 1300), there was a dull roar of a curiously hollow sound which we later came to know only too well as betokening an underwater explosion. Rushing on deck we saw a Motor Minesweeper sinking rapidly by the bow. Her stern tilted rapidly and she soon disappeared beneath the oily and debris-strewn waters. Instantly we were under way and dashing at full speed to the scene. Litter and wreckage of all kinds were drifting about, whilst a boat from an accompanying *MMS* was picking up survivors hanging on mostly to floating furniture, mess-deck tables, packing cases and oars. Hundreds of packets of cigarettes sodden with diesel oil lolled slug-

5. When I visited Ginette and her husband fifty years later, Ginette assured me that her mother was not blond, so the woman that I had met must have been some other member of the household.

6. In a warship, the four-hour watch is divided into half-hour intervals, each interval indicated by the striking of the ship's bell. The first half hour is marked by one stroke, the second half hour by two strokes, and so on, up to eight strokes of the bell at the end of the four-hour watch.

gishly about us, while uniform suits, private papers, photographs strewed the whole area. In the middle was one final survivor, his face and hair blackened with oil, screaming "Help! Help for God's sake!" in a blood-chilling, hysterical tone. The boat picked him up and transferred him to an MMS. A few minutes later their Aldis lamp began to flash a signal to us—"This man is dying. Can you take him to that destroyer?" Seconds later saw us roaring Full Ahead to a U.S. destroyer some three or so miles away, the badly injured man on a stretcher on our upper deck. We transferred him to the destroyer and cursed Jerry in simple sympathy for the wounded man.

2.25 P.M. saw us back alongside *ML143* and continuing our disturbed sleep. Supper over I was standing at the top of the Wardroom companion-way watching mines detonating astern of a U.S. Minesweeper when suddenly she began to heel over. "SOS" flickered from her signal lantern. A hurried shout, a roar of engines, and we and *ML257* were racing to the doomed vessel. Slowly and gracefully she listed over to port and began to settle stern first. We hove to about twenty yards away and lowered scrambling nets, flinging life-belts over the side. The officers jumped leisurely over the side, having first disposed of their confidential papers in weighted bags, and as the bow rose more steeply two ratings appeared from the focs'le hatch and shouting in dismay, leaped into the water.

In the meantime, as the bows and the name YMS 350[7] disappeared from view for ever, the first survivors were already climbing the scrambling net and being helped below. The now familiar smell of diesel oil hung heavily in the air as I went over to the starboard scrambling net to see how the rescue was progressing. Down at the water level was one of the last two men to jump, being gallantly supported by Ordinary Seaman Vincent Ring.

I went down the scrambling net that hung over our side to assist several of the swimming and injured crew members to get to the net to climb on board. Some could not climb, and so I went into the water—as did several of *ML137*'s crew—with ropes to tie around the waists and shoulders of the survivors so that they could be pulled on board. I was wearing my uniform cap, a white shirt, and a pair of gray slacks and sea boots. The water was covered with thick diesel oil from the sinking minesweeper and this got onto everything. Ships when hit by mine or torpedo rarely (if ever) sank at a level angle. The sea poured into the

7. The YMS 350 is officially recorded as having struck a mine and sunk off Cherbourg on 2 July 1944.

hole caused by the explosion and the weight of water tipped the vessel downwards at that point. Hence, a sinking ship usually went down with one end or other sticking up high out of the water before sliding completely down to the depths. As one end of the hull rose out of the water the machinery and boilers in the engine-room would break from their mountings and crash through the interior bulkheads one by one. This was accompanied by the loud, repeated roaring noise of grinding, clanging metal against metal, the sound re-echoing through the chambers of the still visible part of the hull. It was clearly audible at a distance of up to a mile or more. The effect was melancholy.

Ring was patently close to exhaustion as he was bearing the combined weight of himself and the American seaman with one arm, by clinging to the scrambling net. Being fresh and untired, I relieved him on the net, and he clambered inboard to safety. Turning my attention to the unfortunate American, I found that he was in very great pain, and convinced that his end had come. Shouting, to make myself heard above his agonised screams of "Jesus, I'm dying!" and "For God's sake hurry!" I called for a rope which passed around his waist and knotted in a bowline secured him safely. He was hoisted and dragged inboard, and I to my horror, realised my fatigue and perforce let go of the net. A quick immersion in the oily scummy water and I surfaced, to realize, almost surprised, that a cork life-jacket does work. The pleasure of this surprise was tinged with dismay when I saw my one and only decent cap floating away on the oil. The Executive officer of the sunken vessel—still swimming towards the ML, and cheerfully, almost politely, declining any offers of assistance, calmly salvaged the cap, and flung it inboard. Back on the net I was dragged in by Able Seaman R. Varney (of Plymouth) and A. B. A. McLachlan (of Loch Gilphead), sodden with foul and choking Diesel oil. Quickly stripping, washing and changing, I made my way on deck, where the survivors were being dosed with Navy rum and swathed in blankets.

We were headed for an American sweeper and we soon had the victims transferred to their countrymen's care. On orders from a British fleet sweeper, we returned to the debris and made a check search.

Just when we were concluding that all survivors had been accounted for, Varney shouted and pointed towards what was apparently a floating life-jacket. In it was a body. [The diary ends here.]

The body was a sailor from the YMS 350, floating face down in the oily water—head, arms, and legs dangling below the surface, his back and shoulders above water supported by his life jacket. He was surrounded by floating debris. We pulled alongside. One of the crew hooked a boat hook into the straps of the life jacket, and another went down the scrambling net to attach a line to him. That done, two more went down the net and between them managed to get the body on board. There was no sign of breathing; beneath the trickling oil, his face was dirty white. We immediately set course for the distant U.S. destroyer, which would presumably record the man's identity and perform whatever sea burial was to be done.

While we were moving out of the debris—still looking out for any stray mines that might be around—Hutchins decided that we should try artificial respiration. The man was stretched out, spread-eagled, face down, and one of the crew began to press hard repeatedly on his back just behind the lungs. For a short time, nothing happened, but then trickles of black oil began to seep out of his mouth and nose. Crew members relieved each other, and still the oil came. Suddenly, the body gave a shudder, a little more oil came out, and then there was one large intake of breath. The pressing on his back was redoubled, and we cracked on speed to the destroyer. By the time we came alongside, there were more intermittent breaths coming from the rescued man. He was passed over to the destroyer and taken immediately to sick bay.

A couple of days later, we happened to encounter the same destroyer at sea and asked what had happened to the man. He was recovering, and the doctor judged that he was going to be all right.

The first dead bodies that I had seen close up were those of the sailors killed by the explosion of the mine that had sunk their motor minesweeper on 2 July. Two of the dead sailors were floating partly submerged in the oil that covered the water. At first, entangled in the debris, they looked like bundles of rags. Slack and shapeless, they rose and fell with the swell of the sea beneath them. One rolled over slowly; now lying on his back, his face chalk-white and oil-streaked and his eyes glistening dully, he seemed to stare up at the blue sky and white clouds over our heads. With the next lift of the swell, he rolled back once more. The iridescent gleam of the oily scum, mixing with the reflection of the sky, hid him from view as we moved on through the wreckage and looked for survivors. What has persisted from that time was my sense of surprise and horror at the way in which a human body could be so reduced to rubbish in no more than a few moments. I still recall in detail a photograph showing a smiling woman and child, a sailor's family undoubtedly, as it sank slowly. Fingers of diesel oil gradually obliterated the features of the family until the photograph disappeared from sight under the dark spreading scum of the oil slick.

Memory also brings back the incongruous image of two men emerging from the forward hatch of YMS 350, each clutching a fan of playing cards as they scrambled up the sloping bow of their sinking ship. The commanding officer, cool and collected, was holding onto the side of his steeply listing bridge, methodically putting documents in the lead-lined bag to throw overboard.

My clothing (except the seaboots) had been largely rendered useless by diesel oil, and I discarded the shirt and socks. My cap was cleanable, but the gray slacks were resistant to such cleaning techniques as there were to be had—putting them into a bucket with thick bar of soap, scrubbing, and hoping for the best. I could be recompensed for the loss of the uniform items but not for non–uniform items, such as gray slacks. Monksfield hit upon the idea of tying them at the end of a long line to be towed behind us when we returned to England. The wash of the propellers and the general roiling of water in the wake ought to do it. That is what we did—towing the trousers from Cherbourg to Portsmouth. As we drew near Portsmouth, where unauthorized lengths of rope dragging from ships would draw some kind of rebuke, we hauled in the rope to find that the trousers had gone—sunk to the bottom of the Channel somewhere, perhaps to be preserved for the ages in diesel oil.

The minesweeping of Cherbourg was a dangerous and daunting task. Nothing could be done until the mines had been swept from the area outside the harbor. After the events of 2 July, our ship was one of the few minesweepers still afloat from the task force assigned to clearing the approach to the harbor entrance. Good men had died doing this duty, and they had died without fanfare or recognition.

Minesweeping could be tedious and unglamorous, but it was never safe. During the three-week period following 2 July, we entered Cherbourg harbor as part of a group of MLs and other minesweepers to begin the clearance of mines. Some time in July 1944, we had reported a mine in the anchorage area close to the docks and were waiting for the area to be cleared of ships so that we could sweep it. Before that happened, a Liberty ship entered the harbor and proceeded directly toward the anchorage. We began to signal a warning with the lamp, but before her signalman could even read it, her anchor was rattling into the water. The mine immediately exploded, disintegrating the bow and the few men who were doing the anchoring. The ship sank immediately. The water was sufficiently shallow that the upper works remained above water. We had our dinghy in the water and sent it out with two crewmen to look for survivors. Some already had been picked up by other small boats. Our dinghy crew reported pulling out two dead men from the water; both bodies were badly mutilated from the explosion.

Another group of MLs from the Fifth Flotilla was ordered to relieve us and continue the task of mine clearance. The urgency of the task of making the port of Cherbourg usable for the delivery of troops and supplies had been increased by the destruction of the westernmost Mulberry, as mentioned above.

In due course, we returned to Cherbourg to relieve the MLs who had taken our place. It was July, and the weather was hot. The city and docks were in various states of ruination. Supplies were being delivered by freighters that had ventured just inside the breakwater and were being off-loaded by amphibious trucks. The harbor was heavily mined, and it took us some days to clear it enough to be usable. The mines came in all of the familiar types, plus some new variations. One of the most dangerous of the latter—the existence of which we learned the hard way—was the snag line mine. The mine lay on the seabed in the shallow water of the harbor. Attached to it was a long length of thin green line, to which seaweed sometimes had been deliberately attached. Camouflaged by its color and the seaweed, the end of the line floated inconspicuously on the water. Any ship passing over the line would snag it around her propeller, pull the line, and detonate the mine. This would blow off the ship's stern and sink her. Only after several such sinkings did we discover the device.

The only way to sweep these snag lines without snagging our own propeller was to lower the dinghy, equipped with a long line and manned by one officer and one rating. The rating slowly rowed the dinghy up to each piece of floating line or seaweed. In the case of seaweed, the officer felt gently beneath it to see if there was rope attached to it. If not, he pulled out the entire piece of seaweed to avoid the necessity of checking it again. If there was rope, the officer very slowly and gently tied the end of his long line to it, tugged it very slightly taut, and peered at its submerged portion to find out which way the attached mine was lying. The rating then rowed carefully in the opposite direction from the lie of the mine, while the officer paid out his line until he reached its end, about one hundred yards from the mine. There he gave the line a swift, hard pull (usually more than one), and the mine detonated at a safe distance. This procedure was followed with every piece of floating line that they encountered. Mac and I rotated turns on this duty, as did the ratings. We got several mines, a lot of seaweed, and no casualties. It was by far the most nerve-wracking of the procedures that we used at any time. The entire harbor was checked for snag lines in that way.[8]

One of our MLs swept a contact mine with a conventional wire sweep. When the sweeping crew were winching in the wire, they saw that the mine, somehow entangled in the wire, was coming in with it. They paid out the wire again very quickly, and the ship headed out past the breakwater in an attempt to destroy the mine out there. On the way out, the mine banged against the rock foundation of the breakwater but, surprisingly, failed to explode. The mine was very rusty, and the interior mechanism probably had rusted solid long before. The ML finally towed the mine well out to sea, hauled it in closer but at a safe distance, and cut the sweeping wire with an ax. The mine and wire sank to the seabed forever.

In Cherbourg, we had an opportunity to go ashore. Around the harbor, German signs addressed their ships: "Ankeren Verboten," "Rauchen Verboten," and so forth. Entering the immediate dock area, we were surprised to see a huge billboard, on which was printed something to the following effect:

> You are entering Cherbourg courtesy of General George S. Patton.
> The following fines are in force:
> Not wearing steel helmet—five dollars. Not shaving—two dollars.

These words were followed by list of other "offenses" punishable by fines. The not-shaving regulation led to a minor incident. One of our ML captains was stopped by military police, who wished to fine him for having a beard. He refused to deal with them. Many angry telephone calls were made between higher-ups before it was understood that beards were normal in the Royal Navy and nobody was going to pay any fine for having one. The whole idea of having a billboard at all seemed to us to be rather vain—we felt that we were entering Cherbourg harbor courtesy of the efforts and losses of the two navies that had cleared the approaches to the harbor.

---

8. Rear Adm. G. S. Ritchie, RN, in his memoirs, *No Day Too Long,* Durham, England: Pentland Press, 1992, 55, comments on the snag line mines: "A new form of anti-boat mine had been laid by the enemy at Cherbourg. From a mine laid on the sea-bed, green buoyant snag lines trailed near the surface ready to foul a passing boat's propellers. This called for a sharp-eyed look-out in the bows of the sounding boats." At that time, Ritchie was in HMS *Scott,* which, with HMS *Franklin,* was charged with the task of surveying captured ports for wrecks and other obstacles. Formerly Hydrographer of the Royal Navy, Ritchie had previously served in the *Jason* when she had been a survey vessel before her conversion to minesweeping.

At first, the city was dangerous. On my first visit with some fellow officers from the other sweepers, we were advised by a U.S. military policeman to hurry when we crossed a nearby intersection; a German sniper was shooting from one of the houses. From time to time, single rifle shots or short bursts of machine-gun fire could be heard as the troops winkled out isolated German resisters here and there.

We had been issued with "Liberation" franc notes issued by the Allies for purchases in France, with the promise to the French that they would be redeemed for real francs when the war was over. We bought odds and ends of things from such shops as were open—mainly cheap perfume and soap and some faded postcards. Tattered and fading remnants of posters urging the French to volunteer to work in Germany were still on the walls of some buildings.

The dock area itself had been blown up by departing German troops. One huge warehouse with a thick concrete roof had been demolished at the foot of each wall, so that the entire roof had collapsed to the ground as a single piece. U.S. engineer battalions were already on the scene with cranes and bulldozers to get things back into working order, and the harbor became functional in a relatively short time.

German air-listening devices had been abandoned on the breakwater and at various other points. I can still remember the name on the metal labels, "Ringrechtrechtungs hörer." The device consisted of a pair of circular antennae, placed at right angles to each other in a large, shallow, saucer-shaped metal "dish" just about the size of a modern TV dish antenna. The whole thing was mounted on four wheels, with seats for two people who rotated the device with handles. Apparently, the Germans had relied on detecting the approach and direction of aircraft by the sound of their motors, which was amplified through this device. When I considered the level of Allied radar technology at that time, the German device seemed strikingly primitive.

During the first few days, while cleanup was still going on, many of the casual items of battle debris were strewn around the dock areas. Burned-out German vehicles, items of uniform, sheets of paper blowing about in the summer breeze, bits of horse harness, broken fragments of rifles, and piles of indescribable filth were all spread around in confusion, as if the place had been blown apart by a tornado. There were clouds of flies, and the odor of decay and death were pervasive.

Some of our crew managed to get onto the breakwater, and they came back to the ship with souvenirs—German helmets, insignia, and officers' caps. Able Seaman Monksfield brought on board a very large horse's gas mask. The German army made much use of horses for transport, mainly, I suppose, because they were short of gasoline. One of the crew gave me a tiny tunic badge, with the swastika and eagle, and a German bronze eagle service badge with the name of its previous owner engraved on it. I still have both items. German helmets and hats were generally stiff inside with hair oil and gave off a powerful, mixed odor of eau de cologne, sweat, and sometimes the all-pervasive battlefield smell of death and excrement. Several German gunners were said to have been found dead, with no obvious injuries, in the casemates. Apparently, they had been killed by the concussion and asphyxiation caused by the bombardment.

A description of this period of mine clearance is provided by war correspondent Holman. On the evening of 12 July, Holman was instructed to go on board HMS *Franklin*, under the command of Comdr. E. G. Irving, RN. The *Franklin* and her sister ship *Scott* were naval survey ships of the fleet minesweeper type. Holman describes events of the following day:

> Towards midday we sighted the French coast and presently picked out Cherbourg with its long protecting breakwater. . . .
>
> A group of British minesweepers, B.Y.M.S.'s, were sweeping outside the breakwater as we entered the harbour. Inside, smaller M.L.'s had their big red sweeping flags flying as they moved in pairs over these dangerous waters. . . .
>
> It was a tense moment because no ship of our size had crossed the harbour since the departure of the Germans. Constant sweeps had been carried out for several days, but it was known that the Hun had used various types of mine and the question was, "Would we set off something that had evaded the sweeps?". . .
>
> Little more than an hour after the *Franklin*'s arrival her boats were away on their first surveying task, the location of wrecks in the harbour.
>
> As the boats headed away from the ship, the B.Y.M.S., doing a magnetic sweep in the inner harbour, set off a big mine which sent a mighty cascade of water into the air just round the corner of the mole.
>
> The commanding officers of some M.L.'s which came alongside the Survey ship just afterwards, mentioned that they had been over the position of the explosion many times while doing non-magnetic sweeps.
>
> From these young R.N.V.R. officers, whose vessels had been right in the van of the Allied approach by sea to Cherbourg, I heard a thrilling story.
>
> Although they had been sweeping for ten days, whenever the state of the tide permitted, they showed few signs of the long strain imposed by

such duties, beyond a very natural physical tiredness. They laughed and joked about odd incidents during their sweeps and could even see the funny side of such mishaps as getting a mine caught up in a sweep and having to tow it out to sea.

While drinking water was pumped from the *Franklin* into the empty tanks of the M.L.'s, I sat in one of the little ward-rooms, and this is what I heard:

"We were sent to sweep the inner harbour and have been at it steadily ever since we started. There were quite a few mines, as we soon discovered. The M.L.'s between them have collected a nice 'bag' and have suffered no casualties, although there have been a few hair-raising moments."

One of these, I was told, was when a mine suddenly shot to the surface after the sweep had been pulled in close to the boat. A Petty Officer saved the situation because, as soon as he saw what was being pulled in, he grabbed a chopper and in one terrific slash severed the sweep and its lethal attachment. . . .

One flat-bottomed craft, smaller than any of the M.L.'s had met with disaster when she ran right on to a mine. Two of her crew had miraculous escapes, one swimming 150 yards with a broken arm and in a semiconscious condition as a result of concussion.

Lieut. de Lange [Douglas de Lange, RNVR, commanding officer of an ML of the Fifth Flotilla] laughed with the rest when they gave an account of how he had been called to a conference when he was in the midst of clearing an obstruction from one of his propellers. The Commanding Officer himself had gone over the side "in his birthday suit" to work on the obstruction. When the signal for the conference arrived he had to move in a hurry. He just had time to dry himself and then rushed off with a bundle of clothes under his arm, stopping at intervals to slip into a garment. . . .

Much remained for the sweepers to do, odd mines going up all through the following week while I was still in Cherbourg. The harbour has an immense area, and it was clearly beyond the power of the Germans to "cover" it with mines, as first reports had suggested. But the mixture of mines they had put down made it necessary to carry out various types of sweeps over the same area.

The German demolitions in the naval dockyard area, which I saw after my arrival, were almost beyond description. High explosives had been used in vast quantities to bring buildings tumbling down, to break up machines, to sink vessels and to smash and destroy in every direction. . . .

One end of the concrete roof of the E-boat pens had been lifted solidly and a huge twenty-feet thick slab of concrete, with an area larger than that of a tennis court, perched crazily above ruined walls. The pens themselves, which had been built like vast subterranean caverns to allow for the twenty to thirty-feet rise and fall of tide on this part of the coast, appeared to be undamaged.[9]

Channel Convoys

We were ordered back to England to recoup and resupply. We were then briefly employed on convoy escort duties for ships coming from the United States and entering the Channel to proceed to Cherbourg or other areas of the beach. We moved from Portsmouth to Portland, from Portland to Plymouth, then to Falmouth, and finally to Penzance.

While at Portland, we were ordered to join an eastbound convoy of U.S. ships headed for Cherbourg. The ships were just entering the English Channel after their Atlantic crossing. We were to rendezvous with them near Portland and lead them to a point just south of the Isle of Wight. This point, popularly known as "Piccadilly Circus," was the hub of several broad-swept channels leading to various parts of the French coast. From here, we were to lead the convoy down the Cherbourg channel to its destination.

We joined the convoy in the late afternoon. The weather was beginning to blow up, and the convoy was moving slowly. It consisted mainly of tugs and other maintenance or repair vessels. The convoy was under the command of the USS *Owl*, a large oceangoing tug. She was flying a U.S. Army Engineer flag, and her captain held army rank, although he had been a professional sailor much of his life.

In the rendezvous report made by loud-hailer from the bridge of one ship to the other, the captain of the *Owl* reported no losses on the way over and added that many of the crews of the ships in his convoy had just completed training at the Great Lakes naval training station and this was their first ocean voyage.

Everything went relatively smoothly, except the weather steadily worsened. By the time we reached the Isle of Wight, it was late in the evening, pitch dark, with heavy seas. We showed no running lights, of course, and could communicate with the *Owl*, immediately behind us, only by signal lantern. Making the turn to the southbound swept channel in the darkness and heavy weather was likely to be a little tricky with a group of

9. Holman, *Stand By to Beach*, 196–200.

slow-moving ships that had no prior experience in these waters. Nonetheless, we made the turn, the *Owl* followed, and we headed farther out into the weather. Not long afterward, the signal lantern on the *Owl* flickered. Some of her ships were losing formation, and the commanding officer felt (wisely) that it would be better to seek the shelter of Portsmouth for the night and try again to get into the channel the next day in daylight.

We reversed our course and headed north back up the channel and into the Solent. The entrance to Portsmouth Harbor was guarded by an anti-submarine net boom. We arrived at the boom vessel well after midnight, with heavy seas banging us around. The boom vessel slowly opened; the convoy entered and then dispersed around the anchorage for the night. The next day, one ship in the convoy was missing from the anchorage. It turned out that her captain had been unaware of the boom and simply crossed right over it somehow—perhaps the heavy seas had lifted the propeller out of the water at just the right moment. The captain had then proceeded up the inner harbor and brought the ship to rest at a large launching ramp built for loading tank landing craft. He and his ship were unharmed, and he joined the convoy the next day when we were able to make the crossing.

One dramatic incident occurred in the Channel, south and a little west of Portland. Proceeding eastbound, we were escorting yet another convoy; most of the convoy escorts were destroyers. Suddenly, with no warning, there was a tremendous explosion. One of the merchant ships immediately split open in the middle, the bow and stern very slowly beginning to fold up like a V. The crew of the sinking ship took to the lifeboats, and the destroyers immediately began to search for the U-boat—clearly, the ship had been struck by a torpedo, not a mine. As the hull of the ship started to slope, the machinery in the engine room broke loose and began to crash with a grinding and clanking sound through the bulkheads of the vessel. Steam poured out of the upper deck, and the hooter sounded continuously.

In the meantime, the destroyers were scurrying around like terriers. We joined them, and the sonar began to ping. One of the destroyers hoisted the contact flag, and the others formed up near her into a half circle. They moved steadily toward the coast, which was only a mile or so away, and fired depth charges as they went. The U-boat had no place to go. The depth charges were continuous, and the seabed was shoaling rapidly toward the land. We returned to the convoy and resumed our eastward passage. Later, we received the signal that the U-boat had gone aground and been taken by the army. All but a few of her crew were dead from concussion caused by the depth charges.

Sometime in late November or early December 1944, well after the incident with the USS *Owl*, we were ordered to Falmouth to join a convoy proceeding up the Irish Sea. The weather was a full gale—the worst I had ever seen. We went out anyway, of course, and made it to Land's End. Here, we were to alter course around the tip of Land's End, but the full force of the weather on our port beam made it impossible to steer the ship in that direction. After an hour of near capsizes, we radioed in and were told to return to Newlyn, a tiny fishing harbor just inside the spur of Land's End and a few miles from Penzance. We were there for a few days. It was a very quiet place, somehow remote from the war.

Brest

Shortly before Christmas 1944, along with two other MLs of the Fifth Flotilla, we were ordered to proceed to Brittany to sweep the harbor at Brest. We were then in Plymouth, having moved steadily westward from one Channel coast base to another as the spreading liberation of France changed the geography of the war. At this point, U.S. forces under Gen. George S. Patton had moved south from Cherbourg, down through Normandy, and into Brittany. They had driven the Germans out of the port of Brest—an important loss to the enemy as it eliminated a major U-boat base and thereby reduced the capacity of U-boats to refuel and resupply for attacks on Allied shipping in the Channel and Western approaches.

Our course lay from Plymouth to a point south of the Scilly Isles and thence southward to make a landfall with the lighthouse at Ushant. In order to make the landfall by daylight, we proceeded to sea in the darkness of the early morning hours, having arranged for the Start Point light to be turned on to provide a departure fix. We saw the coast of the Scillies in the dawning light and then turned south. It was a dreamlike passage, the opalescent sea rising and falling slowly in the long Atlantic swell.

A lookout called to me excitedly from the bow, "Come down here, Sir. Look at this!" Just ahead of us were porpoises, diving and playing in the bow wave. They accompanied us for some time before they disappeared.

The leg to Ushant was about one hundred nautical miles, and our cruising speed fourteen knots, making for a probable time in passage of seven hours. The entire passage was dependent on dead reckoning. We had no sextant, no radio direction finder, no radar, and no loran; our only aid to navigation was the depth sounder. During the seven-hour passage, the strong Channel tides would reverse themselves, a fact that made it necessary to compute a series of hourly triangles to determine the changes in the course-to-steer that would, in fact, maintain us on a steady course-made-good. This was a pure exercise in dead reckoning straight out of navigation classes. My calculations led to the prediction that we should see the top of the Ushant light rising above the horizon at 1200. A look out spotted the light, just visible, at 1150. The dead reckoning had been only ten minutes out in a seven-hour passage. It is difficult to convey my feeling of elation when my calculations turned out to be correct; this kind of feeling sometimes comes when the analysis of results from an experiment shows that a long-shot hypothesis has been confirmed. Failure is so likely that success is extraordinarily joyful.

We then altered course to enter Brest harbor. The harbor has a narrow mouth, with hilly promontories on either hand. From one of them, we heard the crack of a rifle shot and the whine of a bullet passing our mast about fifteen feet above the bridge. Some last-ditch German sniper apparently was hiding among the scrub vegetation on the northern shore. Lookouts trained their binoculars on the shore, and a man stood ready with the Vickers machine gun to fire at anything suspicious. We increased speed into the harbor, but our invisible enemy did not fire again.

Once inside the harbor, we anchored. On entering the anchorage, we had been struck by the pervasive sweet-rotten stench of decay blown by the wind from the direction of the inner harbor. It came from the corpses of German horses and men still lying in the dock area; the fighting had ended there only a day or two before. Very shortly after arrival, we were joined by a U.S. Navy minesweeper and a British vessel equipped with a saltwater condenser to provide fresh water. The British ship anchored in position and remained there throughout the period of the sweeping operations.

We spent Christmas in trying to sweep Brest harbor and roadstead. Officers of the Free French Navy invited us to the Naval Academy building for Midnight Mass on Christmas Eve, to be followed by a dinner. By common consent (except mine), it was agreed that, as the only person with experience of the Catholic Mass, I should sit in the very front row, so that others could follow me in the incomprehensible (to them) sequences of sitting, standing, and kneeling that occur throughout the service. What they refused to believe was that these sequences always had been incomprehensible to me, too, and to follow them I had simply watched other people or the altar boys. Nonetheless, I was stuck with it. I managed, from time to time during the Mass, to catch a glimpse of what the Free French were doing and do likewise, but there were several mix-ups. Fortunately, the ignorance of my flotilla mates also prevented them from recognizing a quick sit-stand-kneel as an admission of error; they simply regarded it as part of the normal mysteries.

After Mass, we were invited into a dining room containing long tables, with simple chairs and big platters of langoustes. We ate a lot of langoustes and drank the wine that accompanied them. It seemed like a complete banquet to us, but we were surprised to learn that this was just the first course. Many other good things followed. As we sat with the ruins of the port around us and the masts and hulls of wrecks, sticking out of the water, visible as dark silhouettes in the winter moonlight, this was a sight—and an evening—to remember.

Somehow, during our time in Brest, mail got to us once or twice. One of the items that came to me was a package from Aunt Lil (my father's sister in New York). The package contained Schrafft's fruit cake, eaten with great enthusiasm by the group of us, and also a box marked "Melba toast." We each admitted ignorance of what that might be. On opening the box, we found a large quantity of what looked like crumbs. Obviously, the package had been much banged around on its long voyage from New York City to Britain and then to France. There was a general consensus that nobody would make or send a box of crumbs and that this must be an unfamiliar type of American breakfast cereal. We poured it into bowls, added milk and sugar, and were a little dumbfounded to see it instantly dissolve into a soggy pulp. Nonetheless, we ate it, reflected on the interesting differences in food preferences from one country to another, and concluded that it would never capture the breakfast cereal market in the United Kingdom.

Royal Navy MLs were not well equipped for comfort during long periods at sea. We had no refrigerator. Fresh vegetables, milk, and other perishables were kept in ventilated lockers on the upper deck. When these had been consumed (usually within three or four days at the most), we turned to the remaining supplies, which were either canned or dried, canned beans, canned spaghetti, powdered milk, powdered egg, dried potatoes. This led us to spend considerable energy and imagination in attempting to find fresh food ashore wherever possible. During our sweep of Brest, we once managed this by exchanging gasoline for fresh-caught fish with some local fishermen. On another occasion, at the coastal market town of Douarnenez some miles away, we traded gasoline for local vegetables, fruit, and butter. Most of the time, however, we lived on canned food and dried food, the latter reconstituted with water. Powdered egg could be turned into a plausible imitation of scrambled eggs, but powdered potatoes plus water resulted in only a kind of pale grayish slime, rendered marginally edible by the addition of large quantities of salt and pepper. For the rest, we had the inevitable box rations with their dried, compressed food and the packet of five cigarettes.

Brest itself was in ruins—acres of rubble, with occasional walls or parts of buildings still standing. Incredibly, some people had stayed and survived in the chaos, and others who had fled were now beginning to return. The inner harbor had many wrecks, the upperworks showing above the water. Dominating the port area were the huge concrete U-boat pens. A large slab roof, several meters thick, covered a series of concrete interior berths, each large enough to accommodate a submarine. The roof of the pens had been bombed several times, as the craters in it showed, but none of the bombs seemed to have penetrated it.

Sweeping the large anchorage area was relatively easy. There had been no reason for the Germans to mine their own harbors, and they did not have time to do so when retreating. There were a few mines, probably laid by Allied aircraft some time before. Several days after arrival, when we were sure that the main anchorage and bay area were clear, we moved to the dock area and berthed there. As we were tying up our ships to a catamaran float secured to the dockside, a group of people came down to the dock to wave and cheer. We invited them on board, and soon the little ships were crowded with Bretons, old and young, talking and gesturing to us and to each other. They had brought fruit and wine with them, and we supplied gin and Scotch whisky from the wardroom store. One group of young people, about or own age, invited us to visit them at the family estaminet (café) that their parents owned. It was still intact enough for the owners to begin serving customers again.

On the following evening, I went with my shipmate Mac and Sub-Lieutenant MacDonald (of *ML245*, as I recall), to the estaminet to which we had been invited. More or less intact, it stood at a corner of what once had been an intersection but was now a scattered pile of bricks, wood, and broken glass. The door was open, and there were one or two customers inside. We were greeted immediately with great hospitality. Drinks were poured, and neighbors appeared. A young man with a mustache, slicked oiled hair, and a cigarette dangling vertically from one corner of his mouth brought along an accordion. As the evening wore on, he began to play and everybody sang—"La Madeleine," "Aupres de

Ma Blonde," and "Alouette." Our Breton hosts taught us "La Scarlatina,"
which went:

> Ça vaut mieux que d'attraper la scarlatina
> Ça vaut mieux que d'envaler le mort au rat
> Ça vaut mieux que les puisines dans vaseline
> Ça vaut mieux que faire le zouave au Pont d'Alma.

> *That is better than getting scarlet fever*
> *That is better than drinking rat-poison*
> *That is better than flies in the ointment*
> *That is better than sentry-duty on Alma Bridge.*

We introduced them to musical chairs ("les chaises musicales") and the
accordionist played tunes to provide the accompaniment. It was all very
noisy and cheerful, when suddenly a door opened and grandfather, clearly annoyed by the din, appeared in his night attire and robe. Our young
hosts explained who we were, and his expression changed. He turned
back through the door and reappeared a little later, dressed in the uniform tunic of a French Marine officer of the First World War and
holding a hammer. Explaining that this was his uniform from
"quatorze/dix-huit" (fourteen-eighteen), he proceeded to pry up a floor-
board. Under it, wrapped in paper now stained with damp, was a bottle
of champagne. He had hidden this when France fell, with the resolve that
it would not be drunk until France was free. Now was the time. He
poured a glass for each of the company present. We toasted the Allies and
"Vive la France." It was very moving to see him, in pajama pants and
military tunic with faded medal ribbons, holding up his glass for the
toast, his back straight as on parade.

Once, when walking through the ruins of Brest, I came to a church,
from which I heard the faint music of an organ. The walls of the church
were still standing, but part of the roof had collapsed into the nave.
Inside the church, rubble from the roof lay scattered around on the floor
and on the pews, and a thin cloud of dust hung in the air. A broken statue
lay near the door; the baptismal font was half-filled with dust; some
shards of glass crunched under foot. Rays of sunshine slanting through
the empty windows picked out the particles of dust that hovered and
turned lazily in the light.

The notes of an organ rose and fell at the other end of the church. In
the bright daylight that streamed through the open roof, I could see a
priest at the keyboard. He held his head back, his face to the open sky
above him. He moved slightly from side to side as his feet touched the

pedals and his hands slid across the keys. A thin sprinkling of the dust had settled on his shoulders. It was as if I had wandered into another time and place, perhaps into a painting, imagined but never painted. I stood listening for a while. Absorbed in his music, the priest did not seem to notice the intrusion. After some time, I stepped out into the clear winter sunshine. I did not know the music, but it seemed joyful and confident.

During this period, we received orders to survey the inner port, where most of the wrecks were, and to report the extent to which any part of it was usable and the magnitude of the wreck removal that would be required to make all of it usable. To do this meant that we would have to identify any wrecks that might not be visible above water. This, in turn, required us to move slowly over the water surface and, by using the echo-sounder, to create a profile of the bottom of the harbor. We planned to do this by making a gridlike series of passes over the area and marking each pass by a compass bearing on a point on shore. These passes then could be plotted on the chart and the location of any underwater obstacle recorded. As this whole process put the *ML137* at risk of running into a submerged wreck, we first surveyed the harbor from our dinghy. We used the traditional hand lead line to identify any obstacle less than eight feet below the water. Our ship had a draft of six feet, which meant that an eight-foot clearance would be reasonably safe. This task took us two or three days to complete.

It appeared that the destruction of the port facilities by the Germans had effectively prevented any use of them by the Allies within the near future. One historian of this campaign, Correlli Barnett, describes it as follows:

> On 19 September Brest, in the west of Brittany, surrendered after a bitterly fought siege of 40 days which cost the American 3rd Army more than 10,000 men killed and wounded. Here a culminating bombardment by massed artillery supplemented by that ubiquitous and ever-useful old warrior, HMS *Warspite*, did the trick. In the original "Overlord" planning high hopes had been entertained of Brest as a supply port, but in the event the prize went to the German demolition parties. So colossal was the problem presented by all the sunken blockships and the lavish sowing of oyster pressure mines that no attempt to clear Brest was made until 1945.[10]

An attempt *had* been made, and by us. We encountered no oyster mines at this time (which might have been luck). Experience with the

10. Barnett, *Engage the Enemy More Closely*, 846.

oyster mine was to come later. We did conclude that the number and location of the sunken blockships in the inner harbor made it impracticable to try to sweep it. When we had completed what we could of the sweeping of Brest, at the end of 1944, we were ordered to return to England for new assignments. The small sweeping force left together, but the unfortunate water ship, which had laid out two anchors because of the heavy weather in the roadstead, twisted her anchor cables and could not accompany us. We left her behind and proceeded out to sea. Huge Atlantic swells were coming in from the west. As we headed into them, the ship seemed to be climbing uphill to the top of each swell and then sliding downhill on the other side. All that we could see of the other MLs were the tops of their masts sticking out above the crests and rolling wildly from one side to another. We continued in this way until we were well clear of the Island of Ushant and the other little rocky isles that lie near it.

Once well clear of the land, we turned northeastward, which meant that the swells were now coming at us on the port quarter and rolling us like a cork until it seemed certain that the ship would never be able to roll back upright again. On the bridge, we each stood with one leg on the deck and one on the starboard side of the bridge—the angle made it impossible to remain upright otherwise. On one unusually steep roll, the starboard end of the signal yard that lay across the mast, near the top, picked up a streamer of seaweed from the crest of another wave, altogether a hair-raising experience. The seas continued like this throughout the night. It was impossible to sleep with the frame of the ship groaning and creaking and the propeller racing rapidly every time the stern lifted out of the water and then suddenly changing to a labored beat as it hit the water again. On the bridge, we could see nothing other than the white gleam of spume topping the waves. Somewhere to our starboard was the land, and the weather was pushing us slowly toward it.

By daybreak, we could see a stretch of rocky coast. The weather had scattered our little group of MLs, and the others were nowhere to be seen. Hutchins decided that we should seek the nearest port. This proved to be Saint-Malo. The entrance channel to Saint-Malo lies between rocks and small islets. A fisherman came out in his boat to see if we could use him as a pilot. We thought it wise to do so, and a deal was struck. He waived the pilot fee in return for some gasoline and cigarettes. Once in the harbor, we repaired what minor damages had been done by the weather, replenished our water, and reported our position to the Admiralty. A few hours later, we headed out again and turned north for Cherbourg. The weather was a little better, and we reached Cherbourg the next day without incident.

We refueled and replenished our water supply in Cherbourg. After a night's sleep, we prepared to cross the Channel to Portsmouth. The U.S. Naval Weather Station at Cherbourg predicted very heavy weather in the channel and warned us to delay departure. Hutchins, who could be stubborn about anything that sounded like a challenge to his seamanship, promptly decided that we must leave. So, once again, we went out into what developed into a full gale. In the Channel, where the water depth is less than off the coast of Brittany, the incoming rollers break up into turbulent and erratic patterns, and the general direction of the wind is from the west. This meant that we were taking the weather on the port beam again. Steering was difficult, and we rolled and pitched our way toward Portsmouth in increasing discomfort.

Finally, Hutchins decided that to continue on this course was too dangerous (as the U.S. weather people had predicted) and that we would have to take the safer course of heading into the weather. To do this, we had to abandon the plan of going to Portsmouth and, instead head toward Portland. As we approached the South Coast, a Junkers 88 came out of the clouds. The plane spotted our ship and decided to have a crack at us. While it banked and turned for a run-in, our gun crews were already at the Oerlikon 20-mm machine guns. Our fire seemed to have put the German pilot off his aim; the track of his bullets raised a stream of splashes some yards from our side. I don't know whether or not we hit him, but he disappeared into the clouds. The whole thing was so quick that there was no time to do anything except what we had been trained to do. Some time later, as we were entering Portland harbor, I looked casually at the pile of spent brass cartridge cases rolling around the gun platforms. Only then did I begin to feel afraid—with real trembling of hands and knees and the conscious realization that the attack had been close enough that we could all have been killed.

The next day in Portland, I collapsed while eating a meal. The medical officer came to take a look. He examined my gums and pronounced that I had scurvy—the disease that the Royal Navy was famous for having prevented by issuing lime juice on sea voyages as early as the seventeenth century. The medical officer added casually that he had seen several cases of scurvy. It was probably a result of living on a diet of dried vegetables, dried potatoes, dried eggs, and nothing much fresh during the weeks in Brest.

He sent me to a convalescent center near Cerne Abbas in Dorset. This was a requisitioned mansion, in which patients completed convalescence, rather than occupying beds in major hospitals. For about a week there, I was treated with a diet of vitamins, green vegetables, and fresh juice. The scurvy quickly cleared up, and I was soon back on *ML137*, which was still berthed at Portland.

9

General Duties

The test of a vocation is the love of the drudgery it involves.—LOGAN PEARSALL-SMITH

From Portland, we were ordered to Immingham, Yorkshire. We proceeded in convoy up the Channel, past Dover, and northward past the coast of Norfolk. We swept areas around the Yorkshire coast for a week or two and were then ordered to Harwich. En route in this passage, we stayed in Portsmouth Harbour for a few days to refuel and replenish supplies. During this stay, I was ordered to sea in a submarine that was going out for a two-day exercise. It was common to send junior officers on available training exercises as part of their naval education. Such assignments were usually made when officers had a few days available from their usual duties. I had never been in a submarine before. Once outside Portsmouth boom, we submerged and proceeded to the exercise area. The submarine was to play the role of a U-boat for a group of frigates and sloops that would "hunt" us.

Once we were underwater, I went through the procedures for trying to fix the ship's position on the chart by taking bearings through the periscope. This involved slewing the periscope around until I could identify some conspicuous object on the distant coast. If the object was also marked on the chart, it could be used as a point on which to take a bearing. The periscope system permitted one to read the bearing at the eyepiece. With two such bearings, it was possible to get a rather rough fix; with three, the position could be plotted more closely.

There were no heating systems in submarines, and they were very cold when below the surface. The ubiquitous white oiled-wool sweaters were worn at all times except by the engine room crew. Everything inside the submarine was cramped. Pipes, wires, and tubes were overhead everywhere. There was no room to stand up straight, except just under the conning tower where the periscope was positioned. The so-called wardroom was so tiny that it made the accommodation in the *ML137* seem almost comfortable. When I was off watch at night, I slept on a bunk that had a clearance of not much more than two feet between it and the pipes overhead. The occupant had to insert himself horizontally onto the bunk and remember not to sit upright on waking.

The combination of discomfort and danger in the submarine service was, in my opinion, the worst in the Navy. Minesweeping was not a great way to pass the time, but I would choose it over the life of a submariner without a moment's hesitation.

During this time, Mac invited me to go with him when he decided to call on his former housemaster at Christ's Hospital, Horsham, Surrey, where he had been a student before entering the Navy. Horsham was not far from Portsmouth by train. Christ's Hospital was a "Bluecoat" school—students wore long blue coats with a single row of silver buttons down the front, knee breeches, white hose, and black shoes with silver buckles. It was a "public" (i.e., private) school and totally residential. The school had been founded in the early eighteenth century in London but had moved to new buildings in Horsham in 1902. It had long historic connections with the Navy and Army, and sons of indigent career officers might receive scholarships to the school. These scholars usually wore some kind of large metal badge on their coats to indicate the origin of the endowment that supported them. Mac's father had been a career RN officer, and his mother had died when Mac was quite young. He had gone to Christ's Hospital on one of the naval scholarships.

We met Mac's housemaster, had sherry with him, and then lunched in the dining hall filled with serried rows of blue-coated boys. Looking at the boys, their eighteenth-century dress, and the badges of those on the naval scholarships, I could not help reflecting on the long continuities that have sustained the Royal Navy. These were the "Midshipmen Easys" of the future, and their dress proclaimed the unbroken line that linked them to Trafalgar and the Armada.

In February 1945, the Fifth Flotilla was moved to a new base at Harwich. The flotilla was to be engaged in defensive convoy escort patrols and some minesweeping. On passage to Harwich, Mac was officer of the watch while we were eastbound up the Channel in company with two other MLs of the flotilla. It was late afternoon, and the light was failing. Hutchins and I were below in the wardroom. Suddenly, there was a sharp listing turn, followed by a loud thump, and the ship shuddered. Hutchins was up the companionway and on deck in a rush, and I was close behind him. Our first thought was that we had hit submerged wreckage because we had not heard any explosion, but the ship had collided with a large channel buoy. The hull was slightly cracked where it had hit the buoy. Although the buoy was rocking wildly, it seemed to have come to no harm.

The worst damage was to reputation. Hutchins could scarcely contain himself. Mac did not have a watchkeeping certificate nor did I, but we both had been in independent charge of watches at sea for almost a year. Because we lacked watchkeeping certificates, anything untoward that happened during our watches would be blamed on Hutchins, the commanding officer. And this is what happened here. There was a formal inquiry when we docked in Dover. Hutchins was charged with negligence; there was damage to the ship and possible damage to the buoy. Although he was issued only a mild reprimand, Hutchins was furious that this blot had been placed on his record. His previous naval service had been very good, and he nourished hopes of staying in the regular Navy after the war, rather than returning to his peacetime position as a Lloyd's underwriter.

When Hutchins came back on board from the court of inquiry at Dover, he turned on Mac and pointed out that Mac's negligence had damaged his (Hutchins's) prospects. He then handed Mac a watchkeeping certificate, duly signed. He warned that, in future, Mac would be held responsible for his own mistakes. Hutchins seemed to be unaware of the paradox involved in giving a certificate of competence that had been long overdue only after a single, specific instance of negligence. I received my own watchkeeping certificate shortly afterward. Hutchins was unusually pleasant when he handed it over and assured me that it was unrelated to the Mac incident.

After the inquiry, we continued on to Immingham near Hull on the east coast of Yorkshire, where we arrived in a snowstorm. It was quite unclear to me what we were to do there; we stayed for only a very brief time, but I was given a short leave and went home for three days. We were then ordered back south to Ramsgate. The passage south was uneventful except for one incident. While I was off watch and taking a nap below, a fog began to roll in, reducing the visibility to less than a quarter of a mile. We had no radar, and our navigation was mainly dead reckoning and depth sounding. I was awakened by a messenger from the bridge, who said that I was needed there to determine our position. I did so by calculation from the entries in the deck log and figured that we were not very far north of Harwich. We were moving noticeably slower than we had been before the fog came in, and I asked when the reduction of speed had been made, as it was not recorded in the log. Hutchins, who was keeping the watch, admitted that he was not sure. "Some time back," he said. Now we had no reliable way to tell where we were except in the most general terms.

We decided to head west toward the land and take soundings until we came to a depth suitable for anchoring. Not long afterward, the lookout on the bow shouted that there was a fixed red light faintly visible in the gloom. We promptly stopped engines, anchored, and decided to wait it out until the fog cleared. The light suggested that we were opposite a harbor entrance somewhere, but I could not find one on the chart that had a red beacon near it. Somewhere around 2200, the anchor watch came down to report to me that the red light had mysteriously changed to green, and that he could distinctly hear a voice shouting, "All change here! All change here!"

When I went up on the bridge to take a look, I found that the fog had thinned and I could see a beach less than half a mile away; the changeable light was from a railway signal at a small station close to the shore. Depth soundings were now lower, as the tide had been falling, and it was risky to make a long turn that might bring us aground. We weighed anchor and slowly backed out, stern first, until we got into deep water. This incident was the cause of much later amusement and feeble jokes that centered on navigating for the railway.

We entered the harbor in Great Yarmouth on the way south. All that I can recall about our brief stay there is that we went to the cinema and saw an Abbott and Costello movie in which they were doing something farcical in the Middle East.

On arrival in Ramsgate, we were assigned to coastal defense patrolling, plus some short coastal convoy duties. There were still E-boats and U-boats about, and the war had taken a turn for the worse with the appearance of the flying bombs—engine-driven V-1 bombs that flew until their fuel ran out and then, falling to earth, blew up anything that was in the landing area. The V-1 looked like a small plane, with wings, tail, and a motor that sounded much like that of a large lawn mower. Its aim was erratic. Quite a few simply ran out of gas over the sea. One became famous for flying as far as Lancashire, but most of them were aimed at London. The V-1s were usually intercepted by fighter planes that shot them down. Some pilots, however, had developed a "sporting" approach, in which the fighter pilot flew his plane parallel to the V-1, edged near to it, and then tipped it sideways with his airplane's wing. The V-1 then crashed into the sea.

On one of our patrols, we watched a radar-controlled antiaircraft battery on the coast near Aldeborough dealing with V-1s. These batteries generally operated by putting up an intense pattern of flak around the target; it was impossible to fire selective single shots in the hope of hitting a moving plane. With the first introduction of precision radar control, the situation changed, at least for such a nonmaneuverable craft as the V-1. The target in this case came speeding along, its put-put motor clearly audible at sea level. The battery's radar antenna swiveled to follow it. There was a single bang from one of the guns, the flak shell struck the V-1 directly, and it blew up in midair. A few minutes later, another V-1 appeared and suffered the same fate. Watching this kind of action was an impressive change from our previous experiences.

Heavy air raids on Germany were going on day and night. By day at sea off the East Coast, one could see the squadrons of Flying Fortresses reach an assembly point, take up their formation, and then turn eastward when the pathfinder plane fired a bright flare. We also watched them returning, most of them intact, but more than once a solitary plane came in low over the water with one or more of its engines dead. The RAF maintained a fleet of air-sea rescue launches (MLs, originally) with sick bays, surgical nurses, and rescue gear, to pick up downed aircrews along the route of these attacks. The rescue launches were tied up to a navigation buoy, ready to slip their mooring ropes and speed off whenever the message came. We met them frequently.

Most of these Flying Fortresses were U.S. Eighth Air Force planes based in Norfolk and Suffolk. When my wife and children and I stayed in Norfolk more than thirty years later, we saw the runways half hidden in the long grass of the fields.

In Ramsgate, the only social event of note and a rather silly one at that was provided by the Tie-Biters Club at a pub called The Rising Sun, much patronized by local naval officers. This club originated when someone unnamed had undertaken a bet with somebody else that he could bite off the end of the latter's tie with a single bite. This he managed to do. To celebrate this feat, the name of the owner of the amputated tie was inscribed on a card and pinned on a board over the bar, together with the fragment of tie. The challenge caught on; by the time we came to Ramsgate, the bar board had neat rows of cards, names, and tie fragments. Rules had evolved—chiefly, that only someone whose name was already on the board could sever the tie of a newcomer. It was like a laying-on of teeth, so to speak. I was duly initiated by a complete stranger, also in the Navy, but I felt disinclined to pass the favor on to somebody else. (I am amused, looking back at the Tie-Biters Club, to reflect on what Freud would have had to say about it.)

Two rather more serious events took place while we were based in Ramsgate. One evening, when we were in harbor, we received orders to put to sea immediately because a U-boat had been reported to be in the area. Mac and some of the crew were ashore for the evening, and there was no time to find them. Once out of the harbor, we headed in the general direction indicated in the report. It was a brilliantly clear moonlit night, with the water gleaming, a gentle swell, and a slight breeze. Suddenly, the bow lookout shouted, "Object dead ahead!" A small submarine, not much bigger than a torpedo, with a Plexiglas dome, was clearly visible without binoculars. The submarine's upper hull, showing two or three feet above the surface, lay across our bow; it was moving slowly toward the land. With two ratings, I hurried down aft where our depth charges lay on their racks. We turned the priming keys to sixty feet (the minimum depth that could be set) and reported back to the bridge. Hutchins cracked on speed as the submarine dived below the surface. The "Fire" bell sounded. We released one of the depth charges, and it rolled over the side of the ship into the water behind us. We continued to speed ahead to get clear of what was going to happen next. There was a brief wait. Then came a huge vibrating roar; from the sea surface, a white spout of water rose and fell. *ML137* shook and shuddered, and the cups in the galley shattered. We turned around, ready to continue the attack with our remaining three depth charges.

Where we had dropped the first charge, large bubbles of oil gouted up to the surface, followed by a piece of Plexiglas, which rose and sank in one motion. There was little doubt that the submarine had been destroyed. We circled for a while to see if anything more happened—perhaps a survivor would appear or some sign that the submarine was still there. In the meantime, we had sent a radio report to our base. After about an hour of searching and circling, we were ordered back to Ramsgate. Mac and the rest of the crew, chagrined to have been ashore when this had happened, were on the wharf as we entered the harbor. Word of the incident had already spread throughout the Navy ships in Ramsgate. Mac had heard about it in a bar—security must have been getting lax!

Certainly, the submarine was either a one-man or two-man type employed by the German Navy (and by the Royal Navy, too, for a while). One of these ran aground on the Goodwin Sands some days later and was left high and dry when the tide fell. An LST, carrying a bulldozer and some soldiers, was sent out to capture the submarine by towing her in over the LST bow ramp. The two-man crew were in good shape and were relieved to have survived what was normally a one-way passage. This incident must surely have been the first example of a warship being captured by a bulldozer. These small submarines were designed to carry a single torpedo slung below the small hull. Like the V-1 flying bombs, they had only enough fuel for a one-way trip. After firing their torpedo, the crew were to get into a rubber raft provided on board and hope to be picked up by one side or the other.

The second incident was quite different. A radio message had come in from a U.S. Liberty ship at anchor in the Thames estuary. One of the engine room crew had been badly injured when a spinning flywheel fractured and a piece of it hit the man in the stomach. We were given the name of the ship and her approximate location. Once again, the weather was roughish, the night dark, and a slight mist hovered over the area. On arrival at the anchorage, we found that a convoy of about a dozen Liberty ships was there. None of them was illuminated in any way, in keeping with blackout requirements. In order to find the right vessel, we had no choice but to approach them one by one. Communication proved to be very difficult. As we approached each ship, we had to use a loud-hailer to identify ourselves and ask the deck watchkeeper if this was the ship that we were seeking. Just explaining this and why we were asking, in pitch darkness at a distance of fifty feet or so, with both ships rising and falling in the swell, was not easy. We found our ship on about the third try. We came right alongside, with many fenders out to limit banging and grinding against the ship's side. The injured man, bound in a strapped litter, was lowered down to our deck. He had been given morphine and lay motionless, staring upward. We hurried back to Ramsgate where an ambulance was waiting on the wharf. Later, we heard that the injured man was recovering.

Although we had been assigned to the base at Harwich since February, we had yet to spend any time there. Finally, we were moved from Ramsgate to Harwich. Nearly twelve months had elapsed since I had been in Harwich; that had been the occasion when promotion took me from the *Jason* to *ML137*.

On arrival at Harwich, we berthed at Parkeston Quay. The quay was crowded with destroyers, fleet minesweepers, and other larger vessels. Shortly afterward, we were ordered up the River Orwell to a small former yacht harbor at the village of Pin Mill. This became our regular berth between intervals at sea.

10

VE Day: A Victory and a Loss

Death, whither hath he taken thee?
To a world, do I think, that rights the disaster of this?
The vision of which I miss,
Who weep for the body, and wish but to warm thee
and awaken thee?
And the things we have seen and have known and
have heard of, fail us.

—ROBERT BRIDGES, "ON A DEAD CHILD"

On 7 May 1945, *ML137* put into Parkeston Quay at Harwich after a few days at sea on convoy escort duty. Hardly were the lines secured to the bollards on the quay when a sailor from the shore base came on board with the mail and a telegram for me from my parents. It was very brief and simply said something like "Kerry seriously ill. Please come home immediately." No other details. I applied at once for compassionate leave, which was granted on the spot, and I was on the next train to London, which left the following day (8 May, VE day), and thence on to Manchester.

I reached home late that night. The train journey still remains clear in my mind. The war in Europe would end in a matter of hours, and there was an atmosphere of jubilation everywhere—at each station where we stopped and in the faces of passengers on the train. But all that I could think was that Kerry must be terribly ill for such a telegram to come; the noise and good cheer everywhere seemed surreal.

I arrived home to find my parents distraught and my father overwhelmed by what had happened. Kerry had complained of a headache while at Mass the previous Sunday; his pain became so unbearable that my parents left the church and took him home. Shortly after that, he became delirious. The local doctor diagnosed meningitis but decided to keep him in bed at home for the time being. Kerry went into a coma and was taken to the hospital the next day. There, his illness was diagnosed as encephalitis.

Soon after my arrival, my father collapsed and went to bed, where he was to remain for the next few days. He was angry and almost incoherent, demanding of God to know why this was happening, what had he done to deserve this, and begging that God would take his life to spare Kerry. The doctor decided that my father was in serious trouble and that he should not be exposed to any further stresses until he managed to get on his feet again.

In the meantime, my mother and I took the bus to the isolation hospital where Kerry was lying. Because encephalitis is infectious, Kerry was in a bed within a glass-walled cubicle. All that I could see—and the last that I was ever to see of him—was his face as white as the sheets around him, his eyes closed. I could press my own face against the glass, but nothing more. The nurse was kind but frank. Kerry was going to die, and this would be better than surviving the disease, which, she stated, would leave him severely and permanently retarded. So there was no hope, only two dreadful alternatives.

My mother was stoic. I was benumbed and unbelieving. The nurse told us that they would call us whenever "anything happened"—which meant, of course, when Kerry died. We had given her the phone number of the Booths, a family who lived across the street from us, as we had no phone. In any case, the doctor had urged that nothing be done to arouse my father's suspicions that matters had become worse, for my father was still clinging to a desperate hope that somehow it would all work out right.

Sometime in the morning of 15 May, Mr. Booth opened the door without knocking to tell us that it was all over and that Kerry was dead. In two weeks, he would have been sixteen years old. My mother and I went out to the hospital. Concealing the fact of Kerry's death, we had told my father that we were going to visit Kerry. At the hospital, there were arrangements to be made. Both my mother and I kept a face on things until, on the way home, she felt the need to visit the priest who acted as Catholic chaplain to the hospital. She too wanted to know why a merciful God had allowed such a dreadful thing, and the priest, poor man, did his best with the standard phrases of the Church: Kerry was now among the blessed, God's will had to be accepted, His ways were mysterious, He only takes young those whom He loves. These words were no help, of course—how could anything be a help? For my mother, the tears then came, mainly grief, partly disappointment in God. She had now lost three of five children, and the light of her life was dimmed forever. For myself, I was uncomprehending and speechless.

Funeral arrangements had to be made and, for a short while, were kept secret from my father, who was still weeping and cherishing his forlorn hopes in the bedroom upstairs—where the framed certificate testifying to the Pope's blessing and wishes for the happiness of their marriage hung on the wall above the bed.

We managed to conceal the truth from my father for one day. To convince him that nothing final had yet happened, I left the house for a few hours, with the lie that I was going to visit Kerry at the hospital as on the previous days. Still numb, I walked aimlessly around the streets of Swinton, then returned home. My father wanted me to come upstairs to tell him how Kerry had seemed. I could not face him. I turned to look out of the window, with my back to him so that he could not see my face. I told him that Kerry looked about the same, and, with lead in my throat and my chest, I listened to my father's expressions of hope. Later that same day, the doctor finally agreed that my father must now deal with the truth; it could be concealed no longer. My mother asked me to wait downstairs as she went up alone to tell him. I do not know what she said, but I heard his loud cry of grief and disbelief.

My father did not come to the funeral. All that I can remember of the funeral is that Kerry's whole school turned out—his classmates, his Air Training Corps friends in their uniforms, all of the masters, all of the monks in their habits—and scores of neighbors and friends. My mother, her face like a mask, walked as straight and stiff as a ramrod to the grave. I took her by the arm, but I do not know who supported whom.

We had tried to get word to John and to see if he could get leave to come home. He was in a convoy to North Russia. The police had sent a telegram to the Admiralty, who had transmitted an order for him to be given leave. By the time the message reached his ship, the funeral was already over and done with. Two days later, I had to return to duty.

For some weeks, I could not grasp it all. I kept thinking that it was a bad dream and that, when I came out of the Navy, Kerry would be there just as we had always expected. His death devastated my parents. They really never got over it, and, for this reason, the grandparents whom my children knew were different from the parents whom I had known—my mother grieving until she died, my father bitter and self-pitying.

Months later, after I had been wounded and the surgeons had wired my jaws together, I began to have dreams in which Kerry was still alive, but he would be moving into danger—near the edge of a cliff or on top of a roof—and I would try to shout to warn him, but my mouth wouldn't open, and I had to watch helplessly as disaster struck him. I always woke up in a sweat of terror and loss.

I wish I had known Kerry better. John and I were closer to each other than either of us to Kerry, as we were nearer in age. Our distance from Kerry had increased when my parents sent him to Ireland to live with our grandmother when World War II began in September 1939. I'm not sure now, but I remember Kerry as being in Ireland about two years. He had come back to England, with a marked Irish brogue, to go to the school that John and I had attended (De La Salle College in Pendleton, Salford, near Manchester). There, he did very well in everything. He was well liked by his fellow students and teachers, his academic work was excellent, and he was a good athlete, especially in swimming. During the course of his swimming, he had suffered a perforated eardrum, which had caused him no big problems, but was later to be regarded by my parents as a probable origin of the disease that was to strike him.

Hunting through what few documents I have, I came across the De La Salle College Annual for 1944, which mentions Kerry in the class notes as follows:

> Form Upper Five L (Latin): Ciaran Maher is a source of much wonderment to some of his companions owing to his liking for authors like Dickens and Scott; he used to spend much of leisure time trying to decide whether to spell his name "Ciaran" or "Kieran," but he finally decided in favour of "Kerry."

I saw little of Kerry during the years that he spent at De La Salle. By then, I was in the Navy and saw him only on the infrequent leaves that came my way. He had many friends—they were always calling for him at the house whenever I was there—and he and they often went hiking in the Derbyshire mountains. He was also very much involved in the Air Training Corps, the volunteer weekend air cadet system that provided some knowledge of aviation for young men who hoped to enter the RAF if and when they were drafted. Later, my parents told me that he had been writing (perhaps had completed) a novel, but I never saw it myself and don't know any of the details—or even whether this is myth or fact. He was more religious than either John or me and was more serious a Catholic than many boys of his age. He was not "goody-goody" about it and did not display a religious faith just to please our parents. I know that my mother entertained her perpetual hope that he might want to be a priest. She had had the same hope for John and then for me, in turn—in both cases, only to be disappointed.

It has always been hard for me to talk about Kerry's death; even as I summon up the memory now, I feel the pain nearly as keenly as when it happened. I am glad that I was able to be there to help my mother when he died, but, in a cowardly way, I wish that I had not been there to watch his dying.

11

The Last Sweep

New brooms sweep well!—PROVERBIAL SAYING

When I returned to *ML137* after Kerry's funeral, she was undergoing extensive refit at Tough's Yard, a boatyard at Teddington on the River Thames, just a short walk downstream from Teddington Lock. One officer and a small number of ratings were required to be around. When I arrived, Mac went on leave. I was billeted in a private home nearby. The house was a large, three-story riverside Victorian structure; the garden ended at the bank of the Thames. Here, I slept on a couch in the living room. The husband of the couple worked as a cameraman at the nearby Twickenham movie studios of J. Arthur Rank. My host and his wife were already in the middle of arrangements to go to Hollywood some months later. His father owned a small company that made marine instruments, such as speed logs, barometers, and the like (we had them in *ML137*).

Shortly after I came to the house, the father's company threw a victory party—it was still only a few days after VE day—and I was invited. At the party, I was more or less "adopted" by an engineer of the firm. During the following days, he and his wife extended many invitations to me for teas and other social occasions. One day, my hostess felt it wise to caution me that the engineer had been commenting to his friends that I would be a suitable husband for his daughter, who was invariably present on these social occasions. She was a nice and rather shy young woman; she had sparked no enthusiasm on my part, however, and I was slightly aghast at the news. I now noticed that her parents made many efforts to arrange to "leave us alone together" and provided tickets for the two of us to attend local movies and other entertainments. As the daughter herself never hinted at any such thing and my information was all secondhand, it seemed a little impolite to convey to her my lack of interest, given the fact that she had never expressed any in me.

I was appointed first lieutenant of the *ML137*. Hutchins was posted to command a somewhat larger vessel somewhere, and I had a new commanding officer, A. J. Sanderson, who had been first lieutenant of one of our own flotilla MLs. Mac had been discharged from the Navy to permit him to enter Cambridge (Trinity Hall College) as a freshman.

During this time, some of the crew had been given leave. One, a sailor from Glasgow, had been stopped by a naval patrol on his way through London for wearing his cap "flat aback," (i.e., at the back of his head rather than the required position in which the top of the cap is horizontal). Wearing the cap flat aback was much adopted by sailors because they believed that it gave them a kind of "Jolly Jack" carefree look. In due course, a report came to the ship from the Naval Provost-Marshal in London; it was necessary for us to report what punishment had been assigned for this "crime." I was required to conduct the Defaulters, at which this matter was dealt with.

When I asked the rating why he had been wearing his cap in this fashion, he responded, "Ma heid was sweetin,' sir." This explanation mystified me until the accompanying petty officer explained, "He said that his head was sweating, sir." I awarded (that was the word used) the offender three days' stoppage of leave. He had just come back from leave and would not be eligible for more for a while. Also, we were going to sea the next day, and he would have no opportunity for liberty then anyway. Consequently, his punishment was entirely nominal, but we could report back to the Provost-Marshal that the crime had been dealt with. Why the Navy had the time and men to patrol around London and pick on trivial offenses was beyond me then and still is.

After completion of the refit at Tough's Yard, *ML137* was ordered to Rotterdam, Holland, together with two other MLs of our flotilla, to sweep German mines. Just before we left Teddington, I invited the engineer, his wife, and their daughter on board *ML137* for a farewell tea and cake. The daughter brought a gift of books, and her father promised to take a photograph of *ML137*, resplendent in her new paint, as she proceeded down the river the next day. The photograph ultimately reached me and is reproduced in this book.

Our passage down the Thames to Southend was very pleasant. A sunny day, the war in Europe over, the ship newly painted and repaired, and my move to second-in-command as first lieutenant made all seem right with the world. We had retained the original crew, and there was almost a holiday mood. On some pretext or other, we moored for an hour at Westminster Pier—the real reason was to show ourselves off to an allegedly admiring public in sight and sound of Big Ben. Then, we continued down the river to Southend and moored at the pier to await further orders. They came almost immediately. The next day, *ML137* and the two other ships of our flotilla were to proceed to the Hook of Holland and then into the port of Rotterdam to commence sweeping the main Dutch waterways. Some of these had been heavily mined by the Germans, so we were told. Under the terms of the surrender, the mines were to be swept by German minesweepers. In its attempt to sweep the mines, the locally based German minesweeping flotilla had been destroyed. Because there were no more German minesweepers, we were assigned to do the job—not a very encouraging briefing. This was the minesweeping operation during which I would be wounded.

On arrival at the Hook, we moored first in the small harbor of Maasluis. We spent a day there, waiting for instructions. We were something of a curiosity. Many people came down to see the ships and to talk to us. I walked around the village once or twice. I was intrigued by the sight of the little mirrors attached to the outside walls of the houses, just near the windows. The watchers inside could see what was happening in the street without showing their faces too openly while doing so. A slight stirring of the curtains when one walked by indicated the presence of a watcher.

We then went on to Rotterdam and moored to a floating landing stage near a main street along the waterfront. Once again, people came down to see our ships, and there was a great deal of conversation and some bartering. We had flaked out a long rope to dry on the wharf. It had begun to show signs of rot in the core and was probably going to be useless. A Dutchman dressed in a mariner's attire—perhaps a tugboat skipper—offered to buy it from us. We pointed out the defect, but he wanted it anyway. The rope changed hands for some bottles of schnapps.

Several of us were invited to a kind of reception at the home of the harbormaster. He lived in a large apartment at the top of one of the towers supporting one end of a big bridge over the river. From his apartment, he had a view across the entire harbor. We brought our own refreshments because we knew that the Dutch had little available to them. The harbormaster had two daughters, who spoke English well, and we invited the family to come down to the ship the next day. While we were entertaining them, our acquaintance was interrupted by orders for the ship to move to the Dutch naval dockyard. Here, workmen were to install a new kind of sweeping gear; we would then proceed to the Nieuw Meerwade to begin sweeping.

This new sweep was intended to deal with pressure mines, sometimes called "oyster mines." We had no experience with these and had barely heard of them at HMS Lochinvar. Pressure mines are influence mines; they operate by virtue of the fact that when a ship moves through the water, she displaces an amount of water equal to the weight of the ship. The displacement of water by a moving vessel produces a pattern of changes, increases and decreases, in the vertical pressure exerted on the seabed and on any object lying on the seabed. The oyster mine is constructed to take advantage of this fact.

The mine itself lay on the seabed or a riverbed in areas of shallow water. Built into the upper surface of the mine was a structure consisting of two water-filled chambers, one on top of the other. These chambers were divided by a watertight, flexible diaphragm that was sensitive to changes in external vertical water pressure and moved up or down if the water pressure in either chamber came out of balance with the pressure in the other chamber. A small "leak hole" connecting the two chambers permitted rapid equalization of slow changes in pressure, but it was too small to do so if the pressure in either chamber changed rapidly and substantially. Because of this equalizing effect, any slow changes in vertical pressure, such as those caused by the rise and fall of the tide, damped down the movements of the diaphragm. With the occurrence of sudden changes in pressure, such as those caused by a ship overhead, the diaphragm could not be damped down. The resulting differences in pressure between the two chambers activated an internal contact system that detonated the mine.

In order to sweep the oyster mine, the vertical pressure directly over it had to be altered in some way. Several methods had been tried to achieve this. One approach involved towing some large, shiplike, allegedly unsinkable object through the suspected mine field. Allied minesweepers had tried this when clearing mines outside Cherbourg. None of their efforts had been particularly successful; large, shiplike objects are prone to wills of their own, regardless of who is towing them. In one such attempt, the towing vessel had been towed backward out of the harbor that she was trying to enter by the unruly object at the end of her tow line.

A second approach was to try to simulate the pressure signature of a ship by dropping explosives in a sequence timed to reflect the appropriate rapid changes of pressure. To this end, the backroom experts at the Admiralty had invented the X-type sweep. This was the method that we were to employ. The X-type sweep was very simple. The apparatus had a homemade kind of appearance—the cut edges were rough, the welds showed, and so forth. A piece of metal tubing, rather like a drainpipe, was mounted horizontally two or three feet above the deck of the mine-sweeper, with one end projecting a few feet out over the water. This tube was inserted through the center of a steel splinter-shield mounted between the inboard and outboards ends of the tube. The lower half of the inboard end of the tube was slightly longer than the upper half; there was a slit cut along the upper half as far as the splinter-shield.

The purpose of this contraption was to permit the dropping of a pattern of hand grenades into the water. When the hand grenades exploded in the water, it was hoped that the resulting pattern of pressure would detonate the mines. In order to implement this technique, hand grenades were to be loaded one by one into the tube in such a manner that the ring holding the safety pin protruded through the upper slit. Once a grenade was completely in the tube, its ring could be removed without activating the grenade because the firing bar, confined by the tube, could not spring loose; this would happen when the grenade was rammed through the outboard end of the tube. In order to create a gradual buildup of explosive pressure, we were to load a fixed sequence of hand grenades along with one or more cylindrical wooden blocks. When loaded, the whole lot was to be rammed smartly out through the tube with a ramrod. The ramrod was slightly longer than the tube; it was marked on the inboard end with a white stripe, and a matching white stripe was painted on the inboard end of the tube. The idea was that when the white stripe on the ramrod crossed the stripe on the tube and disappeared inside the tube, the end of the ramrod would be protruding from the outer end of the tube. All of the grenades would have been projected into the water and would explode four seconds later. As soon as one load was ejected, the next loading was to begin immediately.

All of this required that our ship move at high speed, which would make her own pressure signature come and go too rapidly for the mine mechanism to operate and permit us to be out of the way when the explosions occurred well astern. At fifteen knots, we were doing one nautical mile every four minutes. This meant that we would cover roughly thirty-three yards in the four seconds that it took for the grenades to go off. These calculations also meant that we had to load and eject the grenades as quickly as possible if we were to sweep all of the area. If we were too slow in loading, there could be gaps that had not been covered by the spread of pressure. The critical component was speed, and we could not wait to check that each load had been fully ejected before beginning to load the next lot. As first lieutenant, it was my duty to supervise the sweeping procedure and especially to make sure that we maintained the right rate of loading and ejecting. One load every forty seconds or so was the requirement.

With all of this made clear to us, we took on board a very large quantity of hand grenades. They came in wooden boxes; these were stacked on top of each other in a hollow square three or four feet high around the space at the inboard end of the tube so that the grenades would be ready at hand for quick loading. We were now ready for the deadly oyster. Leaving the River Waal and heading southwesterly to the River Maas, we proceeded from Rotterdam to the Nieuw Meerwade—a broad waterway that lies some distance east of Rotterdam.

We swept throughout the daylight hours, as we dropped loads of grenades every forty seconds. On the third day, 27 June, we were sweeping at speed. One load of grenades had just been ejected. The white mark on the ramrod had disappeared into the tube, the ramrod had been withdrawn, and the first elements of the next load were already inside the tube. Suddenly, there was a loud flat bang at the outer end of the tube. Splinters rattled on the splinter-shield, and the two grenades and two blocks of wood that had just been loaded were blown back onto the deck. The firing bars sprang off, which meant that we had four seconds before the grenades would explode. I shouted to the men who were working with me to run, and they did.

Trapped on the other side of the tube and surrounded by the wall of grenade boxes, I had no place to go. I dropped to the deck and pressed myself as flat as possible. I did not count; I could clearly see every detail of the grain of the deck planking against which my face was pressed. The two grenades went off together, and I felt a very hard, dull blow to my face and side, not the kind of sharp pain that I had imagined one would feel when hit. I waited and, this time, did count to four. If the boxes of grenades around me were going to explode, they would do so in four seconds and there wouldn't be much left of me to salvage.

Nothing happened. I got to my feet and somehow managed to walk to the bridge. When I appeared, the expression on the faces of Sanderson and the cox'n at the wheel were horror-stricken. I must have been recalling the nonchalance that was standard fare in the heroic war movies of the time as I said to Sanderson, "I think that I'm going to be due some sick leave."

Whether they heard me, I don't know. My articulation must have been a little blurred—a large piece of shrapnel had passed through my cheek and broken my jaw and was now firmly lodged in my mouth. A spray of shrapnel had peppered me down my side. They put me on a bunk in the wheelhouse, injected an ampoule of morphine, and increased speed back to the nearest village. A radio message brought a Canadian Army ambulance to the village. I was placed on a litter that slid onto a kind of rack, and those in my sweeping crew who had been injured were loaded on lower levels of the rack. They had minor injuries; one had a bad cut on his finger, and they all had small shrapnel splinters here and there. Fortunately, we always wore thick cork life jackets when sweeping, and the blocks of cork had absorbed much of the shrapnel.

The ambulance bounced and swerved along the road. I could hear the conversation of the men below me; they did not know that I was in the top litter. "Jimmy doesn't look too good," one of them offered, "I hope that he's going to make it." More remarks in that vein came from the others. "Jimmy," of course, was their term for the first lieutenant. I was in no condition to suggest that they change the topic and, in any case, had already convinced myself that their fears were needless.

The first stop was a convent. We were carried inside and laid side by side on our litters in a large room smelling of convent wax polish. The floor and walls were covered with tiles. The mother superior came forward and sympathized with each of us. The nuns had no medical supplies and could not do anything for us; however, the mother superior did produce a flask of schnapps, from which she managed to pour a little between my clenched teeth—probably not good medical practice, but it helped. The crew members were taken to a nearby field dressing station of the Canadian Army. As I was in worse shape, another ambulance came to take me to a Canadian Army field hospital near Eindhoven. There, they removed my reefer jacket, cut off the rest of my clothes, cleaned me up, and whisked me into surgery.

I awoke in a ward. My teeth were firmly clamped together with wire, and I had a bandage around my head and bandages around my left leg. The shrapnel was gone, other than one or two small pieces deeply embedded in my ankle. They are there still. Another piece embedded in my left eye was not discovered until 1964 in Madison, Wisconsin, when it was removed, but that is another story. I lay in bed for a couple of days— drinking from the spout of one of those mini-teapots that are used to hold liquid food, having dressings changed, getting penicillin injections, trying to read the little pocketbook novels that the hospital handed out, and listening to the banter and stories of my Canadian ward mates. My fellow patients were a fairly lively group. Two of them had been injured when their Jeeps rolled over. Others were recovering from wounds received in the fighting that had driven the Germans out of Holland.

While I was in the field hospital, two officers from the flotilla came to visit me and brought a few of my things—my cap, shaving gear, and other small items. They were accompanied by the harbormaster's daughters, who seemed very distressed and shocked. Not long after their visit, I was allowed to get out of bed to go to the bathroom. There, I saw myself in a mirror for the first time since the explosion. I was not a pretty sight, and I could understand the reason for the reactions of some people when they saw me.

One or two days later, I was told that I was to be airlifted to England. A group of us was driven to an airstrip outside Eindhoven. Lined up side by side on our litters, we waited in the bright sun for an hour or so. Each of us was labeled with a diagnosis and a large tag bearing the dates and times of the many penicillin injections that we had received. We were loaded into an RAF DC-3, known as a Douglas "Dakota" in the RAF. Once again, our litters were racked like shelves in a cupboard. WAAF (Woman's Auxiliary Air Force) nurses were on board, mainly to take care of any emergencies and to give penicillin doses that were due. This was my first air flight, taken under circumstances that were not what I might have expected. As we gained altitude and headed for England, we could see the red-tiled roofs of houses just above the waters, where the Germans had deliberately flooded the land as they retreated. Several small boats, moving around near the houses, were laden with household items that the owners were trying to salvage.

Shortly afterward, we landed at Blackdown Farm, an RAF airfield (in Kent, I think). Some of the patients were taken off there. The rest of us remained for the next leg of the flight, which took us to an airfield in Wiltshire, not far from Swindon. Here, we were carried out and laid in a row on our litters in a shed. Several local lady volunteers, who had been waiting to meet the flight, distributed various things that we might need. When the volunteer who spoke to me found out that I did not really need anything, she gave me a washcloth anyway. She was pleasant and solicitous, and this was a touching welcome home. I was put into another ambulance and was on my way to the RAF hospital at Wroughton, Wiltshire.

Two things surprised me about being wounded. One was that the injury was not especially painful at the moment of impact; real pain came later. The other was that my immediate predominant feeling was one of relief, bordering on euphoria. It was as if all of the unspoken and suppressed fears that accompany minesweeping had now been faced; the worst had happened and I had survived. The nagging and never consciously asked question, "When will my luck run out?" had been answered, and the answer was tolerable. I had done the job, the bad thing had happened, I had had the luck to live through it, and for me the war was really over. What lay ahead was unknown, but it could be managed.

Looking back on the whole thing, I attempted to figure out how the accident had happened. I concluded that the problem must have been that the ramrod was not marked accurately enough. When the white mark had disappeared into the tube, the ramrod had failed to eject the last grenade completely. Instead, the grenade must have jammed part way out of the tube in such a way that the firing bar sprang off, detonating the grenade four seconds later. That had been the first bang, and the blast of that grenade blew the first two grenades of the next load back on board. The combination of crude marking and the requirement for excessive loading speed had come together to produce what happened.

The pressure mine proved very difficult to sweep. The "new broom" had not swept well, and the X-type sweep was abandoned. Towing large, hypothetically "unsinkable" barges or other floating structures over the mine fields proved impractical. After two or three explosions, the structures began to disintegrate; they were also expensive. At some point, individual divers were employed to defuse the mines. In later naval warfare, the introduction of helicopter-towed sweeping improved matters somewhat, but it appears to have been used most successfully in sweeping mines in areas where the locations of the mines were known before the sweep began.

12

Hospitals and Barracks

How many creatures on the earth
Have learnt the simple duties of fellowship
And social comfort in a hospital.
—ELIZABETH BARRETT BROWNING, "AURORA LEIGH"

Royal Air Force Hospital, Wroughton, Wiltshire

During the period when I was in Wroughton, and later Sherborne and Park Prewett hospitals, much of my time was spent in trying to get mobility back into my jaw. At Wroughton, my jaws were wired shut for some weeks as a splint to permit the jawbone to heal. The only way to eat was through a gap left by the loss of a tooth removed by the shrapnel. For much of the time, I sucked milk, soup, raw eggs, Guinness, and other liquids through a straw inserted into the gap. This quickly became quite tedious. Finally, I hit upon the technique of slicing flexible flat food, such as bread and butter, cheese, and fried egg, into very thin short strips. By tilting my head back and dropping a thin sliver into the gap, then gulping it down, it was possible to bring a little variety into my diet.

I counted the days until the wire would be removed. This was done under anesthetic. When I recovered, I found that I still could not open my mouth. After endless attempts to get some movement into my jaw, the surgeons decided that it would have to be forcibly opened and clamped in an open position. After this operation, I woke up with a stainless steel contraption in my mouth that kept it rigidly open. Now, it was possible only to gurgle liquids and continue to gulp-swallow solid foods.

To my intense frustration, when the clamp was removed my mouth would not close. The solution was to close my mouth once again under anesthetic, but this time only partially and with no more clamps or wires. A hinged wedge was fabricated from dental acrylic. A turn screw at the hinge permitted me to widen or narrow the angle of the wedge. Each day I was to insert the wedge and try to gradually force my mouth open a little wider by turning the screw. This strategy worked up to a point, but only later, in the autumn at Park Prewett, did I gain enough opening (19 mm) to get along with normal eating.

When I first came to Wroughton, one of the RAF surgeons had taken some photographs of my face to include in a medical journal article. He was quite excited about it and told me that the photographs would be color slides. Kodak had just developed color photography, and this would be his first time to use it. He gave me two of the slides. This was the first color photography that I had seen, and I still have the slides.

At Wroughton, I was asked by one of the nurses if I would be willing to take the time to chat with an airman in another ward. He was very depressed, and the hospital staff was concerned about him. He was an air mechanic, a corporal, and had been taken into the hospital when he complained of pains rather like those of appendicitis. During X-ray, it had been discovered that he didn't have an appendix. It had been re-moved some years previously, a fact that he had already told the doctor. What the X-rays revealed was a curved surgical needle still inside him, slightly calcified, that was causing the pain. The needle was duly re-moved, and he was stitched up. He kept the needle in a small envelope on his bedside locker. He complained, however, that he couldn't lie flat on the bed without having abdominal pain and adamantly insisted on lying with his knees drawn up. Persuasion having failed, the decision was made to encase his lower abdomen and thighs in a reinforced cast so that he could not draw up his knees. The stitches were apparently healing, and no other cause for his continuing pain could be detected.

This solution left the patient lying flat, but he was depressed and aggrieved—at the first surgeon who had left the needle in him years ago and at everything that had happened to him since. I tried to cheer him up—the war was over in Europe, he would soon be out of the service and going home, and so forth. His sense of grievance never diminished; the plaster cast seemed to have been the last straw. Two weeks or so after my last visit with him, he died. The nurses said that the doctors had reported that there was no medically definable reason for his death.

In my ward was a mix of pilots, navigators, and other aircrew members with various injuries and wounds. A Canadian pilot who came in was badly injured. He was first put into one of the few private rooms, usually a sign that there wasn't much hope. The word from the nurses was that it was all up with him, as he had serious head and abdominal wounds. His British relatives visited him daily. Then the doctors moved him into the ward but surrounded his bed with screens. One day, when the matron was doing her rounds, she stopped to ask him how he was doing. Large and rocklike, the matron held a rank equivalent to an army major. The Canadian, smiling at her, said something to the effect that he was fine and invited her to join him in bed to find out for herself. She must have seen and heard many such things in her career, but even she blushed slightly, smiled, and walked on. The next day, the screens around the pilot came down. A few days later, he was ambulatory and, not long after, on his way home to Canada and a hospital there. This incident more or less coincided with the death of the depressed airman. Both of these outcomes seemed to be medical mysteries.

One particularly cheery and noisy pilot, whose plane had been shot down in the North Sea just before the end of German resistance, had floated in a small raft for several days before being picked up by a Danish fishing boat. The fishermen had taken him to Denmark, and he had been treated there before being sent on to England. He had "immersion feet," which required extensive treatment. On his uniform, he wore a little embroidered gold-braid dolphin. RAF aircrews had invented hypothetical clubs. The best known was the "Caterpillar" club. Its symbol was worn by people who had parachuted to safety (the caterpillar presumably symbolizing the capacity to sprout wings at a crucial moment). The "Dolphin" club was for people who had been rescued from inflatable rafts in the ocean.

Shortly after arriving at the hospital, I was told that my name had been included in a list of wounded servicemen invited to meet the King at a garden party at Buckingham Palace. The surgeons concluded, however, that my fractured and wired-up jaw would not benefit from the long trip to London, and so I was not permitted to go. Royal garden parties for the wounded were a frequent thing, I gathered.

I was informed one day by the RAF doctor that the engineer from Teddington had called to inquire about my progress. He added that it had been decided to grant me a couple of days' leave to visit the engineer and his family in London, as they seemed anxious to have me as a guest. I declined the offer and decided that the time had come to clarify things. I wrote a letter to the daughter and tactfully pointed out that I liked her and hoped and expected that she would find the right person for her very soon, and so on.

Wroughton hospital was situated on the edge of the downs. A short walk from the hospital took one up to a ridge, from which a spectacular landscape could be seen in every direction. I went there often—perching on the ridge, surveying the scene, and listening to the faint sounds from distant farms. The peace that lay over all of this seemed timeless. It was as if the war had ended years before and left little visible trace. Just the hospital itself and a number of abandoned bombers arrayed in an aircraft park offered reminders of what had actually happened.

We had entertainers at the hospital. During the war, an entertainment service, known as ENSA (Entertainers National Service Association) had been formed. It consisted of performers from every level of the entertainment world—theater, vaudeville, opera, and music hall. A troupe came to the hospital while I was there. One of the nurses wheeled me to the auditorium, as I was not yet ambulatory; she left me with a promise to return at the end of the show. The show was terrible. Bad singing, comedians equipped only with dirty jokes, a magician whose tricks never quite came out right, a dog that walked upright and stumbled on and off a little stool, and other such events comprised the program. Unhappily, it was clear that the performers were trying very hard and could do no better.

The audience gradually became restless. Grumbling, sotto voce at first, became louder and persistent. Finally, after one of the comedians had made a particularly obscene joke, an airman patient rose from his chair. Supported by his crutch, he limped to the stage, reached in his pocket, drew out a penny, and threw it down in front of the performer. He turned silently and slowly limped out of the hall. Within minutes, other patients did the same. As the hall began to empty, the entertainers became frantic with embarrassment. The jokes came faster and louder. A juggler, who had been mildly popular with the audience, hurried back to the stage to repeat his act, but it was too late. The patients had decided that they had been insulted and were not to be mollified. I felt sympathy for both sides of this little tragedy—for the entertainers who could do no better and must endure the humiliation of this rejection, and for the patients who had their own pains and deserved better. I wheeled myself back to the ward alone.

Toward the end of the summer of 1945, I was transferred to the Royal Naval Auxiliary Hospital (RNAH) in Sherborne, Dorset, mainly for convalescent recovery before ultimate transfer to Park Prewett Hospital near Basingstoke, Hampshire, for plastic surgery.

Royal Naval Auxiliary Hospital, Sherborne

RNAH was commanded by a surgeon-captain. He maintained the disciplines of the Navy as much as hospital circumstances allowed. From time to time, he did ward rounds. The beds were smoothed, and smoothed again, by the nurses, lockers were lined up, and the patients who were able were required to lie "at attention"—body straight and arms down by the sides. The surgeon-captain passed from bed to bed with some minor comment to each of us. His comments were rarely of a medical nature. More often than not, he solicited our opinions about the oil paintings that hung on the walls. He had done them himself (we had been warned in advance) and evidenced a minor talent for Scottish glens populated by arthritic deer, with an occasional clansman in what appeared to be a checkered café tablecloth around his waist. We expressed great enthusiasm for these paintings.

There were no plastic surgeons at Sherborne and therefore nothing much for me to do except figure out ways to pass the time. I did have one or two minor operations to remove lingering bone fragments from my jaw, but my chief occupation was waiting. During this period, I completed an embroidered naval crest, which I still have. It was either that or make a felt elephant stuffed with kapok. Having noted the pathetic consequences of the latter choice in the tortured products of some of my fellow patients who had opted for the elephant, I think that I made the better choice.

Mac came down from Cambridge to visit me on one occasion. It was a somewhat laborious trip for him, and I was grateful that he made the effort to do so. We went into the town of Sherborne and drank draft cider at one of the pubs. Somehow, the time passed unnoticed until the pub closed at 2300. Hospital "pipe down" time was 2130, so I was now out illegally. When returning after hours, it was advisable to find some way into the hospital other than the front gate. The wards were all on the ground floor, and each had a day room at the end, with French windows opening to a grassy lawn. The solution to the problem of getting into the hospital unobserved was to climb over the fence, open a window to the day room of my ward, climb in, and tiptoe quietly to bed. I followed this plan. All went smoothly until I opened the window and met a flashlight shining in my eyes. The nursing sister, of course, had noticed that my bed was empty and simply waited to apprehend the offender. After a scolding, she commented that there seemed to be no good reason to report this, and she did not.

The incident served to exacerbate my frustration with waiting at Sherborne for the crucial surgery that was to be done elsewhere. I had inquired about this frequently, only to be told that Park Prewett was full and that I was on a waiting list. I decided that I would resort to the permitted step of sending in a request to Commander-in-Chief, Portsmouth, to state my grievance and request some action. This step was not something to be undertaken lightly, as the request itself had to be endorsed and forwarded by the superior officer, in this case the surgeon-captain, about whom I was complaining. When I submitted my complaint, the surgeon-captain called me in and asked me in an unfriendly way whether I really wished to send this petition through to Portsmouth. I told him that I did. He dismissed me, and I went back to the ward.

Within the hour, the ward sister came up to me. "Pack your bags immediately. You are leaving for Park Prewett today. There is a train from Sherborne about an hour from now, and a driver will take you to the station."

I shook hands with my fellow patients, packed my bags, and got into the waiting car. The Wren driver looked at her watch. The train was coming into Sherborne in a few minutes, and we would miss it. Our best chance to catch it was at the town of Milborne Port, a few miles up the line. She drove at great speed through the leafy lanes and pulled up at the little station just as the trained pulled in. Onto the train in a rush, I settled in and was gone from Sherborne forever. The "waiting list" had seemingly shortened dramatically; my complaint was duly consigned to the surgeon-captain's wastebasket.

Rooksdown House, Park Prewett Hospital

The transfer to Park Prewett took place some time in the autumn of 1945. Park Prewett was the main plastic surgery center for officers and men of the Royal Navy and Army. The RAF had had a separate hospital for this purpose since the first casualties of the Battle of Britain in 1940.

The plastic surgery unit was in Rooksdown House. This building stood on a small hill and was surrounded by trees, which (somewhat to my surprise) were home to flocks of rooks. The high ceilings and large windows of the wards, the views across the green-and-gold patchwork of the Hampshire countryside, and the cawing of rooks created an atmosphere redolent of a long weekend at a country house. Rooksdown House was self-contained. It had an operating theater and associated technical rooms, plus a number of small wards, a dayroom, and a kitchen. Many of the patients had been at Rooksdown for some years; the processes of plastic surgery and recovery involved very long periods of time.

The head of the unit and chief surgeon was Sir Harold Gillies, one of the two best-known plastic surgeons in Britain at the time (the other was McIndoe at the RAF Hospital in Sussex). Gillies was a pioneer in some of the newest techniques of that era. He was surrounded by a corps of surgeons who were his associates and, to a significant extent, his students. Although some of these surgeons held naval or other military rank, none wore uniforms while on duty at Rooksdown. Gillies, so the story ran, had decided that none of the nursing staff should be drawn from military units, as he felt that they were unduly impressed with the need for discipline. Hence, the nurses had been recruited from the nursing schools at Westminster Hospital, Guy's Hospital, and other components of the Medical School of the University of London.

A New Zealander of Scottish origins, Gillies was a keen fly-fisherman and an equally keen, but rather bad, painter. He took time to explain to the patient exactly what was going to be done, why it would be done, and what might go wrong. Before my first operation, he sat on the edge of my bed with a pencil and pad and drew a sketch of the proposed surgery. He instilled complete confidence in his skill and honesty. I had to admit to a lack of interest in fly-fishing when he asked me. He was a trifle disappointed because he liked to come into the ward and persuade one of the patients to join him in casting a line down the long corridor outside the ward. The hook end occasionally got tangled up on the nursing sister's desk, but Gillies was very popular and these incidents were taken in good part. Years later, I came across his obituary in a journal of plastic surgery at the Countway Medical Library at Harvard University.

Burn patients were treated by a process whereby a rectangular flap of undamaged skin, called a peduncle, was cut along three sides, with the fourth side still attached to the body. The flap was stitched together into a sausage-shaped tube. The end of the tube was then angled over and stitched to a prepared slit a little distance away. When the stitched end had firmly healed into the slit, the first hinged end was cut and the whole tubular tissue bent over to a new slit. In this way, the healthy skin was turned end over end until it reached the area of burned skin that was to be replaced. For some patients, the process required transferring the peduncle in this way from one part of the body to another remote part.

For example, it was sometimes necessary to bind an arm, from which healthy skin could be obtained, to the shoulder or part of the chest that was to receive it. This meant that a patient's arm might be attached immovably to his chest for a number of weeks before the peduncle would "take." Patients crouched in contorted positions were not unusual at Rooksdown.

In my case, one goal of surgery was to redistribute some facial fatty and muscular tissue to fill out my face in the area where a very deep scar cleft it. The surgeons also repaired the scarred jaw muscles that had created my mouth-opening problem. Finally, there was the task of getting the healed jaw muscles to flex enough to permit opening my mouth. By Rooksdown standards, my case was truly minor.

A photographic museum, which displayed "before" and "after" pictures, was located in the main medical offices. Although the first sight of the "before" pictures was unnerving, the net effect was quite encouraging, even inspiring, to the new patient viewing them. Many of these transformations were incredible, but they often had taken many months or even years to achieve. Some patients had been in the hospital so long that their wives and children had moved to Basingstoke to be near them. Which brings me to Ivor.

When I arrived at Rooksdown, I was assigned to a ward that contained three other patients. Ivor, a Royal Navy aviator, was in the bed next to mine. He had been at Rooksdown for more than two years. His fighter plane had crash-dived into the ground at a naval airfield in Cornwall when its engine failed in midflight. He had been unable to bail out and was still strapped in the cockpit when his plane hit the ground and burst into flame. When rescuers pulled him out of the plane, he was unconscious and badly burned over nearly all of his body. Apparently, the naval surgeons at the air base decided that he could not survive for more than a few hours and placed him on a bed of ice cubes in the morgue. His parents and his fiancée were sent for; the plane crash had occurred shortly before the date for his wedding.

Miraculously, the naval doctors had been mistaken. Somehow, Ivor survived. He was moved from the morgue to a ward, and his burns were treated. When he was ready to travel, he was sent to Rooksdown and Harold Gillies. The only parts of Ivor's body that were not burned were an X-shaped area where his parachute harness and seat belt had pressed against his thighs and upper body and part of the top of his head that had been covered by his flying helmet. Every other part of his body surface was a mass of angry red, with convoluted scars and patches. He had lost one eye, which had been replaced with a glass eye. His eyebrows and eyelids had been scorched away. The disfigurement of his face and features was total.

When Ivor was first allowed to see himself in a mirror not long after he was injured, he became convinced that he should break his engagement and spare his fiancée the difficult, but inevitable, task of getting out of a marriage to somebody now so horrifying in appearance. He withdrew from the engagement, but his fiancée did not. She moved to Basingstoke, found employment as a teacher (they were both graduates of a teacher's college and had met as students), and set to work to convince him that her love for him did not depend on his looks.

Not long before I came to Rooksdown House, they were married in a ceremony held on the ward, in the presence of their families, friends, and most of the hospital staff. His wife came to the ward every evening and had become a kind of sister to all of the long-term patients. She was at my bedside when I came out of the anesthesia after my first operation; she was holding a spout-cup of orange juice to my mouth.

Ivor and I struck up a friendship. A symbolic development occurred in our friendship when he abruptly asked me one day if I would care to see a photograph of him as he had been before his injuries. He showed me a studio photograph taken when he had first graduated as a sub-lieutenant pilot proud of his stripe and his wings; he had been strikingly handsome. When he spoke about this time in his life, his voice had a rending mixture of nostalgic pride and agony of regret over something so much a part of his youth that had been destroyed so soon and beyond any hope of return.

Ivor had taken very little leave during his time in the hospital, partly because he was having so many operations and partly because his looks made him apprehensive about venturing out into the world. His fears were not baseless. On one occasion, four of us—Ivor, two other disfigured patients, and myself—went to Basingstoke to do some shopping, go to the cinema, and have tea in a restaurant. Most passersby glanced at him and quickly looked away. One couple was quite taken aback by the sight; however, the woman turned to her companion with the audible remark: "They ought to keep them in the hospital. It's not right that they let them go out in public looking like that."

After I had known Ivor for some time, I was given a few days' leave to go home. I think that it was near Christmas time, and Ivor had been given leave also. His wife had left a few days earlier to return to their home district of Yorkshire and help both sets of parents get ready for the holiday. Ivor asked me which train I planned to take from Basingstoke to London and what day I would be taking it. When I told him, he said that he had been planning to do the same and perhaps we could travel up together. The evening before our departure, one of the nurses asked him why he had delayed going on leave for a day; he was entitled to have left that morning. He gave some excuse, and I pretended not to hear. He did not want to travel in a compartment of strangers and had delayed leaving so that we would be together.

On the train, he talked about his future. His operations would be finished soon, and he would be discharged from the Navy. He hoped that he and his wife could obtain teaching positions together in a village school in some remote part of the country, preferably the Yorkshire dales, but any isolated place would do. Such a school would require no more than two teachers and have few pupils. He thought that, in due time, a small rural community would come to accept his appearance. We parted ways at Waterloo Station. Soon after my holiday leave, I returned to the Navy for duty and did not see Ivor again.

Another patient at Rooksdown House whom I remember well was Gus, an Army captain, who was in the same ward with Ivor and me. Gus had been hit in the lower face by a fragment of antitank shell at the battle of El-Alamein in North Africa. He had been undergoing repair surgery for a long time; it had been necessary to reconstruct his mouth, lips, and other features, and Gus was still very disfigured. During the time that I was at Rooksdown House, Gus became engaged to one of the nurses. He was still a patient when I was discharged in 1947, and I do not know what happened to him afterward.

Yet another patient, a Royal Navy commander, had been badly burned when a plane crashed into the bridge of his aircraft carrier and he was splashed with flaming gasoline. His face and hands were both scarred. He had great difficulty shaving, and I fell into the habit of shaving him from time to time when matters became especially unpleasant for him.

An Army brigadier, a member of Parliament, was also a fellow patient. I don't know what injuries had brought him to Park Prewett. He was friendly but preoccupied; much of his time was spent in writing letters to his constituents.

Among our number was an Irish civilian, whose case seemed to be very mysterious. He was housed in a private room, and the nurses never discussed him with anybody. Finally, when I had become a kind of regular resident, one of the nurses mentioned that he had been admitted for a sex modification operation—very unusual in those days. He had developed some characteristics of both sexes and wished to be unambiguously male. I chatted with him on a few occasions, but he was naturally reticent about the reasons for his presence in the hospital.

In peacetime, Park Prewett had been a psychiatric hospital. By 1945, many of the buildings had been restored to this use and a number of psychiatric patients had returned. They lived in large pavilions that were spread out around the grounds. Each pavilion had an open space for exercise that was surrounded by an iron railing. One day, Ivor, two other seriously burned patients, and I took a stroll around the grounds. We came to one of the recently reoccupied pavilions, where the patients were at exercise. They shambled along in a serpentine line, eyes on the ground for the most part, some mumbling loudly to themselves, all seeming to us very strange indeed. We approached the railing to see them more clearly. First one patient and then a few more came up to the railing to look at us. We peered at each other. A group of badly disfigured men gazed in wonder at the oddities of the psychiatric patients, and they, in turn, gazed at us and wondered at an even odder and more desperate-looking lot. Many years later, I saw the movie *King of Hearts*; it revived the memory and the drama of the scene and the ironies of our respective views.

Like the "Caterpillar" and "Dolphin" clubs, there was a "Rooksdown" club for everybody who had plastic surgery there. Membership was indicated by a metal lapel button bearing a black rook with extended wings. At Rooksdown House itself, the club was really a framework for arranging the occasional social events organized for the patients. There were dances, of which I can remember only one. It was a costume dance held in a large recreation room. Some of the patients decided to use their disfigurements to create the costume effect. One man who had lost an arm and a leg came as a pirate with hook and wooden leg. Ivor was a pirate with a patch over his missing eye. Others, who were badly burned or scarred, dressed up as Frankenstein, vampires, and other ghoulish creatures. The band played lively tunes, and the nurses danced with the patients. The whole scene had a kind of cheerfully macabre aspect, in which the courageous optimism of the patients defied the damage that they had suffered.

At Rooksdown House, I had three rounds of surgery; each required an interval of recuperation. At such times, I was returned for extended periods to the Navy. During the first interval, I served at RNB Chatham.

Royal Naval Barracks, Chatham

With the war over, life at RNB Chatham (HMS "Pembroke") had returned slowly and partially to peacetime routine. My last service in the barracks had been the short gunnery course that had preceded my entry to Lochinvar. The excited anticipation of those days had vanished. Men returning from sea to be discharged were housed in barracks until the paperwork was completed and they could return to civilian life. Although their time in the barracks would be brief, something had to be done to occupy them. I appeared to be indefinitely available for whatever duties that might occur to the commander of the barracks. My first direct acquaintance with him was not promising.

When I had arrived at the RNAH in Sherborne, I still lacked a regulation naval uniform. The one that I had been wearing when I was wounded was shredded and bloodstained. I arrived at Wroughton dressed in Canadian Army pajamas and my naval cap. The authorities at the hospital issued me with an RAF battle dress, and one of the nurses managed to find a Royal Navy shoulder flash, which she sewed on the jacket. The uniform was totally unauthorized but served its purpose. It had excited curiosity among the RAF patients in the hospital who assumed that I must have been a member of some highly secret naval unit that had collaborated with the RAF.

When I went back into the disciplinary arms of the Navy at Sherborne, it became incumbent on me to get a uniform. I was able to get a naval officer's working rig, a navy blue battle dress, from the hospital, but I had to order a dress uniform from a tailor. In the town of Sherborne, a tailor advertised his status as an approved tailor of naval and military uniforms. His window was largely occupied by hunting jackets and other riding apparel, but the display included an Army captain's uniform of World War I design, with the "pips" of rank on the cuff, rather than on the shoulder strap as currently required. An interesting museum piece, I thought.

After being measured, I ordered a new uniform from this tailor and paid him a deposit. It would take him some weeks to make it, and before it was finished I was moved to Park Prewett. The tailor sent me a letter saying that the uniform was ready and requesting a check for the remainder of his bill. When the package with the uniform came, I opened it but did not try on the uniform. At Rooksdown House, I had little need for a uniform. During the long period covered by these events, my kit from *ML137* finally caught up with me. It contained my second, slightly worn blue uniform, which was good enough for going out around Basingstoke.

The glittering new uniform reposed in its box until I arrived at RNB Chatham. Here, I was required to appear in "No. 1" rig on parade. I put on the uniform and, to my horror, discovered that it had been made from a World War I pattern—a double-breasted reefer jacket, high across the chest, generally worn with a wing collar and small black bow tie—that once had been de rigeur for naval officers. The general effect resembled the drawing of Sir Thomas Lipton on Lipton's tea packets. I had no choice but to wear the uniform on parade. The barracks commander inspected me very closely, but silently, as he moved down the ranks. I breathed a sigh of relief.

After the parade was dismissed, I returned to my office and found a message waiting that instructed me to call the barracks commander. When I did, he explained icily that it was unacceptable in his barracks for an officer to appear on parade in theatrical costume. He demanded an explanation for this misdemeanor. I described the circumstances and detected a mixture of coughing and choking at the other end of the phone. In a pleasanter, but less coherent tone, he told me to leave the barracks immediately and go into Chatham to order a new uniform for delivery as soon as possible. I was to find other duties to keep me off the parade until such time as the new uniform was available.

A naval town for more than two centuries, Chatham had an ample supply of naval tailors who were accustomed to emergencies. Forty-eight hours later, I was able to turn up at morning parade again. I returned the "theatrical costume" to its box and took it home to Manchester. It finally disappeared without a trace. I imagine that my father gave it away to some seemingly deserving person, an act of charity that he tended to perform from time to time, usually without prior consultation.

Barracks routine had resumed the rituals of peacetime. One of these was weekly Mess Night, with a formal dinner, held on Thursdays. Attendance was expected, except for officers on duty. Best uniform and black bow tie with wing collar were required, and formalities of rank were scrupulously observed. The first lieutenant of the *Jason* would have been instantly at home. An admiral or a commodore, other senior officers, and the chaplain were at the head table. The rest of us, one hundred or so, sat at very long tables running the length of the room. On the walls were large, darkened oil paintings of old naval battles—Camperdown, The Saints, Trafalgar, The Nile. Three-decker men-of-war, shrouded in billowing white smoke, blasted broadsides at each other. Broken masts lay over ships' sides, the sea was rough, the skies cloudy with an ominous red telling of blood and fire. In the foreground, a few survivors invariably clung desperately to floating timbers. The details varied, but the theme did not.

Starched and white-coated stewards stood arrayed behind the tables. They wore a faint look of pained disdain, such as might be seen on the face of a professional jockey watching an amateur about to mount a horse for the first time. Their betters were about to embarrass themselves in the matter of fish knives, finger bowls, and other implements, and the stewards knew it.

Dinner began with a grace offered by the chaplain. At the long tables, we watched the high table, alert for the moment at which the senior officer put soup spoon to lips. When this happened, we were free to do the same. This ritual was repeated for each course. After dessert, a silence fell. From the high table came the message: "Gentlemen, you may smoke." This meant that the senior flag officer was getting ready to withdraw to the large lounge/smoking room, always known as the Anteroom. When he retired to the Anteroom, we were free to go there, too, or to leave the mess, as we felt inclined.

Mess Night had been reintroduced not long before I came to Chatham. The constant coming and going of officers from sea on their way to discharge from the Navy meant that the performance was always new to some proportion of the diners present. The first time that I attended Mess Night, there came that point at which plates of dessert fruit were laid out along the tables and finger bowls, complete with tiny napkins, placed before each plate. Several schools of thought emerged about the proper approach to this stage of the meal. The stewards waited and watched with impassive faces and bated breath.

The first diner to take the plunge reached for an apple, washed it carefully in the finger bowl, dried it with the napkin, and bit into the apple. He made some immediate converts, who followed suit. A second tack was taken by a trawler skipper of independent mind, who simply took the finger bowl and drank the water in it. A sophisticate dipped the tips of his fingers delicately into the water, dried them somewhat daintily with the napkin, and sat back waiting for the meal to come to its formal end. It was transparently clear to most of us that this was a truly ridiculous response to the situation; looks of derisive incredulity spread across our faces. Nobody's fingers were dirty, and a little cold water and a napkin were quite inadequate to wash them anyway. The silent stewards had had their entertainment and could count on it again in the weeks to come.

For some reason, naval ratings, who otherwise were likely to be publicly cynical about impractical ideas, were nonetheless prone to believing in ghosts. RNB Chatham had a ghostly visitor. One of the sentries patrolling the ramparts at night returned hurriedly to the guardroom to say that he had seen and heard a ghost. The apparition was described as being dressed in the naval uniform of Nelson's day and walking with a crutch and a wooden leg. The leg made audible thumping sounds as the spirit approached. There was much immediate interest in this report. The petty officer of the guard was alleged to have spit tobacco juice and resumed reading a magazine, but others in the guardroom went out to see for themselves. Conflicting opinions were expressed about having "seen something vague and ghostly that gave me the shivers," but there was unanimity on the sound of the wooden leg. In the course of subsequent inquiries into this strange affair, a plumber pointed out that there had been considerable trouble with a knocking in the stream pipes of the barracks heating system; the problem still existed at the time of the ghostly sailor's visit. The reality of the "thumping" was scarcely in doubt, but the visual part of the sentry's experience seemed more dubious. Events of this kind almost always found their way into the press, and this one did. The journalists preferred the sentry's version to the plumber's.

A duty officer was responsible for dealing with emergencies as they arose. These included possible fires (there was a barracks fire department), injuries, and discipline cases. In order to ensure our alertness, the barracks commander called drills at any time of the night or day, his preference being for night drills. His particular favorite was the emergency fire drill. Calling this in the middle of the night not only allowed him to make sure that the duty officer was alert, but it also prevented the duty fire party from sleeping in the fire station. These calls came to the duty officer by telephone: "Fire on the third floor in Nelson block" (each accommodation block was named after a famous naval person) or in some other location. A record was kept of how many minutes it took for the fire engine and crew to reach the hypothetical blaze. If the time was deemed too long, rebukes were issued to all concerned, especially to the duty officer and the duty petty officer and the duty petty officer in charge of the fire party.

The latter duty was rotated among the petty officers, and they all understood that the petty officer in charge of the commander's office would call ahead to let us know in advance where and when the "fire" was going to happen. Forewarned, the fire party and engine moved into the shadows nearest the designated target a short time before the expected emergency. When the call came, the duty officer answered it, called the firehouse, and then proceeded rapidly to the site of the imaginary fire. In the meantime, a runner from the firehouse dashed to the waiting firemen, who now had only a few yards to drive to get to the scene. Our times were always phenomenally brief and drew suspicious praise from the commander. I sometimes wondered what would happen to a fire crew if a real fire occurred. They would certainly get there promptly but could hardly hope to equal the speed with which we handled imaginary fires.

Another duty, briefly, was that of funeral officer. We had quite a few funerals—the barracks was large, there was a naval hospital nearby, and many ships were at anchor or in the dockyard itself. The occasion that I remember most vividly was when three newly conscripted young sailors, crew members of a frigate in the anchorage, had drowned. During bad weather, they were stranded ashore because they were too drunk and too late to catch the last liberty boat back to their ship. They decided to steal a small rowboat and make it back by themselves. The boat capsized in the heavy seas. The sailors could not swim, and they all drowned. Their bodies washed up a few days later. Each sailor was of a slightly different Christian faith, and hence there were three separate funerals, each with a different undertaker.

I was provided with a party of about forty "mourners," sailors wearing black armbands and carrying reversed rifles; a Royal Marine bugler; and a naval firing party. We went by truck to the cemetery and waited for the first hearse. The undertaker's man was already waiting for us, and I went over the arrangements with him. The hearse arrived, a selection of eight sailor mourners lifted the coffin onto their shoulders and the chaplain led the way. The parents walked directly behind the coffin. There was no one else present who had known the dead men because their ship had already gone to sea. The slow-marching group of sailors and I followed the parents.

The prayers were said and the coffin lowered into the grave. After the rifle shots were fired and the bugler played the long sad notes of "Last Post," the parents turned to me. They thought that I must be an officer from their son's ship and could say something to them about him. I did so. I said that he was a fine sailor, that he was much admired by his shipmates and officers, and that his service and his loss were as much of a sacrifice for the victory that had been gained as if he had died in action. We shook hands, and they slowly walked to the waiting car. I have sometimes wondered if they ever knew the truth. It was the same with the other two funerals. When the last was gone, we got into the truck and drove back to the barracks.

RNB Chatham, with its dockyards and barracks, was permanently closed in 1984. Some of the buildings remain, but others were demolished, and most of the grounds were sold. One of the oldest barracks, Chatham had been one of the main centers (for a long time *the* main center) for the Navy since it opened in 1588.

A Slow Way to Tipperary

At some time in 1946—dates are a little vague at this point—I was given home leave, including permission to spend part of it in Ireland at my maternal grandmother's home, Three Bridges House near Carrick-on-Suir in the County Tipperary. My parents were particularly anxious that I do this. I had lost a lot of weight. Food was plentiful in Ireland but still rationed in Britain, and the plan was that I would spend some time at Three Bridges where they would "feed me up." I took the boat train to Holyhead in Anglesey, North Wales. At the pier, there was a changing room where Irishmen in the British service left their uniforms in lockers and were issued civilian suits for visits to what was a neutral country. Germany and Japan had both been defeated, but for some technical reason there was still a "state of war" and uniformed servicemen were liable to be interned if they entered a neutral country. As an officer, I was entitled to possess civilian clothes and so the locker system did not apply to me. I packed my uniform into a suitcase, changed into civvies, and boarded the boat for Dun Laoghaire (or Kingstown, as it was still generally called). At the other end of the voyage, the Irish customs officer opened the suitcase, eyed my uniform, closed the case, and said "Have a good leave, sir," and I was on my way. So much for the danger of internment.

I stayed overnight in Dublin at a small hotel near Stephens Green and went to Kingsbridge Station the next morning to take a train to Carrick-on-Suir. Ireland was short of coal during the war and for some years afterward, and people had taken to burning peat for many purposes in addition to their traditional cottage fires. At the platform stood two trains. One, the Killarney Express, was beautiful. A green locomotive with polished brass trim stood at the head of a train of glistening passenger carriages. Through the windows of the dining car, I could see the tables, bright white cloths, waiters at the ready, menu cards in little silver holders—all in all, a tempting sight.

I was about to board the train when a small, wizened porter came up to me and said, "Where are ye bound for, sir?"

"I'm going to Carrick by way of Limerick Junction on this train."

"Take my advice," said the little man, "don't get on that train. It'll never get there. Take this train here." He pointed to a small grimy engine and dilapidated carriages, the kind of train that stopped at every village.

Something about his tone must have affected me. I found myself giving him a tip and getting aboard the stop-everywhere train. Settling into a window seat, I felt rather foolish. A few minutes later, the whistle of the Killarney Express shrieked, steam poured from the pistons, and the train began to glide smoothly out of Kingsbridge. A mountain of peat blocks filled the coal tender. Contented faces gazed at me from the dining car as it passed slowly by. The waiters were serving breakfast, and I thought that I could smell the rashers of bacon and other good things that the passengers were about to eat. A survey of my own surroundings revealed dust-sodden seats and faded sepia photographs—one of Dublin Bay in the late Victorian period and another of somebody hanging upside down over the ramparts of Blarney Castle and kissing the Blarney Stone.

After several jerks and stops, my train groaned into action and left the station. One station followed another until we left Dublin completely behind. We began to pick up a little speed and slowed down only when we passed the Killarney Express stopped on the rails. Anemic wisps of steam came from its piston boxes. The diners were still in the dining car, although some had descended to the track to discuss the problem with the engine driver. A fireman was frantically throwing blocks of peat into the faint glow of the firebox. I settled back in my seat as we left the green glory behind. The parting words of the porter came back to me, a whispered comment as he pocketed the tip: "The Killarney Express always runs out of steam. You can count on it."

At Three Bridges, the injunction that I was to be fed heartily was taken seriously. I slept in the master bedroom, the one in which my grandfather, Michael Vincent Power, had slept and finally died. It was a big four-poster laden with quilts and eiderdowns. Each morning, Molly Murphy, the maid, came in with a breakfast tray filled with good things and one bad thing, a black blood pudding. Black puddings had always filled me with dismay and perplexity—dismay at taste and texture, and perplexity that anyone had ever thought it good to create them. What to do with them was the problem. After Molly withdrew, I climbed out of bed, opened a window, and hurled the offending delicacy some distance into the ornamental bushes bordering the front of the house. Undetected, I returned to bed to begin breakfast.

What a fool I was. My grandmother was surprised and delighted that I clearly liked black puddings. There was not a crumb left on the plate when the tray came down to the kitchen. Obviously, I was a black pudding fan of some capacity. Next morning, two of them were on the tray. They suffered the same fate—I was a slow learner. Morning three came, with two more of the odious objects; this time, I left a little fragment of one of them on the plate. The daily offering stabilized at two; each day one and three quarters of them joined their predecessors in the bushes. Surely, those bushes must have grown greener over the years.

This was a brief period away from the Navy and away from anything reminiscent of war. Ireland had benefited from neutrality. Many men and women had gone to Britain to work in the war industries. Although some of their countrymen at home had half-hoped for a German victory on the basis of a wish for some kind of historic revenge on the British, many thousands of Irishmen had joined the British forces, and many had died. By 1946, it was clear what Nazi Germany had been, and Irishmen with earlier pro-German sentiments were now rather quiet about them.

The two weeks passed quickly, and I was soon on my way back to Chatham and the Navy. From RNB Chatham, I returned to Rooksdown House for the second in my series of surgical operations. While recuperating from this surgery, the Navy assigned me to HMS Laughing Water in Kent.

HMS Laughing Water, Cobham, Kent

HMS Laughing Water lay on both sides of the main road from London to Dover, the road taken by young David Copperfield on his way to Aunt Betsy after he escaped from the blacking factory in London. Laughing Water consisted of a group of Nissen huts, a parade ground, a ratings' canteen and other bare essentials of barracks life. It was used to house and train newly drafted cooks, stewards, and other dayman branches of the Navy. A staff of petty officers provided the training.

As an officer in the Seaman Branch, I had nothing much to do with training other than to conduct occasional inspections and deal with such disciplinary matters as might arise. Out of curiosity, I did attend one of the classes, in which future stewards were being taught how to carve a chicken. Chickens were in short supply, and no actual chickens were provided. Instead, a set of rather faded and scratched papier-mâché chickens was employed. They were made in "slices" that could be assembled together to produce an unconvincing facsimile of the real thing. Under the watchful eye of the petty officer, the recruit steward placed a carving knife into the narrow space between one slice and the next and removed the pin that joined them. Lo and behold, a perfect slice fell flat on the platter. This continued until the "chicken" was completely sliced.

At one point, two of the recruits requested permission to fight each other under the "grudge fight" rules of the Navy. The Navy strictly forbade any fighting between men but provided a kind of safety valve through the grudge fight. The fight had to be with gloves, Queensberry rules, with a petty officer as referee and an officer to stop the fight if it was getting too bloody. I was required to perform that function on this occasion. The one special rule was that there were no rounds—once the fight started, it was to continue until one man or the other conceded defeat, was knocked out, or the fight was stopped.

A large crowd of off-duty men formed a ring. The two combatants attacked each other with great swinging blows, mostly missing but some hitting. Both noses began to bleed, but the vigor of the initial onslaught had used up most of the combatants' available energy. In a few minutes, the blows were falling slowly and weakly, and both men were breathing hard. The crowd was disappointed and began to drift away. Neither combatant would admit defeat, but, finally, neither had the energy to lift his arms. I looked at the referee, he nodded, and we stopped the fight. The referee then declared both men to be winners.

We were visited by ghosts at Laughing Water, too. The village of Cobham in Kent lay about a mile or so from the camp. Cobham had two pubs, the Leather Bottel and the Ship. Dickens described the Leather Bottel in *Pickwick Papers*, thereby giving it a kind of fame. In peacetime, the Leather Bottel had been a landmark for tourists, and, reverting to that after the war, it became a rather "upmarket" inn and restaurant. One of our number, a lieutenant (RNVR) known as Dickey, had been at the camp for some time and was engaged to one of the daughters of the Ship's landlord. Consequently, the Ship became the preferred pub of people at Laughing Water.

On one occasion, Dickey announced a séance planned for that evening in the NAAFI (Navy, Army, and Air Force Institutes) canteen. It was to take place after the canteen had closed. In the spirit of a lark, we accepted the invitation to join in. That evening, in a back room, we sat around a table—three officers, two petty officers, and two or three of the women canteen servers, one of whom was reputed to have mediumistic powers. Fingers touched, and a circle formed. Quite quickly, one of the young women began moaning and mumbling: "There she is again. It's a little girl in white. She says she was murdered here years ago." She said much more in the same vein and then collapsed in a kind of faint. The more

veteran of the petty officers, a stoker, also collapsed. The séance broke up. We tried primitive first aid on the fainting casualties—fresh air through an open window and much slapping of the face—and they revived. Feeling rather foolish, we trooped back to the wardroom. Unfortunately, news of this event was soon part of the gossip at the Ship and then percolated throughout the village of Cobham. Somehow, a London tabloid got hold of the story, and it hit the newspapers with sensational headlines, "Naval séance discovers evidence of long-forgotten murder," or words to that effect.

The Admiralty was not long getting into the act. Our commanding officer (a career officer) received a memorandum, which was distributed to all of us. It ran something like this:

From: The Second Sea Lord.
To: Commanding Officer, HMS Laughing Water.
Subject: Appearance of ghosts on HM ships.

Their Lordships' attention has been drawn to reports of a recent visitation by a ghost or ghosts to HM ship under your command. They view this report with displeasure. You are hereby instructed to prohibit all such visitations from now on.

The war was effectively over, and the coastal areas had been opened up for travel again. Motor coaches came down the road quite frequently and generally stopped at a pub in one of the nearby villages if it was lunchtime. The camp itself had the traditional designations of areas as the quarterdeck, fo'c'sle, and so forth. On one occasion, the sentry at the main gate telephoned me to say that there was a problem for which he needed some orders. When I reached the sentry box, he drew himself to attention, saluted on his rifle butt, and said, "I wish to report that some ladies are making water on the quarterdeck, sir." The quarterdeck in question, on the other side of the road, was an area containing some huts fringed at the roadside by a dense screen of bushes. The ladies had disappeared into these bushes when the motor coach driver had accommodated their need for a rest stop. The conversation was loud enough that their purpose had become clear to the sentry.

"Get over to the quarterdeck," I said, "and ask them to leave. You are the sentry and it is your duty to prevent unauthorized visitors to the ship that you are guarding."

"Aye, aye, sir," he said, with visible discomfort. His rifle and bayonet at the attack position, he crossed the road and headed for the bushes. It was only a minute or two before there were loud squeals and some giggling. The sentry returned, his face red.

"Well," I asked him, "Did you get them to leave?"

"Not exactly, sir. They were unfortunately situated, and I had to withdraw. They said they'd leave when they were finished."

The sound of the motor coach starting up terminated our conversation. The guilty parties departed with much laughter, smiles, and waves at the unfortunate sentry. Ignoring them, he stood stoically at his post like a Roman soldier at the ruin of Pompeii.

At some point during my time in Laughing Water, I acquired Smith. Smith was a small-sized whitish puppy. One of the ratings reported that a pup had been left behind in a hut after its owner had been discharged from the Navy and that it seemed very sick. I arranged for the dog to be taken to a veterinarian. The dog was returned to me, together with a bill for the treatment. I paid the bill and discovered that, willy-nilly, the dog was now mine. I called him Smith as a kind of feeble joke, the idea being that, whenever I called "Smith," several people were bound to respond.

Smith slept in a box at the foot of my bed. He soon became a pet of the whole camp and was grossly overfed, overpetted, and generally spoiled. I had been careful to keep Smith out of the wardroom, but, once in a while, he found his way in and headed for the stewards' pantry where good things were to be had. The end of that came one evening during a game of billiards involving the commanding officer. As the CO was sighting down the cue to take his shot, an expression of surprise gradually appeared on his face and quickly gave way to mild fury. Smith had peed on his trouser leg, and it was seeping into his shoe.

I admitted that I was the dog's owner, "in a manner of speaking, sir," and was promptly ordered to get rid of him. With the help of some of the ratings, Smith was kept out of sight for the next few days at a safe distance from the wardroom. One of the departing sailors decided that Smith could come home with him; in due course, the sailor left Laughing Water with his kit bag on his shoulder and Smith trotting along on a leash.

One evening, a naval truck carrying an officer and two armed ratings pulled up at the gate. The officer reported that they were transporting cases of documents and other items removed from the headquarters of German Admiral Raeder. The items were on their way to London for analysis; some of them were later used in the Nuremberg trials. As the officer in charge of the escort was under orders to keep this cargo under armed guard at all times, he requested overnight accommodation and a secure placement of the truck under constant guard. We complied with this, of course. The next day, the truck headed toward London and left us a little puffed up by this brief encounter with History with a capital "H."

From Laughing Water, I returned to Rooksdown House for my third and final surgery. During my recuperation, I was assigned to Kitchener Barracks (another satellite of RNB Chatham) as first lieutenant. While at Kitchener, my personal living quarters were in RNB.

Kitchener Barracks

When I was first assigned to Kitchener, the commanding officer was a Lieutenant Thomas, RN, a former commissioned warrant officer who had, as the phrase went, "come aft by the hawse pipe"—that is, he had risen through the ranks from the lower deck. He was due for retirement from the Navy, and this was his last assignment. He lived in Chatham and was free to go home every night.

While at Kitchener, I was promoted to lieutenant in the RNVR on 31 October 1946, my twenty-second birthday. I learned of this promotion when I received a call from the office of Commander of Barracks on 1 November. The caller informed me that the commander wished to point out that I was "once again" improperly dressed—presumably referring to my "theatrical costume" of some months before. Respectfully requesting to be told what was wrong with my uniform now, the answer was that I should have a second stripe on my cuff, and that, when I had added it, the commander would be obliged if I would join him for a drink. Thomas retired soon after, leaving me as senior officer and CO of the barracks.

In Kitchener Barracks, the main problem continued to be how to keep people occupied as they waited for discharge. There really wasn't much in the way of useful work to be done. A few men were assigned to join working parties in the barracks or the naval dockyard, but most were essentially idle. In a discussion with the chief bosun's mate, it came up that a spare billiard table, in storage somewhere, could be placed in the ratings' recreation room (a wooden hut). The weight of the table, however, was more than the floor of the hut would bear, and the floor would need reinforcement. A formal request to have brick or cement pillars placed under the floor where the table legs would be was inevitably refused. In brief, we could have the table, but we couldn't do what was necessary to make it usable.

On my daily trips to and from the main barracks, I had noticed a construction project in progress on naval property. Later, in another casual conversation with the chief bosun's mate, I commented on the small number of bricks that we needed compared with the large number stacked at the construction site, on the ease with which one man might carry one brick under his greatcoat, and on the high probability that somewhere in Kitchener there was a former bricklayer. Less than a week later, the chief reported to me that "further testing of the floor" of the hut indicated that it could now safely bear the weight of the billiard table. The table was delivered and went into instant use. Nothing was ever said, although the brick pillars under the floor were plainly visible from a side view.

Team sports were another way to keep people occupied. We organized soccer and field hockey teams. Although I played on both teams, the high level of skill of the ratings who made up the teams always gave me the strong suspicion that I had been placed on the teams as a gesture of good will. We played teams from other Navy and Army bases in the area and did rather better than worse. The most memorable and violent game was a field hockey contest between Kitchener and a mixed Army team. The latter included two or three brawny women from the Auxiliary Territorial Service (women's Army service). While I was trying to defend our end of the field from a charging Army onslaught, one of the women raised her hockey stick to some height and banged me on the head. The incident interrupted the game at a crucial moment. I was stunned for a few minutes. Returning to consciousness, I looked up at the blue sky and saw several concerned faces peering down at me. Hockey has never appealed to me much since then, not even as a spectator sport.

Kitchener housed a number of newly drafted recruits, in addition to the men awaiting discharge. Although the war was over, the draft, known as the National Service, was still in force. These national servicemen were retained in Kitchener while waiting for sea assignments. They were separated from the men awaiting discharge by the common disdain of the veteran for the recruit.

Naval regulations permitted a rating to complain about food and to request to see the OOD about it. This did not happen very often, and never from the men coming in from wartime sea service. One day, the petty officer of the day knocked at my door to inform me that two national servicemen had objected to the food and wished to lodge a complaint. I asked him to bring in the first one. As he opened the door, both came in. They looked very annoyed. The petty officer ordered the second man to wait outside, but he ignored the order. In chorus, the two complained that the food was "disgusting" and not fit to be given to human beings. I asked them about their length of service. Both had been drafted out of Oxford University as undergraduate students; they had been in the Navy eight weeks and did not like it; and they were counting off, day by day, the eighteen months' service that lay ahead of them. They were articulate and quite confident, even elegant, in manner. The petty officer, standing behind them, looked keenly at me.

I asked them whether they were familiar with the definition of mutiny. They responded "No," with a "what's that got to do with anything" tone.

"Well," I explained, "when two or more ratings combine to make a complaint, in disobedience to the order to do so individually, that is mutiny."

The two men seemed dumbfounded. They had reason to be—I think that the general principle was roughly correct, but I wouldn't have bet money on it. In wartime, I went on to explain, the punishment for mutiny is very serious and can be the death penalty. At that point, both requested permission to withdraw the complaint, which I granted with feigned reluctance, and away they went. The petty officer permitted a smile to cross his face, and the great meal mutiny was over. In fact, the food at Kitchener wasn't bad—much better than *ML137*.

Stephen Crane, in *The Red Badge of Courage*, tells how, during the American Civil War, Union soldiers who had seen battle and those who had not were divided by a gulf. It was expressed in the question, "Have you ever seen the elephant?" Presumably, this was a reference to the Confederate Army (something gray and dangerous). Those who had not seen the elephant were innocent novices and could not cross the gulf until they had personally experienced it. Although we did not use that phrase, the psychological distinction was the same. It was quite independent of rank and formed a tacit bond between officers and men who had seen action.

The two complainants had not "seen the elephant." They had never been to sea in a gale, had never been under fire, had never seen a ship sink beside them. In the eyes of those who had, the petty officers and their messmates with long service, the two recruits were possessed of an inferiority that could be overcome only by having those experiences. Education, accent, and self-confidence had nothing to do with it. The very fact that they complained about the food was further proof that they did not know what naval service was; hence, they had no moral right to be heard.

Night watches as OOD rotated among the three or four officers assigned to Kitchener. In a barracks, the watchkeeping system required that one officer be assigned as OOD for each eight-hour period of the day; the officer on duty from 0001 to 0800 slept in the duty office on a camp bed and was wakened if anything required his presence.

My brother John visited me at Chatham during my time there. He was then a paymaster sub-lieutenant and had just returned from sea duty. We had dinner together in the wardroom. I was duty officer that night, and, after dinner, I departed to spend the night in the guardroom at Kitchener. John slept in my cabin in the officers' quarters at the main barracks. At that time, he had a beard, but I was clean-shaven. The next morning, as was the practice, a Wren steward brought in a cup of morning tea. She was mystified to find a bearded face above the blanket, where just the previous day the face had been clean-shaven. John told me that she left the room and then came back to ask him his name. He told her that it was Maher, which confused her even more. Finally, the petty officer steward was brought in to clear up the confusion.

While Mac was at Cambridge, I managed to invite him to lunch at the RNVR Club (now the Naval Club) on Hill Street in the West End of London. Arriving by cab, he jumped out of it with many whoops and shouts. He was wearing a suit topped by one of the old Thomas Lipton naval caps that his father had given him. The Naval Club was (and still is) rather particular about the behavior and dress of members and their guests. The club could not really object to him, but the other occupants were not happy with the hilarity and decibel count that Mac brought to the dining room.

After Mac graduated from Cambridge, he was taken into a management training scheme by the Lyons Company, a big catering chain in London. The training involved learning the trade from the kitchen up; at some point, he spent a week or two selling ice cream from a tricycle (echoes of the navigation exercise at Lancing). I never found out what happened to him after that. One story was that he had decided to go into the ice-cream business for himself.

During our time together in *ML137*, Mac and I had become good friends. He had experienced a series of crushes on various Wrens encountered at such places as Dover and Portland. One of these was Tatania, a young Czechoslovakian woman who was a Wren at Dover. Mac was often downcast by her apparent indifference to him, but he recovered through a new interest in Helen, a Wren at Plymouth. That interest did not fare much better. When last I saw him, he had no replacement in sight. I hope that something good happened to him.

At Kitchener Barracks, when it was established that my medical treatment had been completed as far as was possible, I was granted discharge leave beginning 2 January 1947. Before I left Kitchener and the Navy, the petty officers invited me to a farewell tot of rum in their mess. At the end of the little ceremony, they gave me an engraved cigarette lighter as a token of appreciation. I left Kitchener with pleasant memories.

At the end of the war, there was a distribution of "prize money." Throughout its history, the Royal Navy had paid the officers and men of its ships who captured enemy vessels (known as "prizes") a sum of money in return for the fact that the Navy acquired ownership of the prize vessels. Captains of warships during the seventeenth, eighteenth, and nineteenth centuries could accumulate sizable personal fortunes if they managed to capture a number of prizes, especially enemy merchant ships filled with cargo. The practice was carried on into World War II, after which it was terminated. During World War II, the Admiralty put all of the prize money into a single fund, which was shared out after the end of the war to all officers and men of the Navy. Shares varied by rank and years of service. Sometime in 1947, I received a check for about £40.

Medals awarded for specific service (i.e., in recognition of acts of bravery or endurance) were given in two ways. After performing a very conspicuous act, an individual was recommended for an award. Such medals (decorations, as they were called) might be given at any time and always to named individuals. After major operations, such as D-Day, the Admiralty awarded a "ration" of decorations to a unit. The senior officer of the unit provided the names of individuals to whom these should be given. Some time after D-Day, the Fifth ML Flotilla was notified of a small ration of decorations. I forget the exact number—perhaps three for the thirty officers, plus ten for the two hundred ratings. Campaign medals were awarded to everybody who had taken part in a particular campaign. For service on D-Day and later, the France and Germany Star was awarded to everybody who had put in at least six months' service in that combat area. At the end of the war, each person who had served in the military forces or in various civilian organizations (such as civil defense, police and fire services) was awarded a Victory medal.

13

Discharge

Goodbye, brothers! You were a good crowd.
As good a crowd
as ever fisted with wild cries the beating canvas of a
heavy
foresail; or tossing aloft, invisible in the night gave
back yell
for yell to a westerly gale.

—JOSEPH CONRAD

On 26 February 1947, I was discharged from active duty in the Navy and appointed to the rank of lieutenant in the permanent RNVR. I was officially attached to HMS Eaglet, the stone frigate that constituted the Liverpool shore base of the RNVR in Northwest England. From 1947 to 1950, I was an undergraduate at the University of Manchester. My duties to the RNVR required me to do a certain number of weekend drills in Eaglet. As a student, I was excused from the requirement to spend two weeks at sea every summer. Upon graduation from the university in June 1950, my exemption terminated. I was assigned to HMS *Boxer* for two weeks in July as my summer sea-time requirement in the permanent RNVR.

The *Boxer* was in dock at Portsmouth when I joined her. Like all former tank landing ships, the *Boxer* had a big, ungainly hull and was built with a large internal hold designed to carry many tanks. She had little cabin structure above decks. I had a private cabin, several decks down. Arrays of radar antennae and transmitters bristled on her upperworks. Her hold had been converted to a radar fighter-control room. A bulkhead displayed a large, illuminated glass map of Northern Europe, with longitude and latitude lines. In front of this were banks of radar screens, at which operators in training sat during sea exercises. These exercises consisted of cruising slowly up and down a course in the Channel, while the Fleet Air Arm sent out planes from various distant points. The radar operators were supposed to detect these planes and plot their altitude, speed, course, and direction on the glass map. During the war, radar operators and fighter-control officers had been engaged in tracking enemy aircraft and directing our own fighters to positions from which to intercept the enemy.

Our schedule required us to go out each day, Monday through Friday, to conduct these training exercises. A permanent ship's company had the task of working the ship as the radar people came and went in training groups each week. Something of the technical revolution that had overtaken naval science was reflected in the transition from my own experience of service in the aging gunnery training cruiser *Cardiff* to service in the *Boxer*, where men learned how to direct fire from the air onto unseen targets.

During the second week of my duty in the *Boxer*, we were sent to anchor some distance off the end of Brighton pier, a very long and famous example of Victorian piers. The city of Brighton was having a celebration, and our ship was to represent the Navy during the celebration. This sort of thing, usually described as "showing the flag," apparently occupied a not insignificant part of naval duty during peacetime. We were to lie off Brighton for three days. On the first day, I was with one watch of officers and men who went ashore via motorboat to the pier. We had been given complimentary passes to various events. I went with one or two others to watch an ice skating show. We had dinner and then returned to the ship.

The next day, the commanding officer went ashore with other officers to a formal dinner with the mayor and other dignitaries. The officers shone in their dinner-dress uniform—bow ties, gold epaulettes, and so forth. As the evening wore on, the weather began to pick up; the waves increased and the wind freshened from the south. The anchor watch reported that the anchor seemed to be dragging, and it soon became obvious that we would have put out to sea to avoid being driven aground.

A message was sent to the captain, who left the dinner immediately. the motor launch was sent to the pier to get him. By the time he arrived back on board, the seas had risen to the point that no more motorboat trips could be made. The rest of the crew would have to be left in Brighton. We weighed anchor and, with half a ship's company of officers and men, headed to sea to ride out the weather.

We had been out only a few hours when a stoker petty officer came to the wardroom to report that one of the stokers was very ill. He had a high temperature and dizziness and was finding it hard to breathe. The sick-berth attendant was ashore in Brighton, and the ship carried no medical officer. The captain called me in to inquire what I was studying at the university. When I told him psychology, that seemed good enough for him. He ordered me to take charge of the stoker's medical problem.

The stoker was put in the sick bay. I took his temperature and looked in his mouth. The back of his throat seemed suspiciously whitish. There was a Navy medical manual on a shelf, and I consulted it. I concluded that the stoker had one of two things—strep throat or diphtheria. As the latter was clearly the worse of the two, that was the one to treat. All that I could do, however, was to follow the instruction that everybody on board should gargle with a disinfectant made from a solution of water and a blue fluid, identified by a label, in a bottle in the drug locker. Two ratings mixed up buckets of this stuff, and everybody on board (captain included) came to the sick bay to gargle with it. The solution tasted nasty; hence, everybody was confident that the right thing was being done.

I had communicated my alternative diagnoses to the captain, who radioed a description of the situation to the Royal Naval Hospital at Haslar, Portsmouth. The response was to order the *Boxer* back to Portsmouth immediately so that the stoker could be admitted to the hospital. In a near full gale, we pitched and rolled our way to Portsmouth. As we entered the harbor, just about where the boom-net used to be in wartime, an ambulance tender came to meet us, but the weather was too rough for her to come alongside. Our stoker was strapped into a Robinson stretch-er consisting of long, flat strips of wood and canvas straps that effectively trussed him up all around into a cylindrical shape. A small rocket carry-ing a line was fired to the ambulance tender. A crew member of the tender grabbed the line and attached a thicker, stronger rope to it. We pulled this back to the *Boxer* and attached it to the stretcher. Hands on the tender began to haul in the line, as we eased it out.

Both ships were rolling, with a distance of about one hundred feet between them. When the ships rolled away from each other, the line went taut as a bar, straight from one to the other. When they rolled toward each other, the line went slack and dipped down to water level. The necessity of keeping the stretcher out of the water meant that, at each end, the hands hauling the line had to heave in quickly to avoid the dips and ease out equally fast to prevent the line from breaking when it was rising taut. The stretcher slowly dipped and jerked its way across the chasm. When it was finally secured on board, the tender headed immediately for Haslar.

We made our way into Portsmouth. Waiting on the jetty was the rest of the crew, who had come by train from Brighton. The officers looked quite scruffy. They were unshaven and their gold finery was crumpled from sleeping on the train. My own tour of duty came to an end a few days later. Before I left the *Boxer*, we received a report from the hospital that the stoker had strep throat.

This was my last service in the Royal Navy. In September 1950, I left Britain for the United States and graduate study at Ohio State University in Columbus. For the academic year 1950–51, I was technically on leave from the RNVR. In 1951, I resigned my commission, thereby terminating my connection with the Navy.

One year later, I married a fellow graduate student, Winifred Barbara Brown. After completing the Ph.D. degree at Ohio State in June 1954, I returned to England. Barbara joined me in November, having collected the material for her own doctoral degree. I worked briefly as a psychologist in the Prison Service in Wakefield, Yorkshire. Our first child, Rebecca, was born in Leeds. A few weeks later, we returned to the United States in the aging Cunard liner *Samaria*. Barbara graduated from Ohio State, and I began an academic career that continues to the present.

The years have been good to us and to our five children. Barbara and I have collaborated from time to time in scholarly writing. The present work owes far more to her encouragement, persistence, and skills than can be expressed in a simple acknowledgment.

The *Cardiff* and *Jason* passed into the hands of the shipbreakers many years ago. Once in a while, I come upon a Fairmile "B" motor launch still in use, the last time at a wharf in Mahone Bay, Nova Scotia. I do not know what happened to *ML137*, but perhaps she, or part of her, is still afloat in some corner of the world.

Epilogue: Return to Normandy

His voice speaks plain the words which you would say
If to your shipmates you could bid farewell:
"Across the steep seas where I met my end
The ships sail on; and sail thou on, my friend."
—JOHN MOORE, "SONNET FOR DEAD COMRADES"

The D day landings at Normandy are commemorated fifty years later, in June 1994. This is an opportunity to see what has happened to the places that I had known half a century earlier. So, with the support and urging of my wife, I fly to England and meet my brother John and his son-in-law Mario. We take the catamaran ferry from Folkestone to Boulogne on 6 June.

A misty fog hangs over the waters of the English Channel. The white cliffs near Folkestone are visible, but the distant cliffs of Dover are hidden somewhere in the mist. We choose to take this route because of a threatened strike of French dock workers, which would stall the more direct ferry services to Normandy. The sea is choppy, and not much shipping is visible—a sharp contrast to that other passage of fifty years ago. Arriving at Boulogne, we pick up a rental car and drive to the center of the city. After much "to-ing and fro-ing" with one-way streets, we find a bank, change our currency, and head out of town in the general direction of Normandy. At Abbeville, we stop to eat at an estaminet. The barmaid recommends Neufchatel as a good place for overnight accommodations, specifically, the Chapeau Rouge.

Neufchatel is a charming old town—"City of Cheeses," it announces proudly as one enters. Being too far from the nearest beach, Neufchatel had played no part in the D-Day landings. The Chapeau Rouge is in the town square, directly opposite the church. It identifies itself as founded in 1621, but it is locked up tight—no sign of life and no sign that it has been in business any time recently.

We find rooms at the Hotel de Grand Cerf nearby and enjoy an excellent dinner, with Bouzet wine in a souvenir bottle for the D-Day anniversary. And then to bed, with the church clock chiming the hours and the bell echoing through the quiet and peace of the town.

The next morning, we press on to Ouistreham, the easternmost edge of Sword Beach and the point toward which we had navigated on D-Day. Driving via Dives and Cabourg, we intend to pass along the east bank of the Orne River and cross the Orne canal at Pegasus Bridge. Once in sight of the bridge, we join a traffic jam of cars, buses, and restored World War II vehicles. The bridge is raised to permit a vessel to go through toward Caen, and no traffic is moving.

We park the car at the edge of the road and walk up to see the bridge. At a small stall, a young man is selling souvenir T-shirts emblazoned with gaudily printed emblems. Gray-haired British veterans are strolling around in blue blazers, gray pants, berets with regimental badges, and regimental ties. One of them comes up to me when he notices the RNVR tie that I am wearing and introduces himself as a former RNVR sailor. Too young for D-Day, he did not join the RNVR until after the war, but he had come to Normandy to commemorate the event anyway. Maj. John Howard, frail in his wheelchair, is escorted by a platoon of paratroopers. Some sort of ceremony has just ended, and the paratroopers are dismissed. Falling out of their ranks, they lift Major Howard into a wheelchair van.

Across the river, we can see the Pegasus Café (originally the Café Gondrée but later renamed Pegasus in honor of the badge of the Parachute Regiment that had taken the bridge). The area is rigged up for a sound and light show. Deactivated German guns stand in their original positions, and the place where the gliders landed is marked with concrete strips to identify the exact tracks that they had made. Here, we see a few of the many hundreds of World War II vehicles that we are to meet later on: two Jeeps, two motorcycle and sidecar combinations, and an ambulance. A cruise ship passes downstream from Caen and is followed a little later by the Norwegian Royal Yacht *Norge*. A uniformed figure on the

bridge—presumably, the Norwegian prince—waves to the spectators as the ship passes through the drawbridge.

When the bridge closes, we return to the car and wait to cross. A man comes down the line of cars and hands out reproductions of the *New Testament*, which had been given to the Allied troops about to embark for the D-Day assault. He says that they are surplus from a supply provided at a memorial service held on the previous day at the British–Canadian cemetery. We take some as souvenirs for children and grandchildren, who some day might have reason to think of the men who had taken part in that famous day.

No traffic has moved, and the bridge opens up again. We conclude that the short route across the bridge to Ouistreham will take longer than driving the long route into Caen and crossing the Orne there. We leave the line of traffic and turn south toward Caen. This has been a brief but convincing demonstration of why the Allied possession of Pegasus Bridge was so effective in preventing a German counterattack on Sword Beach.

My feelings are chiefly of astonishment at the boldness of the glider attack and the speed of its success. I think of the courage that it must have taken to run across the bridge under machine-gun fire, with the knowledge that there were no other Allied troops yet on French soil, and to do so under orders to hold the bridge at all costs until relief came.

Sword Beach

I don't know what to expect as we enter Ouistreham. Fifty years ago, what little I had been able to see from seaward were occasional glimpses of buildings that emerged briefly and disappeared into the obscurity of smoke and dust. The memory of the artillery bunker and its guns that had shelled us remains clear, and I wonder what has happened to the bunker. Through the years, these images have remained like black-and-white photographs in an old album rarely opened. The sharper edges fade as sepia pales the print, but some details remain fixed forever.

What we see is a newer and bigger town. At the ferry terminal, lines of cars and trucks stand ready to board for the voyage to Southampton. Sidewalk cafés are crowded with gray-haired veterans and their wives. They sit and talk together—perhaps of times past, perhaps of comrades who died on the beach or in the town, perhaps of good times since then. Many have walking canes, one or two are in wheelchairs.

In the streets of the town, we come across clusters of restored military vehicles. There are trucks, Jeeps, amphibious DUKWs, ambulances, half-tracks, and even an artillery piece. Shining paint and refurbished divisional insignia tell of the care and pride that has gone into the preservation of these survivors. A young man and woman sit in the front of an amphibious vehicle; behind them, a baby reclines in a car seat. A picnic chest lies next to the baby. Parents and baby are smiling.

Finally, we reach Sword Beach. Pastel-colored villas line the road that runs along the inner edge of the dunes. The beach stretches westward into the haze. In the middle distance is a casino flanked by a row of bathing huts. The original casino had been a point of strong enemy resistance on D-Day and was eliminated by French commandos only after bitter fighting.

Beyond the casino, half-hidden in the dunes, is a concrete gun emplacement. We walk along the beach to look at it. From this emplacement had come the shellfire that compelled us to cut the sweep wire on the morning of 6 June 1944. The roof of the emplacement, dislodged by naval shellfire, has partially collapsed and lies steeply aslant. It looks oddly like a failed layer cake. Nearby, a riding stables uses the surviving parts of the emplacement for storage. Standing by the ruined emplacement, I look out to sea and try to imagine how it must have looked to the German gunners who attempted to destroy us.

The sea is shimmering and pale in the bright sun, as if it too has changed. I meander slowly down to the water's edge and grasp a handful of the coarse golden sand. Mingled with the grains are the iridescent fragments of seashells that give this stretch of coast the name Côte de Nacre. I put the sand in my pocket and look back toward the sound of voices. Some yards away, three French youths are laughing and joking with each other. One of them approaches me, holds up a camera, and asks if I will take a photograph of the three of them. They want to be pictured together on this famous beach, he explains. Smiling and happy, they stand shoulder to shoulder with their backs to the silver-blue sea.

The picture taken, the owner of the camera comes up to thank me. He asks if I had been there on D-Day and then asks, "How do you feel about the Germans now? Can you ever forget? Don't you still feel. . . ." Here, language fails him. He clenches his fist and shakes his arm in a gesture of anger.

My answer does not come quickly. "The Germans I know were not even born when all this happened," I reply. "It is not possible to forget or forgive what happened in World War II, but the people most responsible are now dead. It would be unjust to blame their children and grandchildren now for things that happened before they were born."

"I understand," the boy says. "There is a past that must not be forgotten, but also a future to think of."

As we are speaking, one of his companions shouts, "Take a picture of me, take a picture of me like this!" He begins a slow, graceful, balanced cartwheel against the backdrop of sand, sea, and sky, carefree in the enjoyment of his agility. He finishes, standing upright. At first, I feel uncomfortable and slightly angry; it seems that there is something almost irreverent in his frolicking in a place where so many other young men had fallen, never to rise again. But then, I reflect, this is indeed a part of what it was all really for—so that people can take pleasure in their freedoms. Resuming their stroll along the beach, the youths wave and salute as they leave. This sword, at least, has become a ploughshare.

With another look at the sea, I rejoin my companions and we head toward a building known as the "Grand Bunker." This bunker was the control center for the German batteries in 1944. It stands intact, two or three blocks back from the houses lining the beach. A facade designed to look like the front of a house disguises the appearance of the side of the bunker facing the sea. We approach the building from the rear. There are few signs of damage to the structure. It is now a museum, and for twenty-five francs each we are admitted. A narrow rising passage and a bend in the stairs bring us face to face with an internal machine-gun position, the gun aimed down the passage ready to shoot any invaders coming from that direction. At different levels, there are exhibits: the "Maschinerum," where the generators and ventilation fans and ducts were activated; in another compartment, a uniformed model of a German radio operator and his equipment; in yet another, a Skoda cannon, photographs of the construction of the Atlantic Wall, models dressed as British infantrymen, a German soldier, and a soldier/construction worker of the Organization Todt. Cases display rifles, pistols, grenades, and many rusted rifle parts—the wooden stocks and butts long decayed and lost in the sand that must have held them buried for so many years. There is a hospital room with a narrow bunk, an operating table, and surgical instruments.

In a room at the very top of the bunker is a range finder aimed seaward, vision being through narrow slits in the concrete. The range finder is now fixed in position, and the view through the twin eyepieces shows a target grid on which a picture of a freighter has been pasted—nothing can be seen of the calm of the sea and beach outside. With this range finder, the German observers passed ranges and firing orders to the batteries situated at various points covering the beach. They must have been controlling the gun that fired at us from the beach defenses fifty years ago. Somewhere at a higher level, perhaps on the roof, is an antiaircraft gun position, accessed through a hatch at the top of a short steel ladder, but it is closed to visitors.

Returning to the entrance, we chat with a former British Army major, a veteran of the Normandy campaign, who had accepted the surrender of the bunker from the Germans. His account of this, which he gives gladly to anybody interested, is that some time after the beach and town had been secured, he was ordered to take the bunker. All of the batteries controlled from the bunker had been destroyed by the assault forces, but the bunker itself had not been attacked. The major took a few soldiers with him and, opening the door at the bottom of the bunker, waited with grenades and submachine guns to deal with any resistance. He shouted through the open door for everybody inside to come down with their hands up. A voice replied in fluent English, "You come up here, Tommy."

The major repeated his demand that they come down. In reply, he was told there were fifty Germans in the bunker. They were waiting to surrender and would, indeed, come down and give themselves up—which they did.

We go for a last look at Sword Beach and take some photographs. About half a mile to seaward, a French warship moves steadily toward the port entrance. It is the only reminder that fifty years ago something magnificent and terrible happened here.

We find a restaurant for lunch and then continue westward along the coast road through Courseilles to Juno Beach at Arromanches. To the right, the remnants of the Mulberry harbor are clearly visible from the road. We run into a traffic jam at the top of a hill. On a bluff overlooking the sea is a tall framework tower erected to provide a bird's-eye view for a television camera. Around the base of the tower and all across the road are television trailers, recreation vehicles, and a crowd of people who have come to see whatever is happening. A quick U-turn brings us back down the hill, and we turn into a narrow dead-end lane to the beach itself. We park the car, and John strolls a little way down the beach to where he can sit and watch.

The tide is out, leaving some of the Mulberry caissons dry on the sand. Mario and I step out across the beach and wind our way among the streams flowing down to the sea. Tiptoeing across the shallows, we finally come to a caisson. It is encrusted with seashells around the base; the concrete is pitted here and there, and some minor damage is visible. Nonetheless, the caisson appears to have weathered the storms of half a century quite well. Other caissons, farther out, have suffered more damage.

Two French fishermen are flicking their fishing rods and dipping their nets into the tidal pool around the base of the nearest caisson. Across the sand behind us, a DUKW filled with tourists whirs along parallel to the dunes. A World War II ambulance fitted out as a camper-van stands some distance away, the occupants standing around chatting with the owners of two World War II Jeeps parked nearby. Overhead, a modern helicopter flying low carries sightseers along the water's edge. A sand-surfboard, with a brightly colored sail, glides rapidly along in the distance. Away at the west end of the beach, we can see the bluffs that border the eastern edge of Omaha Beach.

We leave the beach and return to the car. Our route takes us to the edge of Bayeaux, where we run into a traffic jam. A parade of World War II vehicles is leaving the town. Two gendarmes dance and wave the traffic one way or another. Blue police wagons and motorcycle police by the score are heading eastward out of town—perhaps some formal ceremony involving VIPs has just been concluded. Finally, through the jam and around the edge of Bayeux, we head down the road for Carentan. We modify our plans when we realize that, at best, we might get to Valognes. Perhaps it is more sensible to find lodging for the night in Carentan.

Saint-Vaast-la-Hougue

After a night in Carentan we wind along back roads, bordered by high hedges, toward Saint-Vaast-la-Hougue. When we come to the harbor itself, I find it changed beyond recognition. I walk along the main quay to locate the place where *ML137* had berthed in June 1944. Brightly painted fishing boats line the quay; lobster traps are piled on the decks of the boats and in pyramids on the quay itself. In the middle of the basin, the floating pontoons of a yacht marina are laid out in a fishbone pattern. Sloops, ketches, yawls, and a multihull or two are arrayed in rows. Fiberglass hulls are polished to a shine, and aluminum spars gleam dully in the bright sunlight.

Most disorienting of all is the fact that, outside the harbor, the tide is out and the edge of the sea lies some distance beyond a stretch of glistening sand. Inside the harbor, the water level is high and the fishing boats and yachts ride gently on the water. What has happened to the low tides that left the harbor dry fifty years ago? The answer is soon clear. A tidal gate now keeps the water level in the harbor basin high at all stages of the tide. Boats wishing to leave can moor to an outer jetty to wait for the tide to rise.

Cafés line the quay, tourists stroll the sidewalk, and the French flag flaps gently in front of the Tourist Bureau. As we explore the quayside, I try to remember something, some detail, that will trigger recognition. At which estaminet had we sipped Calvados with the fishermen? Which, indeed, is the village square? There seem to be several places that might be so described. Had there ever been a Bordier family and, if so, what has happened to them? We decide to find out.

The young woman at the Tourist Bureau speaks little English but manages to communicate to us that the way to find the Villa Madeleine is to inquire at the Post Office. At the Post Office, a helpful clerk checks a directory and tells us that there is no such house as the Villa Madeleine and nobody by the name of Bordier lives in Saint-Vaast. "However," she adds with polite pessimism, "Monsieur might try the Mairie."

Our inquiries at the Mairie seem to spark the enthusiasm of the officials: "When did you visit here in 1944?" "What age did the young Bordier woman seem to be?"

I guess twenty-two years old. A clerk disappears to a cabinet and returns with two bound volumes, registers of births and deaths. With a note of happy triumph, she points to an entry—Mlle. Genviéve Bordier, once of Saint-Vaast, but long married and living in Luxembourg. Her name now is Madame de la Morvonnais, and she and her husband still maintain a villa in Saint-Vaast, which they visit only occasionally. With the new address in hand, we head for the Villa La Coquille not far away.

Through the wrought iron gates, we see a man on a ladder. He is pulling ivy out of the windowsills. I ask him if he can tell me anything about the family de la Morvonnais. He carefully comes down from the ladder and asks what we want with the family. I explain. He leads us to the door of the house, pushes it open, and calls out, "Ginette, there are people here to see you." In the hallway, plumbers are busy pounding on pipes and peering at plaster where winter leaks have stained the ceiling. We wait at the foot of the stairs, and, in due course Ginette descends.

Explanations and introductions follow. Ginette ushers us into the drawing room. A tray with glasses and Calvados appears, remembrances improve, and Ginette talks of the days of the liberation as they were for herself and her family, both before and after the Germans were driven out. She describes seeing the parachutes slowly descending "like white flowers opening up against the dark of the sky." She speaks of a neighbor who cycled back to Saint-Vaast on the morning of D-Day after leaving the scene at Utah Beach. White-faced and benumbed, he had repeated over and over, "All those poor boys, those poor boys—they lie in rows on the beach, one next to another like logs of wood."

We take photographs and exchange information about our families and children. We hope that some day our two families will get to know each other. Some neighbors come in, and there is much warm handshaking and smiling. Ginette mentions that she also kept a diary of those days, but that is is in the attic. Perhaps some day she will find it and see what she had entered in it for the days when *ML137* was in port.

She urges us to stay for lunch, but our time is limited and we must make our way back to Boulogne. She accompanies us down the drive to the iron gates and gives me an affectionate farewell embrace. I tell her that I hope that we have not intruded in their vacation time at Saint-Vaast, and she assures me that the visit has left her thankful. I leave with a feeling of having achieved a passage back in time.

Later, driving back to Boulogne, I reflect on the events of fifty years ago. A good friend, Col. David Yates, U.S. Army (Ret.), who has read this work, remarked on the contrast in our experiences. As a young career officer, he fought the Japanese in the invasion of the Philippines, was taken prisoner, and survived under deadly conditions. "We lacked the traditions you describe and had to make them up, or change what was generally accepted to confront the totally unexpected situations." He was right, of course. Fortune had been kinder to me than to him. D-Day was a masterpiece of planning and preparation. The leaders had reason to be proud.

Pride comes first, but then sadness close to grief. I cannot forget the other men and women, young and old, civilian and soldier, who did not have the years of peace that their lives had bought and that we have been privileged to enjoy. During these past years, it has been gradually fading in memory, as with a book read long ago. Coming back to Normandy reopens the pages. I look again on the shining sands and the water's edge where so many died; gaze out over the sea where the mines and guns took the lives of sailors and up to the clear summer sky where the airmen fought and fell. Tears come, as they had not then, for it has taken the years of peace and happiness to show me the enormity of the price that they paid. We have a duty to see that this time and its deeds are never forgotten. We must ensure that our children and their children remember those who did these deeds and why they were done.

At Folkestone, our journey back home takes us near the entrance to the Channel Tunnel. Machinery and the debris of construction are everywhere, but I am told that the tunnel is open. The passage to Europe now lies under the narrow seas and the weather is of no concern. This, perhaps more than anything else, speaks of a new beginning in history. If so, it is a beginning made possible by men and women, many of whom have lived to make the proud return to the beaches, many of whom lie unmarked on the bed of the restless sea, and many whose names are graven on the headstones that stand in neat white ranks throughout the cemeteries of Normandy and the other places embroiled in that desperate struggle.

Appendix A: Ranks and Uniforms of the Royal Navy during World War II

Ratings

Ranks below that of commissioned to warrant officer consisted of the following:

- *Substantive ratings:* Ranks of leading seaman and up wore badges signifying rank. The badges used a mixture of anchors.
- *Nonsubstantive or specialist ratings:* Ratings with specialist skills were identified by the wearing of rating badges.

Seaman Branch ("Square Rig")

- *Ordinary Seaman (O/S):* Ordinary seaman was the entering rank; no skills relevant to naval service were expected. Uniform consisted of bell-bottom trousers, jumper, and round cap. Before the war, the cap had the name of the sailor's ship on a ribbon around the rim; during the war, for security reasons, the name of the ship was removed. No badges of rank.
- *Able Seaman (A/B):* An able seaman must have learned a set of skills essential in naval service, such as handling ropes, knot tying, and boat handling, and passed an examination on these. Uniform, as above. No badges of rank.
- *Leading Seaman (Ldg. Sea.):* A leading seaman, equivalent to a corporal in the Army, was in charge of a group of working parties of O/Ss and A/Bs.

Uniform, as above. Badge of rank: a single anchor on one sleeve of the uniform jumper.

- *Petty Officer (P/O):* A petty officer was usually promoted from the rank of leading seaman on the basis of experience, work efficiency reports, length of service, and examinations. A petty officer was in charge of a larger proportion of the crew than was a leading seaman (e.g., a petty officer of the watch, working under the officer of the watch, was in charge of the watch). Uniform consisted of bell-bottom trousers, jumper, and round cap with the name of the ship on a ribbon around the rim. Badge of rank: crossed anchors on one sleeve of the jumper. After a petty officer had been in that rank for one year, the bell-bottom trousers and jumper were replaced by the "fore-and-aft-rig" trousers, single-breasted jacket with brass buttons inscribed with crown and anchor, peaked cap, white shirt, and black tie. Badge of rank: crossed anchors on one sleeve of the jacket and a cap badge with small crown and anchor.
- *Chief Petty Officer (CPO):* Uniform, as above. Badge of rank: three brass buttons on the cuff of both jacket sleeves, with anchors gone, and a slightly more ornate cap badge.

Note: If in a specialist branch, able seamen and petty officers wore a specialist rating badge. For example, a CPO whose specialty was signaling (chief yeoman of signals) wore two small flags crossed on the lapel of the jacket; a CPO whose specialty was gunnery (chief gunner's mate) wore two old-fashioned naval guns crossed on the lapel of the jacket.

Dayman Branch

The Dayman Branch of the service included writers (i.e., clerks), cooks, stewards, supply assistants, sick-berth attendants, and others not directly involved in the handling of the ship. Uniform: all ratings, from the lowest rank up, wore a jacket and trousers. The daymen referred to themselves as "gentlemen of the lower deck" because they wore a collar and black tie. For example, a supply assistant wore trousers and a jacket with a badge consisting of a star and incorporating the letter "S," indicating his rating, on one sleeve; if promoted to the next higher rank, he became a leading supply assistant and wore an anchor on the other sleeve of his jacket.

There was a police branch of the Navy on larger ships. A naval policeman at the rank equivalent to leading seaman was called a leading patrolman; at the rank of petty officer, regulating petty officer; and at the rank of chief petty officer, master at arms.

In all of the specialties, a new system of ranks began above chief petty officer.

Warrant Officers

A warrant officer (W/O) was always referred to as "Mister"; for example, if an officer said, "Present my compliments to Mr. X and tell him to come to the bridge," Mr. X was obviously a warrant officer. Warrant officers were typically referred to by their specialty; thus, the gunner was a W/O in gunnery; the torpedo gunner, a W/O in torpedoes; and the bosun, a W/O in the Seaman Branch. Uniform was a commissioned officer's uniform, consisting of trousers, double-breasted jacket, peaked cap, white shirt, and black tie. Badge of rank consisted of one thin stripe of gold braid on the cuffs of both jacket sleeves, larger brass buttons with crown and anchor, and a cap badge with oak leaves on each side of a crown and anchor. No specialist badges were worn.

Commissioned Officers

- *Commissioned Officer:* All commissioned officers wore an officer's uniform; double-breasted jacket, trousers, white shirt, black tie, and peaked cap with badge with oak leaves, crown, and anchor. On ceremonial occasions, all officers at the rank of sub-lieutenant and above were entitled to carry a sword; midshipmen and warrant officers carried a dirk. The gold lace stripes worn on the cuffs of officer's uniforms differed for the RN (Royal Navy career officers), RNR (Royal Naval Reserve officers), and RNVR (Royal Naval Volunteer Reserve officers). RN officers wore straight stripes, RNVR officers wore wavy stripes (which led to the Volunteer Reserve being termed the "Wavy Navy"), and RNR officers wore two thin stripes, plaited in crisscross fashion, that were equivalent to one regular stripe.

  Specialties at the warrant officer rank and higher were indicated by a colored band next to the gold braid on the cuffs of both jacket sleeves (e.g., a red band was worn by surgeons, pink by dentists, green by electricians, purple by engineers, light blue by instructors, white by paymasters). With the exception of warrant officers, these specialists had usually acquired their training before entering the Navy. Officers with specialties acquired by additional training in the Navy itself, such as navigators or gunners, were not indicated by badge or color. The specialty was indicated by the addition of a bracketed initial in the title of rank. For example, a qualified gunnery officer was designated as Lt.(G) and a navigator as Lt.(N). (Sometime after World War II, both naval reserves were combined into a single reserve and the standard straight stripe was adopted for all officers' uniforms.)
- *Commissioned Warrant Officer (CWO):* A warrant officer could be promoted to this rank, which was equivalent to that of sub-lieutenant. Badge of rank was one thick stripe of gold lace on both jacket sleeves. A commissioned

warrant officer was still called "Mister." CWOs were rarely found except on very large ships or in naval barracks.

- *Midshipman (Midn.):* Midshipmen were commissioned officers under the age of 19½ years. In the days of sail, when they were likely to have been even younger, midshipmen came to be known as "snotties" because of their youth. The traditional claim was that three brass buttons were put on the cuff of the midshipman's jacket sleeve to prevent him from wiping his nose on it. Although the age limit had changed, the nickname remained. Badge of rank was three brass buttons on the cuffs of both jacket sleeves and, on each lapel, a colored tab (purple, RNVR; blue, RNR; white, RN) to which was stitched a small brass button and a loop of gold braid. Midshipmen in the specialist branch wore the colored band signifying their specialty around the cuff of the jacket sleeve. Although midshipmen, if they performed satisfactorily, were routinely promoted to sub-lieutenant, they were actually inferior in rank to CWOs.
- *Sub-Lieutenant (Sub-Lt.):* Badge of rank was one stripe of gold braid, wider than that worn by warrant officers, on the cuffs of both jacket sleeves.
- *Lieutenant (Lt.):* Badge of rank was two stripes of gold braid on the cuffs of both jacket sleeves.
- *Lieutenant Commander (Lt. Comdr.):* Badge of rank was three stripes of gold braid (known as a "two and a half" because the middle stripe of gold braid was thinner) on the cuffs of both jacket sleeves.
- *Commander (Comdr.):* Badge of rank was three broad stripes of gold braid on the cuffs of both jacket sleeves; the front edge of the cap visor was trimmed with gold braid oak leaves. Commanders and up were known as "brass hats" because the gold braid on their cap visors was made of brass wire.
- *Captain (Capt.):* Badge of rank was four broad stripes of gold braid on the cuff of both jacket sleeves; the front edge of the cap visor was trimmed with gold braid oak leaves.

Flag Ranks

Flag ranks began with commodore and ascended to admiral of the fleet.
- *Commodore:* Badge of rank was one very broad stripe of gold lace on the cuffs of both jacket sleeves; the front edge of the cap visor was trimmed with gold braid oak leaves.
- *Rear Admiral (Rear Adm.):* Badge of rank was one very broad and one normal-width stripe on the cuffs of both jacket sleeves; the front and inner edges of the cap visor were trimmed with gold braid.
- *Vice Admiral (Vice Adm.):* Badge of rank was one very broad and two regular stripes on the cuffs of both jacket sleeves; the cap visor was the same as for rear admiral.

- *Admiral (Adm.):* Badge of rank was one very broad and three regular stripes on the cuffs of both jacket sleeves; the cap visor was the same as for rear admiral.
- *Admiral of the Fleet:* Badge of rank was one very broad stripe and four regular stripes on the cuffs of both jacket sleeves; the cap visor was the same as for rear admiral.

Miscellaneous Wartime Badges

- *War service chevron:* These small red chevrons were to be worn vertically on the cuff of the jacket sleeve. Each chevron signified six months of wartime service. They were not popular and rarely worn.
- *Wound stripe:* This was a short, narrow vertical stripe of gold wire awarded to men who had been wounded. It was worn on the cuff of the sleeve. Men wounded on separate occasions received additional stripes that were added laterally to those already worn.

Traditional Colloquialisms in the Royal Navy

Certain specialist ratings were given traditional nicknames:
- *Buffer:* A chief bosun's mate who was in charge of all work around the ship—rigging, painting, rope work, ship's boats, and so forth. When entering or leaving harbor or during action, the buffer was usually at the helm, while the captain gave the steering orders from the bridge. The *Cardiff* had a buffer.
- *Bunts:* A signalman, or "bunting tosser."
- *Chief:* The chief engineer.
- *Chips* or *Chippy-Chap:* A ship's carpenter.
- *Crusher:* A regulating petty officer (a naval policeman at the rank of petty officer). The name was said to refer to the alleged large size of the crusher's feet and boots.
- *Guns:* The chief gunnery officer.
- *Jack Dusty:* A supply assistant; the name derives from the flour dust associated with the storeroom in which he worked.
- *Jaunty:* A master at arms (a naval policeman at the rank of chief petty officer). Jaunty is a corruption of the French "gendarme."
- *Killick:* A colloquial term for a leading seaman. A killick is a small anchor, similar to that on the badge worn on a leading seaman's sleeve.
- *Number One:* The first lieutenant.
- *Pilot:* The navigating officer.
- *Schoolie:* An instructor officer.
- *Scratch:* The secretary to the commanding officer of a large ship or shore base. This position was occupied by a commissioned officer of the Paymaster Branch.
- *Scribe:* A writer (clerk).

- *Sick-Bay Tiffy:* A sick bay attendant. The term "tiffy" was abstracted from "artificer," a term used officially for engine room artificers and applied rather loosely to some of the trades in which a specialist wore the dayman's uniform.
- *Snotty:* A midshipman.
- *Sparks:* A radio telegraphist.

Traditional nicknames were also given to certain men, both officers and ratings, who had particular last names, such as "Pincher" Martin, "Knocker" White, "Nobby" Clark, "Hooky" Walker, and "Dusty" Miller.

Appendix B: Allied Ships Mentioned in This Book

Royal Navy

First Minesweeping Flotilla

Ships of the First Minesweeping Flotilla were all of the *Halcyon* class. The *Jason* and other ships of the flotilla were attacked from the air by friendly fire during the invasion of Normandy; several of the officers on the bridge of the *Jason* were wounded or killed, including the midshipman who had been sent to take my place. The *Jason* survived. The report that filtered back to us was that, on 27 August 1944, the ships had been attacked off Le Havre by Allied aircraft. The leading pilot of the aircraft had seen the ships and radioed back to his base to ask if they were British. He was told that no British ships were operating in that area; the ships must be German and should be attacked. The pilot made another pass over them and reported back that they were flying the White Ensign. He was told that this must be a German ruse and he should attack them anyway. His squadron did so, sinking the *Britomart* and *Hussar* and damaging others, including the *Jason*.

The other ships of the flotilla, the *Gleaner, Halcyon, Harrier, Salamander, Seagull,* and *Speedwell*, survived. The *Harrier* was badly damaged;

a number of her company were killed or seriously wounded, including the commanding officer. At that point, the *Jason* became flotilla leader because Commander Crick was now the most senior of the surviving commanding officers in the flotilla.

Warships

In the descriptions that follow, it should be noted that ships of the same class often differed from each other in minor respects. I have also found minor discrepancies in descriptions of their histories as recounted by various authors.

HMT *Alexander Scott: Castle*-class trawler, built in 1917. The *Alexander Scott* served as a danlayer with the First Minesweeping Flotilla, 1939–44; she survived the war.

HMS *Alresford: Albury*-class minesweeper. All twenty-five vessels in this class were built at the close of World War I. Displacement, 700 tons; length, 231 feet; speed, 16 knots; ship's company, 73. The *Alresford* was sold in 1947.

HMS *Archer: Archer*-class escort convoy aircraft carrier (prototype of her class), built in Chester, Pennsylvania. Displacement, 4,500 tons; carried twenty-one airplanes.

HMS *Argonaut: Dido*-class cruiser. Displacement, 5,400 tons; length, 506 feet; beam, 50.5 feet; speed, 33 knots; main armament, ten 5.25-inch guns. The *Argonaut* was scrapped in 1955.

HMS *Aries: Algerine*-class minesweeper. Equipped for all three types of sweep, acoustic, magnetic, and contact, the seventy-six vessels in this class were built in the United Kingdom, United States, and Canada during the war. Displacement, 800 tons; length, 225 feet; ship's company, 104.

HMS *Belfast: Edinburgh*-class cruiser. Displacement, 10,000 tons. The *Belfast* was the flagship of Rear Admiral Dalrymple-Hamilton during the invasion of Normandy and is now moored as a museum ship in the River Thames, near the Tower of London.

HMS *Blackpool: Bangor*-class minesweeper. The *Blackpool* survived the war.

HMS *Bootle: Bangor*-class minesweeper. The *Bootle* survived the war.

HMS *Boxer:* Tank landing ship built by Harland and Wolff, Belfast, in December 1942. Displacement, 3,260 tons; length, 390 feet; beam, 49 feet; main armament, eight 20-mm guns. The *Boxer* was a fighter-direction ship in 1944 and a radar training ship in 1947; she was sold to Ward of Barrow, 12 January 1958.

HMS *Bramble: Halcyon*-class minesweeper. The *Bramble* served with the First Minesweeping Flotilla; she was sunk in a battle with the German battleship *Hipper* during an escort of the convoy *JW 51.B* to Murmansk.

HMS *Britomart: Halcyon*-class minesweeper. The *Britomart* served in the First Minesweeping Flotilla; she was sunk by friendly fire from Allied aircraft off Le Havre, 27 August 1944.

HMS *Cardiff:* C-class light cruiser built in December 1917. Displacement, 4,190 tons; length, 425 feet; beam, 43 feet; main armament, five 6-inch guns, two 3-inch guns, 20-mm Oerlikon rapid-fire machine guns, 40-mm Bofors antiaircraft guns. The *Cardiff* served in the 6th Light Cruiser Squadron during World War I and took part in the battle of Heligoland and a major raid in the Kattegat Strait. Her wartime service culminated with the honor of leading the German Grand Fleet into Scapa Flow after Germany surrendered in 1918.

HMS *Chant 67*, Royal Fleet Auxiliary: *Chant*-class channel tanker (fuel or water) built in 1943–44. Displacement, 400 tons; speed, 7 knots.

HMS *Clarkia: Flower*-class corvette. Displacement, 925 tons; length, 205 feet; beam, 33 feet; speed, 17 knots; main armament, one 4-inch anti-aircraft gun; ship's company, 80. The *Clarkia* was scrapped in 1947.

HMT *Colsay: Isles*-class trawler built in 1943. The *Colsay* served as a danlayer; she was sunk off Ostend by a German human torpedo in November 1944.

HMT *Craftsman* (previously the *Coriolanus*): Trawler, recruited into the Royal Navy in 1940 and renamed the *Craftsman*. The *Craftsman* served as a danlayer for the First Minesweeping Flotilla; she was returned to civilian use in October 1944.

HMS *Danmark*, Royal Fleet Auxiliary: The *Danmark* was a Danish vessel in service as an oil hulk for the Royal Navy, 1942–46.

HMS *Demeter* (formerly the *Buenos Aires*), Royal Fleet Auxiliary: The *Demeter* was purchased for use as a store-carrier in June 1941, became an ammunition hulk in October 1945, and was sold in 1949.

HMT *Elena* (formerly the *Viola*): Trawler. The *Elena* was employed in minesweeping during World War I under her original name, *Viola*; she was taken back into the Royal Navy in 1939, renamed *Elena*, and again employed in minesweeping.

HMS *Empire Battleaxe: Empire*-class infantry landing ship; ships of this class, designed to carry infantry and a large number of small landing craft, were built by the Consolidated Steel Corporation, Wilmington, Delaware, and transferred to the Royal Navy from the U.S. Navy. Displacement, 11,650 tons; main armament, one 4-inch gun. The *Battleaxe* survived the war and was later returned to the United States.

HMS *Empire Broadsword: Empire*-class infantry landing ship. The *Broadsword* was sunk by a mine off Normandy on 2 July 1944.

HMS *Empire Halberd: Empire*-class infantry landing ship. The *Halberd* survived the war and was later returned to the United States.

HMS *Franklin: Halcyon*-class survey vessel (see HMS *Halcyon*).

HMS *Fraserburgh: Bangor*-class minesweeper built in 1941. The *Fraserburgh* served with the Fifteenth Minesweeping Flotilla; she was scrapped in 1948.

HMS *Gleaner: Halcyon*-class minesweeper. The *Gleaner* was built originally as a survey vessel, was converted to minesweeper in 1939, and served in the First Minesweeping Flotilla; she was scrapped in 1950.

HMS *Halcyon: Halcyon*-class minesweeper (prototype of her class); all twenty-one *Halcyon*-class minesweepers were built as survey vessels between 1933 and 1938 and converted to minesweepers in 1939. *Warships of the World* (1946) gives the displacement as 815–75 tons, but the *Jason*, a *Halcyon*-class minesweeper, had a displacement of approximately 1,300 tons; the book was either wrong or reported a peacetime displacement that was increased by equipment added during the war. Length 245 feet; speed, 17 knots; main armament, one 4-inch gun mounted forward, several 20-mm Oerlikon antiaircraft machine guns, and smaller-caliber machine guns on the bridge; ship's company, approximately 80 in peacetime, increased to 125 during the war. The *Halcyon* served in the First Minesweeping Flotilla.

HMS *Harrier: Halcyon*-class minesweeper (see HMS *Halcyon*). The *Harrier* was senior officer in the First Minesweeping Flotilla; she was severely damaged by friendly fire in August 1944.

HMS *Hussar: Halcyon*-class minesweeper (see HMS *Halcyon*). The *Hussar* served in the First Minesweeping Flotilla; she was sunk by friendly fire of Allied aircraft off Le Havre, 27 August 1944.

HMS *Isle of Jersey:* No information available.

HMT *Isle of May:* Trawler. The *Isle of May* served in the Royal Navy, 1940–44.

HMS *Jamaica: Fiji*-class cruiser. Displacement, 8,000 tons; length, 538 feet; beam, 62 feet; speed, 33 knots; main armament, twelve 6-inch and eight 4-inch guns. The *Jamaica* took part in the defeat of German forces in the New Year's Eve battle in the Barents Sea, 1942, and in the sinking of the *Scharnhorst* off the North Cape, December 1943; she was scrapped in 1960.

HMS *Jason: Halcyon*-class minesweeper (see HMS *Halcyon*). The *Jason* was half-leader (second-senior commanding officer and ship) in the First Minesweeping Flotilla (number J. 99); she was scrapped in 1950.

HMS *King George V:* Battleship. Displacement, 35,000 tons; speed, 30 knots; main armament, ten 14-inch guns. The *King George V* took part in the sinking of the *Bismarck*, May 1941.

HMS *Largs:* French merchant ship *Charles Plunier,* converted by the French to armed merchant cruiser. She was seized by the British destroyer *Faulknor* off Gibraltar, November 1940, and renamed *Largs*. The *Largs* served as landing ship headquarters (LSH) during the invasion of Normandy.

HMS *Londonderry: Leith*-class sloop, built in 1935. Displacement, 990 tons; speed, 16.5 knots. The *Londonderry* was scrapped in 1948.

HMT *Lord Ashfield:* Trawler. The *Lord Ashfield* was used as a minesweeper in the Royal Navy, 1939–45.

HMS *Milne: Milne*-class destroyer (prototype of her class), built in 1941. Displacement, 1,920 tons; speed, 36 knots. The *Milne* was transferred to Turkey in 1959 and renamed *Alp Arslam*.

HMS *Orion: Ajax*-class cruiser. Displacement, 7,000 tons; speed, 32.5 knots.

HMS *Petunia: Flower*-class corvette. The *Petunia* was transferred to China in 1945 and renamed *Fu Po;* she was lost in 1947.

HMS *Pickle: Algerine*-class minesweeper. The *Pickle* was sold to Sri Lanka in 1959 and renamed *Parakarama;* she was scrapped in 1964.

HMT *Pierre Andrée:* French trawler. While berthed in Portsmouth in July 1940, following the fall of France, the *Pierre Andrée* was taken into the Royal Navy. She was returned to France after the war.

HMS *Plover:* Minelayer (only one of her class). The *Plover* was scrapped in 1969.

HMS *Princess Iris:* Train ferry (No. 1), purchased by the Royal Navy in 1940 to serve as a landing ship and renamed *Princess Iris* in 1942. She was returned to civilian use in 1946.

HMS *Repulse:* Battle cruiser. Displacement, 32,000 tons; speed, 31.5 knots; main armament, six 15-inch guns. The *Repulse* took part in the sinking of the *Bismarck*, May 1941; she was sunk by Japanese aircraft at the end of 1941.

HMS *Rochester: Shoreham*-class sloop. The *Rochester* survived the war.

HMS *Royal Oak: Royal Sovereign*–class battleship. Displacement, 29,150 tons; length, 620 feet; beam, 101 feet; speed, 22 knots; main armament, eight 50-inch and fourteen 6-inch guns; ship's company, 1,100. The *Royal Oak* was sunk by *U-47*, a German submarine, at Scapa Flow in October 1939.

HMS *Salamander: Halcyon*-class minesweeper (see HMS *Halcyon*), built in 1936. The *Salamander* served in the First Minesweeping Flotilla; she was scrapped in 1947.

HMS *Savage: Saumarez*-class destroyer. The *Savage* took part in the sinking of the *Scharnhorst* off the North Cape, December 1943.

HMS *Scorpion: Saumarez*-class destroyer. The *Scorpion* took part in the sinking of the *Scharnhorst* off the North Cape, December 1943.

HMS *Scott:* Naval survey ship of the fleet minesweeper type. Displacement, 800 tons.

HMS *Scylla: Dido*-class cruiser. Displacement, 5,450 tons; length, 485 feet; beam, 50.5 feet; speed, 33 knots; main armament, eight 4.5-inch guns. The *Scylla* was the flagship of Adm. Philip Vian during the Normandy invasion; she was damaged by a mine on 23 June 1944 and scrapped in 1950.

HMS *Seagull: Halcyon*-class minesweeper (see HMS *Halcyon*). The *Seagull* served in the First Minesweeping Flotilla. She was converted to a survey vessel in 1945.

HMS *Sheffield: Newcastle*-class cruiser. Displacement, 9,100 tons; length, 591 feet; beam, 61.5 feet; speed, 32.5 knots; main armament, twelve 6-inch and eight 4-inch guns; ship's company, 700. The *Sheffield* took part in the sinking of the *Bismarck*, May 1941; in the defeat of German forces in the New Year's Eve battle in the Barents Sea, 1942; and in the sinking of the *Scharnhorst* off the North Cape, December 1943.

HMS *Speedwell: Halcyon*-class minesweeper (see HMS *Halcyon*). The *Speedwell* served in the First Minesweeping Flotilla; she was sold in 1946 and renamed *Topaz*.

HMS *Thetis:* Submarine. *Thetis* was sunk, with loss of all hands, during trials in Liverpool Bay on 1 June 1939. She was raised, refitted, and renamed *Thunderbolt* in 1940. Again, she was sunk (by the Italian corvette *Cicogna*) north of Sicily, 13 March 1943.

HMS *Tyne:* Depot ship for destroyers, built in 1940. Displacement, 11,000 tons. The *Tyne* was scrapped in 1972.

HMT *Valmont:* Trawler. The *Valmont* served as a minesweeper in both world wars.

HMS *Victorious:* Aircraft carrier. Displacement, 22,000 tons; speed, 31 knots; carried seventy-two airplanes. The *Victorious* took part in the sinking of the *Bismarck*, May 1941; she was scrapped in 1969.

HMT *Wallena:* Trawler. The *Wallena* served as a minesweeper during the war; she was transferred to service as a boom-gate vessel in 1945.

HMS *Warspite:* Battleship of the *Queen Elizabeth* class. Displacement, 31,000 tons; speed, 24 knots; main armament, eight 15-inch guns. The *Warspite* was sold in 1946 to be scrapped; she was wrecked while in tow to the shipbreakers, 23 April 1947.

HM *MLs:* Fairmile B–class motor launches. Displacement, 65 tons; length, 112 feet; beam, 18 feet; speed, 20 knots maximum speed and 17 knots steady cruising speed; main armament, two twin Oerlikon 20-mm machine guns, one 3-pounder gun, and two twin Vickers machine guns; ship's company, 3 officers and 17 ratings. A detailed description of the duties performed by these ships during the war is given in chapter 6. The following, equipped for minesweeping, served with the Fifth ML Flotilla: *137, 138, 140, 141, 142, 143, 189, 237, 257,* and *293.* There were twelve *MLs* in all, but a complete list of numbers is not available.

Stone Frigates

Naval shore bases given ships' names include the following:

HMS *Beehive:* Naval base, Felixstowe.

HMS *Boscawen:* Naval base, Portland.

HMS Dolphin: Royal Navy submarine research and training establishment, Portsmouth.

HMS Drake: Royal Naval Barracks, Devonport.

HMS Eaglet: Royal Naval Volunteer Reserve training depot, Liverpool.

HMS Hornet: Small ships' base, Portsmouth.

HMS King Alfred. Officer Cadet Training Unit. The headquarters of King Alfred was in Brighton and the remainder of the establishment in Lancing.

HMS Laughing Water: An outlying camp of HMS Pembroke located in Cobham, Kent.

HMS Lochinvar: Minesweeping School, Granton, near Edinburgh.

HMS Pembroke: Royal Naval Barracks, Chatham.

HMS Raleigh: Naval training establishment for newly joined seamen.

HMS Tadpole: Naval base, Poole.

HMS Vernon: Torpedo training and research headquarters of the Royal Navy, Portsmouth.

HMS Victory: Royal Naval Barracks, Portsmouth. The HMS *Victory*, Nelson's flagship at the Battle of Trafalgar, is a part of the Royal Naval Barracks and is the symbolic flagship of Commander in Chief, Portsmouth. The *Victory* is the oldest warship still in commission. To the USS *Constitution* belongs the distinction of being the oldest warship in commission still afloat. The *Victory* is permanently preserved in dry dock and is maintained as a museum ship by the Royal Navy. In peacetime, she is open to the general public. In wartime, the *Victory* was used to house officer cadets who were judged to require further training before receiving their commissions.

HMS Wasp: Naval base, Dover.

U.S. Navy

USS *Arkansas:* Battleship. Displacement, 29,000 tons; speed, 20 knots; main armament, twelve 12-inch guns; ship's company, 1,650. The *Arkansas* was the oldest battleship in the U.S. Navy; she took part in the invasion of Southern France, August 1944, and in the landings at Iwo Jima, February 1945.

USS *Augusta: Northampton*-class cruiser. Displacement, 10,500 tons; speed, 32.7 knots; main armament, nine 8-inch guns; ship's company, 1,200-plus. The *Augusta* was the flagship of the U.S. Atlantic Fleet, 1941–42, and the scene of the Roosevelt-Churchill meeting between President Franklin D. Roosevelt and Prime Minister Winston Churchill in Argentia Bay and the signing of the Atlantic Charter, 1941. She was the flagship of Rear Adm. Alan G. Kirk during the Normandy invasion; took part in the invasion of Southern France, August 1944; returned to the United States, September 1944; and carried President Harry S Truman to Europe on his way to the Potsdam Conference, July 1945.

USS *Barton: Sumner*-class destroyer. Displacement, 22,000 tons; length, 376 feet; beam, 40 feet; speed, 35 knots; main armament, six 5-inch guns; ship's company, 350. The *Barton* was slightly damaged during the bombardment of German shore batteries near Cherbourg, 25 June 1944.

USS *Chimo:* Auxiliary minelayer (former U.S. Army vessel). Displacement, 700 tons; speed, 10 knots.

USS *Laffey: Sumner*-class destroyer (see USS *Barton*). The *Laffey* was slightly damaged during the bombardment of German shore batteries near Cherbourg, 25 June 1944; she was hit by two bombs and four kamikaze planes off Okinawa and seriously damaged, 16 April 1945.

USS *O'Brien: Sumner*-class destroyer (see USS *Barton*). The *O'Brien* was hit by an 8-inch shell while engaged in the attack on Cherbourg; she was damaged by a kamikaze attack off Okinawa, 27 March 1945.

USS *Owl:* Oceangoing tug classed as an auxiliary tender (former minesweeper of the *Bird* class). Displacement, 840 tons; length, 187 feet; beam, 35 feet; speed, 14 knots; ship's company, 75.

USS *Raven: Auk*-class minesweeper. Displacement, 890 tons; speed, 19 knots; main armament, one 3-inch gun; ship's company, 100.

USS *Texas:* Battleship. Displacement, 30,000 tons; speed, 21 knots; ship's company, 1,314. The *Texas* took part in the invasion of Southern France, August 1944, and in the landings in Iwo Jima, February 1945.

USS *LST* 133: Landing ship tank. Displacement, 1,490 tons; speed, 10 knots.

USS *YMS* 350: Yard-type minesweeper. Displacement, 214 tons; speed, 12 knots; main armament, one 3-inch gun; ship's company, 50. The YMS 350 was sunk by a mine while conducting a magnetic sweep outside Cherbourg breakwater, 2 July 1944.

Index

About the Author

Brendan A. Maher was a junior officer in the Royal Naval Volunteer Reserve during and immediately after World War II, ending his active naval service in 1947 as a lieutenant.

His postwar career brought him to the United States to attend graduate school (on a Fulbright fellowship) at Ohio State University, where he earned his Ph.D. in 1954. A professor of psychology at Harvard University for many years, he is the author or editor of several books and numerous articles and essays.

The **Naval Institute Press** is the book-publishing arm of the U.S. Naval Institute, a private, nonprofit society for sea service professionals and others who share an interest in naval and maritime affairs. Established in 1873 at the U.S. Naval Academy in Annapolis, Maryland, where its offices remain today, the Naval Institute has more than 85,000 members worldwide.

Members of the Naval Institute receive the influential monthly magazine *Proceedings* and discounts on fine nautical prints and on ship and aircraft photos. They also have access to the transcripts of the Institute's Oral History Program and get discounted admission to any of the Institute-sponsored seminars offered around the country.

The Naval Institute also publishes *Naval History* magazine. This colorful bimonthly is filled with entertaining and thought-provoking articles, first-person reminiscences, and dramatic art and photography. Members receive a discount on *Naval History* subscriptions.

The Naval Institute's book-publishing program, begun in 1898 with basic guides to naval practices, has broadened its scope in recent years to include books of more general interest. Now the Naval Institute Press publishes about 100 titles each year, ranging from how-to books on boating and navigation to battle histories, biographies, ship and aircraft guides, and novels. Institute members receive discounts of 20 to 50 percent on the Press's nearly 600 books in print.

For a free catalog describing Naval Institute Press books currently available, and for further information about subscribing to *Naval History* magazine or about joining the U.S. Naval Institute, please write to:

Membership & Communications Department
U.S. Naval Institute
118 Maryland Avenue
Annapolis, Maryland 21402-5035
Telephone: (800) 233-8764
Fax: (410) 269-7940